Marrying Out

THE MODERN JEWISH EXPERIENCE

Deborah Dash Moore and Marsha L. Rozenblit, coeditors
Paula Hyman, founding coeditor

Marrying Out

Jewish Men, Intermarriage & Fatherhood

KEREN R. McGINITY

INDIANA UNIVERSITY PRESS   Bloomington & Indianapolis

This book is a publication of

INDIANA UNIVERSITY PRESS
Office of Scholarly Publishing
Herman B Wells Library 350
1320 East 10th Street
Bloomington, Indiana 47405 USA

iupress.indiana.edu

Telephone   800-842-6796
Fax   812-855-7931

∞ The paper used in this publication meets
the minimum requirements of the American National Standard for Information
Sciences – Permanence of Paper for Printed
Library Materials, ANSI Z39.48–1992.

*Manufactured in the
United States of America*

*Library of Congress
Cataloging-in-Publication Data*

McGinity, Keren R.
  Marrying out : Jewish men, intermarriage,
and fatherhood / Keren R. McGinity.
    pages cm. — (The modern Jewish
experience)
  Includes bibliographical references and
index.
  ISBN 978-0-253-01315-6 (eb) — ISBN
978-0-253-01319-4 (pb : alk. paper) 1.
Interfaith marriage—United States. 2.
Jewish men—United States. 3. Jews—
United States—Identity. I. Title.
  HQ1031.M3937 2014
  305.38'8924—dc23
                              2014004438

1 2 3 4 5 19 18 17 16 15 14

To my fathers

MICHAEL AND MYRON

and brothers

DAVID, JEFF, AND JOSH

with love and understanding

In our life there is a single color, as on an artist's palette,
which provides the meaning of life and art.
It is the color of love.

—Marc Chagall

Who is rich? He who is happy with what he has.

—*Pirkei Avot* (Ethics of the Fathers) 4:1

Contents

Preface		*xi*
Acknowledgments		*xiii*
	Introduction: Of Mice and *Menschen*	*1*
1	Professional Men	*31*
2	Sex and Money	*63*
3	Shiksappeal	*100*
4	Heartbreak Kid	*141*
	Conclusion	*192*
	Notes	*207*
	Suggested Reading	*257*
	Index	*261*

Preface

RESEARCHING INTERMARRIED JEWISH MEN HAS BEEN DISTINCT from any other endeavor I have undertaken for several reasons. I had to step outside my comfort zone as a woman and try to see the world through men's eyes. In the process I dismantled some of my own beliefs that I came to realize were, like so much else about gender, socially constructed and engrained. When I first began my research, I thought that it would be difficult to find male subjects willing to talk to me. This idea assumed that men are not good verbal communicators, which, it turns out, could not be further from the truth. My initial request for study participants immediately netted dozens of phone calls and e-mails from gentlemen eager to be interviewed. They were pleased that someone was taking an interest in their side of the intermarriage story and, although pressed for time, happy to schedule an hour or more to meet. The only incentive was the opportunity to express themselves behind closed doors. My findings led me to reinterpret feminist theory. While working on this book, I came to realize that it is much harder to be an intermarried Jewish man than an intermarried Jewish woman, because ethnic gender ascriptions assigns descent to women while simultaneously distancing men from their own heritage.

As I progressed with my research and writing, I began to notice that people reacted differently to what I was doing. In academic circles, when I said I was working on intermarried Jewish men, my colleagues laughed. A single woman at the time, I can understand why my office neighbors would tease me that my door seemed to be revolving with men coming and going in rapid succession. In Jewish feminist circles, when I told people I was working on Jewish men, I was greeted with laughter and the question: "Aren't we all?"[1] When I mentioned being interested in Jewish masculinity to relatives, friends, or acquaintances, invariably the men responded in one of two ways: either they immediately burst out in a big grin as if we were sharing an inside joke and asked something akin to, "Is there such a thing?" which perhaps subconsciously echoed the historical notion of Jewish men as physically feeble; or they simply stared at me with a completely blank expression as if I had just told them that the sky was green and therefore I must be totally out of my mind. Conversely, women would nod their heads, conspiring with me about the desperate need to better understand Jewish men. Whenever I mentioned Jewish fatherhood, the response was a request to repeat myself, as if the listener thought I said "motherhood" and they had misheard. The highest compliment I received during this six-year project was when a man called me "the Jane Goodall of the Jews."[2]

Conceiving and writing this book have convinced me that chronicles of American Jews must incorporate analyses of both genders. While the field of men's studies has gained a presence on college syllabi, it lags far behind women's studies with regard to ethnicity. Jewish men's studies as a sub-field occupies an even smaller space, with only a half dozen or so titles on the bookshelf. Just as coming to understand the feminine mystique led to a breakthrough in understanding women's experience, so too does the exploration and discussion of the Jewish masculine mystique. The goal of this book, however, exists far outside any classroom and in the homes of Jewish husbands, fathers, and sons. I wrote this book about men primarily for men and for the women who love them, whether they are wives, mothers, sisters, daughters, or other relations. If you, the reader, find the language on these pages accessible, then I have done my job as I defined it. Books that are passed from parent to child, and from friend to friend, have lasting influence beyond measure. I sincerely hope this book qualifies.

Acknowledgments

MY DEBTS OF GRATITUDE RUN DEEP AND WIDE. IT TOOK A
generous philanthropist and a visionary scholar to bring this book to fruition. Bill Berman funded the Mandell L. Berman Postdoctoral Research
Fellowship in Contemporary American Jewish Life, which called me to
Ann Arbor, where I conducted the primary research. His support and
interest extended beyond my fellowship term, for which I am most grateful. Deborah Dash Moore, whose hands were already quite full directing
the Frankel Center for Judaic Studies, served as my steadfast mentor.
She believed in this project from proposal to printer. Her critiques provided wisdom, inspiration, and unparalleled commitment to excellence.
Fifty-four men and women made this history of Jewish intermarriage
possible by sharing their experiences and emotions. I hope that they will
read it and feel heard. Sarai Brachman Shoup was a superb liaison between my work and the Berman Foundation, as well as an ethical friend.
The Lucius N. Littauer Foundation offset the expense of transcription
of the interviews. Indiana University Press proved exceptionally dedicated and supportive. Janet Rabinowitch, Peter Christian Froehlich,
Dee Mortensen, Sarah Jacobi, June Silay, and Dave Hulsey, along with
anonymous reviewers and keen-eyed copy editor Debra Hirsch Corman, ensured that this book would resonate well beyond academia. I
am deeply honored that it is included in the Modern Jewish Experience
series. The extraordinary legacy of founding coeditor Paula Hyman, *z"l*,
emboldened me every step of the way.

Living and working in the city locals call "A2" was a profoundly positive existence in the most stimulating of environments. The University of Michigan campus was fertile ground for reaching across disciplines and fields. I received numerous social invitations before I'd even finished unpacking my books, a welcome change from New England, where invitations are extended more sparingly. My colleagues became friends, and my friends became family. Oren Gutfeld, whose Israeli accent I cherished hearing through the wall that separated our offices, became like a brother. David Schoem and Magda Zaborowska provided a web of intellectual engagement and encouragement. Numerous individuals graciously discussed my project and offered cogent suggestions. Michal Kravel-Tovi, Vanessa Ochs, Hana Wirth-Nesher, and Chava Weissler, Frankel Fellows at the time, included me in their discussions. I am also thankful to Gabriele Boccaccini, Todd Endelman, Elliot Ginsburg, Mikhail Krutikov, Julian Levinson, MacDonald Moore, Anita Norich, Regina Morantz-Sanchez, and Geneviève Zubrzycki. The Frankel Center staff members Tracy Darnell, Stacy Eckert, Kim Kunoff, and Cheri Thompson were invaluable. Many members of the Ann Arbor academic and Jewish communities gave freely of their time and insights. My thanks to Michael Brooks, Rabbi Robert Dobrusin, Greg Dowd, Karla Goldman, Rabbi Bob Levy, Lisbeth and Mike Fried, Ed Rothman, David Shtulman, Arland Thornton, and Alford Young. The Chervin, Eichner-Portnoy, Levin, Helton-Kaplan, and Steiner families were wondrously hospitable, and Amanda Fisher taught me how to cook by example.

I was fortunate to also have conversation comrades around the country. Kirsten Fermaglich, Ethan Segal, Ken Waltzer, and Steven Gold hosted me for a guest lecture at Michigan State University in Lansing and offered useful feedback. Caryn Aviv, Tobin Belzer, David Bernat, Simon Bronner, Sergio DellaPergola, Eric Goldstein, Harriet Hartman, Bethamie Horowitz, Debra Kaufman, Shaul Kelner, Helen Kim, Josh Lambert, Noah Leavitt, Rebecca Kobrin, Rachel Kranson, Lori Lefkovitz, Bruce Phillips, Riv-Ellen Prell, Randal Schnoor, Ira M. Sheskin, Ron Simkins, and Jennifer Thompson all contributed in tangible ways. Rabbis Braham David, Ralph Mecklenburger, Chuck Simon, Keith Stern, and Andrew Vogel shared insights about their congregations and movements. Eli Valley and Paul Golin enriched the text. Stuart Blumberg and Rena Joy Blumberg Olshansky generously shared their thoughts about

Keeping the Faith. Many more people were helpful and are named in the chapter notes.

If one has to leave Ann Arbor, joining folks at Brandeis University in Waltham, Massachusetts, was a good move. Jonathan D. Sarna's expertise and close reading of an early draft of the whole manuscript resulted in many improvements. My thanks to Len Saxe for reviewing everything having to do with Birthright and to all of my colleagues at the Cohen Center for Modern Jewish Studies, especially Ellie Aitan, Matt Boxer, Fern Chertok, Deborah Grant, Charles Kadushin, Annette Koren, Daniel Parmer, Amy Sales, Ted Sasson, Michelle Shain, and Emily Sigalow. I am immensely grateful to Shulamit Reinharz for her unflinching support and trailblazing leadership at the Hadassah-Brandeis Institute. Sylvia Barack Fishman, Michelle Cove, Lisa Fishbayn Joffe, Joanna Michlic, and Debbie Olins made my experience there all the more rewarding. I was lucky to overlap at HBI with Anne Lapidus Lerner, Nina Lichtenstein, and Rivka Neriya-Ben Shahar. Joyce Antler, a stalwart mentor, invited me to teach in the American Studies program, affording me the opportunity to add Steve Whitfield and Tom Doherty to my list of esteemed colleagues. Ellen Smith assisted me with a wayward *yad*. Diverse groups of Brandeis students were among the first to hear and react to some of my findings.

The Barth, Jawitz-Leikind, and Katz families made daily life a celebration in Boston. Jared Gollob provided astute feedback on an original draft of the introduction, and David Miller made the choicest dinner plans during the final revisions. David Kaplan made me feel like "one of the guys" at the Federation of Jewish Men's Club retreat. The Inner Strength and JP Centre Yoga communities challenged me to breathe deeply, surrender, and find my edge, which were equally beneficial off the mat as on it.

Five members of my family stayed closest to me during this lengthy project. My cousin Nancy, *z"l*, validated my feelings and choices. I will carry her *joie de vivre* with me for the rest of my days. My father always asked how my work was going and made me laugh with his comment, "Gender shmender, as long as you love your mother." My mother's love gave me the strength to move to Michigan as a single parent, and my love for her eased my way back to Boston. My stepfather cheered through a Michigan-Wisconsin football game in the "Big House" and made sure my one-hundred-year-old house still stood when I returned to it. Shira, my amazing daughter, crisscrossed the country with me, switched schools, made new friends, and convinced me that bringing home a kitten from the Ann Arbor farmer's market was a mitzvah. She inspired me to be the best mother and teacher-scholar I could—even when she really wished I'd stop writing, produce a sibling for her, and open a gelato store. Hopefully by the time she is an adult embarking on her own life, women and men will be truly equal partners.

Marrying Out

Introduction

Of Mice and *Menschen*

In every bit of honest writing in the world there is a base theme.
Try to understand men; if you understand each other you will be
kind to each other. Knowing a man never leads to hate and nearly
always leads to love. There is writing promoting social change,
writing punishing injustice, writing in celebration of heroism,
but always that base theme. Try to understand each other.

—John Steinbeck

A Jewish boy comes home from school and tells his mother he's been
given a part in the school play. "Wonderful. What part is it?" the mother
asks. The boy says, "I play the part of the Jewish husband." The mother
scowls and says, "Go back and tell the teacher you want a speaking part."[1]
This joke may play on an old stereotype about passive Jewish men and
domineering Jewish mothers, but it also illustrates the current argument
regarding intermarriage in America that Jewish husbands are ambivalent about Judaism and less proactively vocal than their Christian wives
about how children will be raised.[2] According to one sociologist, "Intermarried men who have negative feelings about Jews and Jewishness
are the 'weak link' in contemporary American Jewish life."[3] The fact is
that the majority of American Jews do not report that religion is "very
important" to them, yet intermarried Jewish men continue to be singled
out as having the least interest.[4] One need only think of the scene from
the television show *Sex and the City,* in which Jewish Harry Goldenblatt
peers around Jew-by-choice Charlotte York to watch televised baseball

Harry Goldenblatt (Evan Handler) and Charlotte York (Kristin Davis)
in *Sex and the City,* the movie (2008). *New Line Cinema/
The Kobal Collection/Craig Blankenhorn.*

as she earnestly recites the blessings for Shabbat. Her retort, "I gave up
Christ for you and you can't even give up the Mets?" says it all.[5] That
scene, and more importantly, what it implies, is popular culture's version
of what some social scientists contend about this issue. One must listen
to men's voices and hear their stories, however, to truly understand them.

Throughout the twentieth century, rabbis and other Jews deeply
involved in Jewish life commonly believed that Jewish men who intermarried were "lost" to the Jewish community. Some Jewish advocates
assumed that those who intermarried had essentially forsaken their
Jewishness; their Jewish identity was no longer important to them and
would never be again. The 1997 statement made by Alan Dershowitz,
distinguished law professor and Jewish activist, illustrates this perception. In his book *The Vanishing American Jew* he wrote, "A decision by a
young Jewish man or woman to marry a non-Jew is generally a reflection
of a well-established reality that their Jewishness is not all that central to
their identity."[6] The 2009 ad campaign in Israel urging Israelis to report

Diaspora Jews they feared were in danger of assimilation, including the intermarried, similarly reveals that the equation of intermarriage with loss to the Jewish people is not limited to the United States. Los Angeles writer Esther Kustanowitz condemned the use of missing-person signs in this advertising blitz because of the association with 9/11: "Invoking that image to refer to people who are not dead, but presumed 'lost to Judaism' because they 'married out,' seems somewhat inappropriate," Kustanowitz wrote.[7] The title for this introductory chapter, "Of Mice and *Menschen*," is borrowed from John Steinbeck's novel *Of Mice and Men* (1937), which was frequently the target of censors for what critics claimed was racist, sexist, violent, and vulgar text. Although intermarried Jewish men have not been banned from participating in organized Jewish life, prevailing assumptions—that their Judaism is not particularly important to them and that they play little role in shaping their families' spiritual lives—likewise threaten to silence their actual experiences.

That men who intermarried could maintain vibrant Jewish identities or that their Jewishness might even deepen during their lifetimes has been persistently beyond belief. Next to the fate of Israel, "continuity" is the number one concern in the organized American Jewish community and has been for at least the past two decades. The rising rates of intermarriage over the twentieth and twenty-first centuries in America seem to suggest that total assimilation draws nearer with every passing decade as fewer and fewer Jews are marrying fellows Jews.[8] The numbers alone warrant concern about the future of American Jewry. Two assumptions color these concerns: that an intermarried Jew becomes fully assimilated into the majority Christian population, religion, and culture; and that an intermarried Jew will not raise Jewish children. However, in recent years research about intermarried Jewish men and women has begun to undermine these assumptions. Nevertheless, they continue to follow Jewish men who intermarry, which make their experiences all the more important to understand.

Heretofore, intermarried Jewish men have only been the subjects of interest to sociologists, celebrity biographers, journalists, and mass media producers. There are brief references to Hollywood giants who married non-Jewish women, a slew of fictional representations on tele-

Marc Mezvinsky and Chelsea Clinton with their *ketubah* in Rhinebeck, New York (July 31, 2010). Rabbi James Ponet and Methodist Rev. William Shillady co-officiated the ceremony. *Genvieve de Manio Photography.*

vision and the silver screen, and several sociological studies illustrating a gender imbalance in religious and communal life. The tabloids cover interfaith romance as a hot topic, informing us that Jared Kushner, an Orthodox Jew, married heiress Ivanka Trump, who converted to Judaism shortly before they wed in 2009.[9] The summer 2010 nuptials between Marc Mezvinsky and former first daughter Chelsea Clinton similarly garnered attention in the national media and the Jewish community; likewise the summer 2011 marriages of David Lauren to Lauren Bush (niece and granddaughter of two former presidents) and of Vice President Joe Biden's daughter Ashley to Howard Krein in the spring of 2012.[10]

Edwin Schlossberg with his fiancée Caroline Kennedy, her brother John F. Kennedy, Jr. and her uncle Ted Kennedy departing wedding rehearsal at Our Lady of Victory Church in Centreville, Massachusetts, July 18, 1986, the day before he wed. *United Press International.*

These four examples indicate the extent to which Jewish men have become eligible husband material in the most upper echelons of American society. Moreover, the inclusion of Judaism in the wedding ceremonies (including rabbinic co-officiants for Clinton and Biden) suggests that a lot has changed since Edwin Schlossberg wed Caroline Kennedy in 1986, when there was no mention of his faith.[11] Even reality television has joined the interfaith act. The final episode of *The Bachelorette* that aired in August 2011 filmed J. P. Rosenbaum proposing to Ashley Hebert and her accepting.[12] Despite the plethora of popular-culture examples, little is actually known about the hearts and minds of intermarried Jewish men. A true void exists when it comes to contemporary historical analysis of intermarried Jewish men and fathers. This book seeks to share their narratives.

This qualitative look at intermarriage combines a study of ethnicity and religion with an analysis of gender to uncover the meaning of cross-religious marriage to and for Jewish men. Although statistical evidence is useful in gaining a general sense for how widespread the practice of marriage between groups became over time and whether individuals who intermarried followed certain behaviors such as synagogue or church attendance, a quantitative analysis that focuses on the rate of intermarriage tells us little about the actual lives of those men (and women) who intermarried and leaves many questions unanswered about the cultural significance of their actions. As historian Virginia Yans-McLaughlin writes in her work on Italians, "Census and statistical data inform us of structure, not content."[13] By asking men, "What does being an intermarried Jewish father mean to you?"—not "How Jewish are you?"—this study considers the "invention of ethnicity." It looks at intermarriage and fatherhood as historical processes during which men defined and redefined their own Jewish identity, that is, the ways in which they belonged to an ethnic or religious group, as well as how others perceived them as belonging.[14] Recognizing the fluidity of ethnicity, the openness of American society, and the role of personal choice, a man's "ethnic identity" is described and analyzed as his subjective orientation toward his Jewish religious origins.[15]

Intermarried men's identities bring to light a uniquely Jewish mystique. American masculinity is a culturally created concept that people apply to men and their role in society. Although the specifics tied to what makes a man masculine may change over time and generations, some expressions seem to have particular staying power—for example, "Winning isn't everything, it's the only thing," and "Nice guys finish last."[16] These and similar statements allude to the idea that American men are and should be competitive, both with each other and in general, and that being a "good guy" is not worth striving for because it lacks cultural currency. This junction, between achievement and being a *mensch*, is where a more generic American masculinity clashes with Jewish values, creating in the process what I call the Jewish masculine mystique. Like the women Betty Friedan described in her book *The Feminine Mystique,* Jewish men suffer from an unnamed malady; in their case, however, it stems from competing priorities and communal disenfranchisement rather than overeducated and underutilized minds.[17] Overall, Jewish men must play by the same "rules" as other American men. In the process, there is the risk of forgetting or losing the commandment of *gemilut hasadim* (committing acts of loving-kindness). Yet when talking to Jewish men, it is readily apparent that while they want to get ahead as much as the next guy, they also want to do their portion to help make the world a better place. How should intermarried Jewish men make sense of these supposed traits of masculinity that appear to be at odds with each other? They are adult "nice Jewish boys" grappling with proving themselves as modern American men. This particular conundrum is specific to modern times, and yet earlier historical periods, too, have challenged what it means to be a Jewish man.[18]

I argue in this book that intermarried Jewish men offer insight into a form of gendered ethnicity stemming from their religious and cultural heritage that increases their ability to raise Jewish children equally effectively as intermarried Jewish women. When Jewish men marry Christian women, their Jewish identities are cast into high relief. The process of becoming fathers further accentuates manifestations of their Jewishness. Hence the dual experiences of intermarriage and fatherhood interact in such a way as to foreground the cultural meaning of Jewish identity and gender. The dynamic relationship between intermarriage and fatherhood illuminates a new concept of American Jewish identity in the twenty-first century that is intimately tied to gender perceptions and roles. Understanding intermarried Jewish men's experiences as husbands and fathers is a key step toward establishing gender equality, so that both sexes may finally live up to their full potential as human beings. Jewish husbands are not alone navigating manhood and fatherhood within the broader American context.

Intermarried Jewish men's struggle to shape their own sense of fatherhood is part of the larger ongoing movement in America to encourage men to become more involved parents. On Father's Day 2009, President Barack Obama launched a national dialogue about fatherhood. In a public service announcement (PSA) by the Ad Council and the

who are you spending
your quality time with?

Be a dad.

**National
Fatherhood
Initiative®**

www.fatherhood.org

Department of Health and Human Services Administration for Children and Families, he stated, "Things can get busy, and sometimes we all fall short, but the smallest moments can have the biggest impact on a child's life. Take time to be a dad today."[19] Based on research about the ramifications of absent fathers in children's lives, whether due to work schedules, divorce, or incarceration, the billboards and PSAs all equated manhood with involved fatherhood. While Obama emphasized "Take time to be a dad today," the message on billboards and subsequent PSAs by the National Fatherhood Initiative became "It takes a man to be a dad." The biological is apparent in the double message, yet the relationship between robust masculinity and active fathering is clearly the intended emphasis. Breadwinning and its related obligations bind men across race and class, as depicted by other ads showing dads of all colors taking time to participate in their children's lives. The president's communication about Father's Day 2010 reiterated the importance of fathers' involvement in their children's lives. The subject was "The Most Important Job," and President Obama made explicit the connection between men's financial roles and fatherhood. He acknowledged that "no government can fill the role that fathers play for our children . . . what we can do is try to support fathers who are willing to step up and fulfill their responsibilities as parents, partners and *providers*" (emphasis mine).[20]

METHODOLOGY

This book aims to contribute to a topic that has heretofore received sparse attention from historians, sociologists, and Jewish studies scholars by looking at the intersection between religion and gender in the post–World War II period, 1945 to present, through the lens of a cohort of intermarried Jewish men. Some of the questions it investigates include: How do intermarried men feel about being Jewish, what does Judaism mean to them, and how have both their feelings and relationship to Judaism changed over time? What is the relationship between how men envision fatherhood and self-identify as Jews? How did intermarriage influence

(*facing*) Public service announcement by the National Fatherhood Initiative. *National Fatherhood Initiative/Vincent DiCaro.*

their ethno-religious identities? Lastly, what roles did Jewish men play in shaping their families' spiritual lives? It is a multigenerational study that interweaves traditional archival research with fifty-four in-depth oral history interviews: forty-one interviews with born-Jewish men who married women who were not "born Jewish," some of whom have since become Jews-by-choice, and thirteen interviews with their wives. It is common for people to sometimes mistake qualitative research for having "too small a sample to be representative," but that is not the intention here. This sample does not strive to be random or representative, but rather selectively sheds light on the complex histories of some Jewish men who intermarried. This sample size is large enough, however, to illustrate some common experiences (patterns) among men who intermarried and the meanings these experiences generated at varied points across nearly sixty years. Drawn from an academic community, these men are in the vanguard of intermarriage illustrating a variety of responses to the "dual pressures of ethnicity and intellectualism," as sociologist Milton Gordon wrote in *Assimilation in American Life: The Role of Race, Religion, and National Origins* (1964). This particular sample suggests that previous theories about marital assimilation insufficiently accounted for the nuances of the social milieu that influence how intermarried Jews live and identify. These intermarried Jewish men characterize what Gordon called the "marginally ethnic intellectual"; "he wears his ethnicity lightly, if not in his own eyes at least in the eyes of the world. Whatever his social psychology, he finds ethnic communality unsatisfactory and takes his friends, and probably even his spouse, where he finds them, so long as they share his fascination with Kafka. . . ."[21] Citing mid-century studies of the academic communities in Champaign-Urbana, Illinois, and New Haven, Connecticut, where Jewish faculty, physicians, and psychoanalysts intermarried extensively, sociologist Marshall Sklare contended that they held to an "Academic Commitment" where "a supernatural deity had no place . . . that man—through understanding the consequences of his actions—can build a better world."[22] This sample of intermarried Jewish men illustrates the dual influences of gender dynamics within their families and of becoming fathers. It also indicates that intermarried Jews in Ann Arbor have considerably less in common with Jews who do not participate in Jewish organizational life at all.

It is important to understand the population that composes this subcommunity. The men who participated in this study represent a spectrum of Jewish identity, from secular to Orthodox. Participation was purely voluntary; there was no incentive or compensation. The majority of men learned about the study through their synagogue or Jewish community center. Approximately a quarter of the men saw the call for participants in either a local monthly publication or the weekly newspaper, and a quarter heard of the study by word of mouth. Because they self-selected, the sample may be skewed toward men with more of an attachment to Judaism or Jewishness than had the sample been randomized. To balance the sample, I conducted snowball sampling by asking participants to suggest someone who was not formally affiliated with any Jewish organization. I conducted all of the interviews personally either in my office or, in a handful of cases, at the participant's place of employment. The interviews lasted an average of seventy-five minutes each and occurred between November 2008 and April 2010. During this period, Michiganians saw the election of the first African American president; the Madoff investment scandal broke; the economic recession deepened, including the federal bailout of two of Detroit's largest automakers; home prices fell; and Pfizer's research center and the original Borders bookstore, both in Ann Arbor, closed. Despite these politically and financially stressful times, study participants showed up for their interviews. In every instance, we were behind closed doors and the men free to speak their minds in absolute privacy. It was not unusual for men to tell me things that they had never uttered aloud before, and more than one commented on the therapeutic effect of the interview process, even joking that I should have a couch in my office. Although some men consented to the use of their actual name, some did not and I respect their wish for privacy. I also found that people are considerably more open about the most intimate details of their personal histories if their real names will not appear in print. With the exception of an illustration caption and reference to a well-known Ann Arbor businessman, I use pseudonyms for all participants to protect confidentiality. The lives of famous intermarried Jewish men, from Eddie Fisher (who wed Elizabeth Taylor) to William Shatner (and his "Irish rose"), are public information and are unique due to their celebrity status, hence I use their actual names.[23]

Although one chapter does discuss celebrities, this book primarily seeks to understand "ordinary" men, non-celebrities whose lives more closely resemble neighbors, family members, and friends.

Intermarriage can be defined in various ways, including interfaith, interethnic, and interracial. Even when a marriage is between two co-religionists, it can still be a form of "intermarriage" for the individuals involved and their families. Consider these combinations in the case of two Jews: Reform and Orthodox, Sephardic and Ashkenazi, former USSR and American, Israeli and American, East Coast and West Coast American.[24] Demographers studying the American Jewish population usually define intermarriage as follows: "An intermarriage is a marriage in which one spouse was born or raised Jewish and currently considers himself/herself Jewish and the other spouse was not born or raised Jewish and does not currently consider himself/herself Jewish."[25] However, none of the extant definitions take into account the role that gender plays in the case of intermarriage or religious conversion nor do they consider the tenacity of Jewishness. Statistically, more women convert to the religion of husbands than husbands convert to the religion of wives. Hence, studying Jewish men who intermarry and Jewish women who intermarry calls for different definitions of "intermarriage" because many more of the men's relationships are what Judaic scholars call "conversionary marriages," between a born Jew and a Jew-by-choice. Most men involved in these marriages and their born-Christian wives who converted, either formally or informally, continue to consider their unions intermarriages. To describe what is a conversionary marriage according to Jewish law as an intermarriage in the everyday sense will be considered problematic by some. Rabbis might even prefer the term "mitzvah marriage." *Halacha* (Jewish law), after all, makes no distinction between in-marriages between two persons born or raised Jewish and marriages involving a born Jew and a born Christian who converted. Just as the Jew-by-choice is to be treated identical to a Jew-by-birth, so too should marriages involving a Jewish convert be considered an in-marriage, many believe. Nevertheless, social scientists do make a distinction between in-marriages and conversionary marriages to study aspects of marital choice and its influence on Jewish behaviors.[26] However, the vast majority of people consider the rabbinic and sociological labels less important than the reality of lived religion and culture. Hence, in this book the term "intermarriage" applies to men who married women born or raised Christian *whether or not they converted later in life.* While I could devise a new term to describe this scenario, it would likely add more confusion than light. So with fair warning to the reader, all of the men and women who participated in this book are intermarried by my definition: based on their religion at birth.

Marriage, too, can be defined several different ways: between a man and a woman, between two men, and between two women. I focused my research on heterosexual couples to be able to compare this study of intermarried men with my previous study of intermarried women that consisted of male-female unions sanctioned by U.S. law. Interfaith gay and lesbian partnerships deserve scholarly attention and I hope will be the focus of future studies. Research will yield significant findings, for example, about how the gender of the Jew in a same-sex couple influences the religious life of a family and about transmission of Jewish identity to children. A staff member of Keshet, an organization working for the full inclusion of lesbian, gay, bisexual, and transgender Jews in Jewish life, spontaneously asked me to hold a sign when I marched in the 2013 Boston Pride Parade wearing a T-shirt with the word "Shalom" on the front. The sign said, "My son is gay and single." The word "gay" was spelled with letters emulating Hebrew. The smiles and shouts from parade onlookers, including "Where is he?" "What's his number?" "I'm a doctor!" "Here's a lawyer for him!" suggested three things: Jewish mothers are expected to meddle in their sons' romantic lives, homosexual Jewish men are in demand, and the imperative of professional success cuts across sexual orientation. Although this book is about heterosexual couples, my commitment to equal rights includes advocating that LGBT couples are indeed part of the Jewish intermarriage story in America that must be told.

Most of the marriages described in these pages were first marriages, although some were not, and I acknowledge these unions accordingly. Scholars have found that while there are several factors that contribute to a first intermarriage, namely biological sex, denominational family background, religious education, age, and academic attainment, only two (academic attainment and age) are significantly related to intermarriage in remarriage. According to the authors of "Exogamy in First Marriages and Remarriages," Jews' higher academic attainment increased the likelihood of in-marriage in first marriage, but out-marriage in remarriage.[27] I refer to this groundbreaking work when it pertains to a particular Jewish man's intermarriage yet do not delve into deep discussion about the man's marital history. My goal is to analyze this cohort of intermarried Jewish men and what it can tell us about gendered ethnicity; hence, whether the intermarriage represents the man's first marriage or not is less relevant for me than it would be for someone writing a definitive history of Jewish men who intermarry.

WHY STUDY SMALL MIDWESTERN CITY DWELLERS?

The conceptual framework for this study of Jewish men takes a regional approach to a universal theory. That is, although the intermarried men I interviewed all lived in one location at the time I met them, Ann Arbor, this particular locale holds many things in common with similar university towns across the United States. The Kerrytown shops, Main Street, State Street, and South University business districts are all within walking distance of the university's central campus, creating a seamless urban landscape blending city and academic life. Ann Arbor has a large number of PhDs and professional degrees in the population; it was named the second most educated city by *U.S. News and World Report* in 2011.[28] As such it represents an ideal case study to test Gordon's hypothesis that ethnic intellectuals interact in patterned ways so as to form a subcommunity, connected to other subcommunities by the concept of "transferability"; the sum of the subcommunities, interlaced by national institutions and organizations, constitutes a subsociety.[29] Ann Arbor is not unique, however, because it shares qualities with other similar university "towns," such as Boulder, Colorado; Madison, Wisconsin; and Berkeley, California. Yet it must also be understood as an anomaly within the state of Michigan. Some people who live in Ann Arbor describe it as "28.7 square miles surrounded by reality." While many people move to Ann Arbor to attend school or to advance careers, significantly more leave Michigan permanently, especially during economically depressed times. Between 2001 and 2009, outmigration cost

Michigan 465,000 people.[30] Detroit's population had decreased by 25 percent since the 2000 census.[31] In 2013, with only 700,000 residents remaining of the over 1.8 million in the 1950s, Detroit became the largest city in U.S. history to file for bankruptcy protection.[32]

In addition to the demographic changes, Ann Arbor is characterized by different socioeconomic, political, religious, and cultural terms than Michigan as a whole. In 2009, estimated median household incomes in Ann Arbor were about five thousand dollars more than in Michigan generally, and estimated median house or condo values were twice as much.[33] Approximately the same amount of whites and Hispanics live in Ann Arbor (72 percent and 3 percent, respectively) as in Michigan overall (77 percent and 4 percent). But there are significantly more Asians in Ann Arbor, 14 percent compared to 2 percent, and half as many blacks. There are also more mixed-race individuals in Ann Arbor.[34] Politically, Ann Arbor went from being a Republican bastion in the 1960s to heavily Democratic by the 1990s. Mayor Bill Brown, a Republican stalwart, was in office for six terms (1945–1957). An important change in electoral policy in 1969 gave out-of-state students the right to vote in local elections, initiating what some have called the Revolution: Robert J. Harris, a University of Michigan law professor and Jewish Democrat won the mayoral position, Robert Faber won the Second Ward City Council seat by a landslide along with four other Democrats, making a solid majority for the first time in thirty years. The counterculture, civil rights, and anti-war movements made a major presence in Ann Arbor, where the first meetings of the Students for a Democratic Society occurred in 1960 and the first U.S. teach-in against the Vietnam War in 1965.[35] A weeklong confrontation in June 1969 between University of Michigan students, administrators, and police became known as the "South U Riots." The White Panther Party, SDS, and Rent Strike Committee demanded that South University Street be made into a pedestrian mall for the city's youth and that the police be put under "Community Control so the Fascist Pigs won't continue to run amuck." University president Robben Fleming interceded and facilitated communication between young Ann Arborites and those with badges and nightsticks, allowing tensions to dissipate. "Reefer madness" contributed to the passing in 1972 of the Marijuana Ordinance that made use of marijuana a minor

civil infraction rather than a criminal offense, catalyzing an annual pot
rally called the Hash Bash on the University of Michigan Diag that still
draws thousands of people.[36] The Human Rights Party, a left-wing political party, championed a city-wide anti-discrimination ordinance, banning discrimination based on race, national origin, sex, age, religion, and
eventually adding sexual orientation, the first of its kind in Michigan.[37]
The transformation from a conservative city to a liberal college town fostered an atmosphere of cultural acceptance where a variety of religions
flourished. Illustrating the spiritual openness and diversity, the Ann
Arbor guide to area churches, synagogues, and religious fellowships lists
over a hundred houses of worship in Ann Arbor, including Apostolic,
Assemblies of God, Baha'i, Baptist, Buddhist, Catholic, Christian Science, Church of Jesus Christ Latter-Day Saints (Mormon), Congregational, Episcopal, Greek Orthodox, Hindu, Jehovah's Witness, Jewish,
Lutheran, Mennonite, Methodist, Muslim, Neopagan Druids, Pentecos-
tal, Presbyterian, Society of Friends (Quaker), Seventh-Day Adventist,
Unitarian Universalist, and United Church of Christ, among others.
Some meet in buildings designed for religious purposes; others meet
everywhere from coffee shops to community centers.[38]

While Detroit has a larger Jewish population (estimated to be 72,000
individuals living in 30,000 households) than Ann Arbor and was ranked
in 2005 as the twenty-first largest Jewish community in the nation, it
actually represents a smaller percentage of the Greater Detroit population—just 2 percent. By 2010, the number of Jews in the Detroit area had
decreased by 5,000, and it became the twenty-third largest Jewish community in the United States; however, the Jewish households held steady
at 1.9 percent of the total Detroit population.[39] Ann Arbor has a relatively
large Jewish population for a small city. In 2000, the total population
numbered just over 114,000 people including 40,000 students, with
slightly more females than males.[40] It is only the sixth largest in Michigan after Detroit, Grand Rapids, Warren, Sterling Heights, Lansing, and
Flint, according to the 2010 census.[41] David Shtulman, executive director of the Jewish Federation of Washtenaw County, estimates the Jewish population to be approximately 7,000–8,000 individuals, 7 percent
of the total population in the city. This figure does not include students;
the University of Michigan ranks high among public institutions for

having the highest number of Jewish students and a robust Hillel. Many of the people currently living in Ann Arbor are not originally from here; they come because of some connection to the university, expecting to leave. There is a "transient community attitude"; however, lots of people fall in love with Ann Arbor and stay. There are 1,400 affiliated families: approximately 700 at Temple Beth Emeth; 400 at Congregation Beth Israel; 75–100 at Chabad House/Orthodox Minyan, whose imposing building on Hill Street houses a mikvah and hints at the many religious services and learning opportunities offered; 75–100 Reconstructionist; and 75–100 Jewish Cultural Society. There are numerous Israelis who live in the community, too, many returning to Israel after spending some time at the university. Shtulman believes that the number of affiliated families is not higher because many Jews do not join anywhere because they do not have roots here, whereas in Detroit they do. Detroit is "a whole other world."[42] Transience is a distinctive characteristic of Ann Arbor, due in part to its shifting population of students, academics, and professionals, in contrast to suburban Detroit with its multigenerational communities. Eighty-eight percent of the Jewish population in the Detroit metropolitan area resided there for twenty years or more.[43] It is possible that there are "hidden *yidden*" in Ann Arbor, Jews who prefer to remain under the communal radar, perhaps due to previous experiences with antisemitism elsewhere in the United States.[44]

The greater Jewish to non-Jewish ratio in Ann Arbor contributes to the communal feeling in a city where one is likely to run into someone from shul at Hiller's supermarket or at Zingerman's deli, which *Saveur* magazine named as having the best rye bread in America.[45] The Jewish circles in Ann Arbor overlap each other, just as the organizational tables stand shoulder to shoulder at the annual "Apples and Honey" event at the Jewish Community Center. Some Jews have affiliations with multiple Jewish congregations or have children who attend the Hebrew Day School, or both. HDS, whose total enrollment hovers around eighty students, is located within the single-level cinder-block JCC building, a former public elementary school, on Birch Hollow Drive.[46] Having only one Jewish day school fosters mingling among Ann Arbor Jews, secular to Orthodox. The school's policy that eligible "students come from families where *either parent is Jewish*" (emphasis mine) speaks to its inclusiveness and sensitivity with respect to gender.[47] One respondent explained, "Ann Arbor's a small community so you know other Jews in the community... either by knowing them or at least being familiar with them."[48] Morton Langfeld, who returned to Ann Arbor after law school and intermarried in 2008, acknowledged the lack of anonymity and remarked, "Everybody knows each other."[49] This sense of knowing other Jews, either personally or indirectly, contributes to intermarried men's awareness of, if not involvement in, Jewish communal events.

Intermarriage may be the most significant Jewish communal distinction between Ann Arbor and Detroit. In the 2005 *Detroit Jewish Population Study*, demographer Ira M. Sheskin found that the couples intermarriage rate in Detroit was 16 percent and the individual rate just 9 percent, the fourth lowest of about fifty-five comparison Jewish communities.[50] A 2010 study showed Detroit in the same place comparatively.[51] Although there is no comparable quantitative study about the Jewish population in Ann Arbor, the popular understanding is that the intermarriage rate there is very high. Certainly among the participants in my study most believed that being intermarried was commonplace, if not normative, in this community. Stuart Kamden, who intermarried in 1976, noted that his Jewish friends from high school in New England almost all eventually married Jewish women, while almost all of his friends in Ann Arbor were intermarried. "So," Stuart remarked, "the concept of being intermarried in Ann Arbor is a very different concept than it might be elsewhere."[52] He speculated that there are probably more intermarried than non-intermarried people there. Morton Langfeld believes that the freedom he experienced in Ann Arbor contributed to him and his three siblings intermarrying: "If we would have been in West Bloomfield," where the "big city Jews lived, yeah ... I think that would have made us all, you know, marry within."[53] Groundbreaking research examining the effects of Jewish community size on Jewish identity by sociologist Matthew Boxer contends that parents in small Jewish communities more readily accept that their children will develop close social relationships with non-Jews, including intermarriage.[54] Even without statistically significant data about intermarriage in Ann Arbor, people who live there believe that the open marital environment is something missing in the Detroit suburbs.

Episcopal cross and Star of David sculptures outside of Temple Beth Emeth
and St. Clare's Church. *Photo by author.*

Many of the respondents commented on what they believed to be
the characteristics of Ann Arbor that contributed to their intermarriage experiences. These characteristics are likely to be found in other
communities with similar Jewish-general population ratios, progressive
politics, and a thriving intellectual milieu. As respondent Larry Rush
described, "Ann Arbor is very much built around the university. Any
time you have a university, you're gonna have a lot of eggheads. Any
time you have a lot of eggheads, you're gonna have a lot of Jews in the
group. I think what binds the Jewish community together here more
than anything else is the university, is the life of the mind . . . you've got
a bunch of academics."[55] Although some, but not all, of the participants

in this study were professional academics, those who were not academics were likely influenced by living among them. Ben Levine, a physician with an academic appointment who intermarried in 1969, commented, "I think here in Ann Arbor, since we're a university community, people are very accepting about whatever you do within reason."[56] Lauren Apteker described the sense of cosmopolitanism that Ann Arbor possesses: "It's less dominated by one ethnic group.... Because of the university, there's much more of an international kind of perspective."[57] For someone who moved to Ann Arbor at age seven in the 1960s, there was very little Jewish youth group programming. As a result, Gary Brodin, who had previously attended an Orthodox day school in Miami, did not socialize with other Jewish children his own age, leading to a sense of isolation.[58] That experience was repeated by the son of one of the respondents who attended a public school and confided to his dad that some kids at the public elementary school were beating up Jewish kids. When the father concluded that his son would also get beat up, the son corrected him: "No, they don't know I'm Jewish."[59] Attendance at a multicultural public school meant that the son could "pass" for Christian to avoid discrimination. Allan Benjamin had lived in Ann Arbor for decades without participating in the local Jewish community, until he met his future wife.[60] What Ann Arbor may have lacked in terms of ecumenical awareness in the 1970s and 1980s, it more than made up for in the 1990s with the creation of Genesis, which teamed up a Jewish Reform congregation with a Protestant Episcopal one. Mark Entennman described his and his wife's reactions: "We were driving down Packard Street and saw an Episcopal church with a Jewish synagogue in the same building and said, 'How cool is this?'"[61] The tall cross and Star of David sculptures outside apparently resonated with their then-interfaith marriage (she subsequently converted to Judaism).

Many of the men drew distinctions between Ann Arbor and the large suburban Jewish community forty-five minutes to the northeast. They specifically contrasted the importance of wealth and property ownership, which signaled different types of Jews. Where you lived mattered and indicated a range of values—personal, cultural, and political. According to Michael Bellow, for example, "A Jew from West Bloomfield is a different kind of Jew." Admitting that this statement was prejudicial,

Bellow explained that in the suburbs Jews were wealthier; their homes were more grandiose, and their Jewish congregations highlighted the significance of deep pockets by putting donors' names on doors and stained glass windows. In contrast, his congregation in Ann Arbor did not put donors' names on plaques; the lay leadership was "more interested in having everybody participate in our service . . . even if they can't afford the dues. . . ."[62] His subjective perspective contends that a congregation that draws attention to wealthy people also draws attention, by default, to those with less, thus creating what he described as socioeconomic class distinctions. Having visited some of the suburban congregations, Bellows reflected how he felt out of place, awkward: "Knowing I would never be a big contributor, I feel kind of an outsider."[63] Although there may in fact be more wealthy Jews living in the northwest suburbs, in truth one must likewise have considerable means to live in Ann Arbor, where rent can equal that in Boston (I write from personal experience). Walter Chatham thought West Bloomfield Jews were "cliquish," whereas Ann Arbor Jews were not because the community was more transient.[64] Yet for all its transience, the Ann Arbor Jewish community can feel provincial to someone who was born there, moved away to live in a major city such as Atlanta, and then moved back. Provincial, however, did not mean unprogressive. Felix Garrison, born in 1950, moved to Ann Arbor when he was twelve and has lived there ever since; he believed that he would not feel comfortable in a politically conservative Jewish community. Comparing Ann Arbor with Bloomfield Hills, Garrison explained that he felt at home in the Ann Arbor Jewish community in part because the rabbis there are members of Rabbis for Human Rights, a group that acts to protect the human rights of all people.[65]

Increasingly, as the twentieth century came to an end and the twenty-first century began, the cultural diversity in Ann Arbor that was a by-product of inhabitants' mobility contributed to a greater appreciation for religious multiculturalism. The "new Jew cool" was part of that trend.[66] Jewish Americans who were part of generation X (born between 1964 and 1977), like other so-called hyphenated Americans, could better appreciate their heritage and also be better appreciated by their non-Jewish neighbors. As Paul Chazen described, Ann Arbor was much like the well-known "Happy Valley" of Western Massachusetts. There were

many educated people who had come to Ann Arbor from someplace
else, contributing to an environment not just tolerant of difference but
actually interested in it. Paul's example illustrates his point: "Oh, you're
Baha'i? I never met a Baha'i person. That's really cool. What do you do?"[67]
Rather than being threatened by people who were different, including
Jews, Ann Arborites were drawn to the diversity. The benefits of living in
a religiously diverse community extended from interfaith couples to interracial couples and same-sex couples. Morris Aker, who moved to Ann
Arbor in 1951 and taught social science at the university there, described
how his relationships with clergy of different faiths over the years enhanced his appreciation for Judaism. He credited Ann Arbor with being
a community where the different houses of worship were less concerned
with whether someone joined them or went somewhere else and more
interested in helping the person find what was right for him (or her).[68]

"JEWPANESE"

A book about Jewish men and intermarriage would be incomplete without some modicum of discussion about men who marry Asian women.
Couples consisting of Jewish men and Asian women have received a fair
amount of media attention in the recent past. One of the most notable,
perhaps, was the May 2012 nuptials between Facebook founder Mark
Zuckerberg and Priscilla Chan, a Chinese American, the day after his
company had its initial public stock offering.[69] Although none of the
men who participated in my study married Asian women, this particular
combination deserves more scholarly attention. Nationally, interracial
marriage has reached an unprecedented high: 15.1 percent of new (2010)
U.S. marriages, according to a Pew Research Center study published in
2012, more than double the 7 percent in 1980. Asians intermarried the
most, and Asian women intermarry significantly more than Asian men,
36 percent compared to 17 percent.[70] This fact might help explain why
there seem to be more Jewish male–Asian female couples than Jewish
female–Asian male couples. High-profile marriages such as Zuckerberg's
cause angst in the organized Jewish community, with negative assumptions about his commitment to Judaism based on his decision to intermarry. "How did we lose him?" asks Rabbi Dana Evan Kaplan in the

Mark Zuckerberg and Priscilla Chan (AP photo/Facebook).
Noah Kalina Photography.

Forward days after the wedding.[71] The gendered undertone of the article
smacks of judgment against intermarried Jewish men and pays no heed
to Zuckerberg's apparent practice of *tikkun olam* through combating
cyberhate and creating the "Share Life" online tool that facilitates organ
donation.[72] Moreover, Zuckerberg was the nation's second-biggest charitable donor in 2012, suggesting that he understands the commandment
of *tzedakah* (justice or righteousness traditionally manifested by acts
of charity).[73] Considering that Jewish identity, connection, and observance are fluid and can change over the life course, it remains to be seen
whether, how, and to what extent he maintains and transmits his Jewish
heritage to any future children. For now, the Zuckerberg-Chan couple
debunks the stereotype of the Jewish man who likes Asian women because he thinks they are demure and submissive.[74] Chan kept her own
name, has a career in medicine, and was influential in Facebook's addition of the organ-donation tool.[75]

Highlighting Jewish-Asian intermarriage in the mainstream press, the article "Orthodox Paradox" by Harvard law professor Noah Feldman appeared in the *New York Times Magazine* in July 2007. Feldman described attending his tenth high school reunion at Maimonides, a modern Orthodox day school in Brookline, Massachusetts, with his Korean American fiancée. A group photograph was taken including them; when the alumni newsletter was circulated, however, they were not included in the photograph chosen for publication.[76] Subsequently, Feldman sent biographical updates about his marriage and the birth of his children to the school's alumni director for inclusion in the "Mazal Tov" section of the alumni newsletter. None of his joyous news was printed. Feldman used this non-recognition as a framework for explicating the inherent challenge of "reconciling the vastly disparate values of tradition and modernity."[77] His article stirred controversy, prompting angry responses from the Orthodox Union, the chancellor and former president of Yeshiva University, and many readers.[78] Ultimately, what is pertinent here is that Feldman did *not* abandon Judaism. In his words, "I have tried in my own imperfect way to live up to the values that the school taught me, expressing my respect and love for the wisdom of the tradition while trying to reconcile Jewish faith with scholarship and engagement in the public sphere. As a result, I have not felt myself to have rejected my upbringing, even when some others imagine me to have done so by virtue of my marriage."[79] For scholars and Jewish parents alike who advocate that formal Jewish learning is the best bulwark against intermarriage, Feldman's piece drew attention to the fact that even a dozen years spent earning a modern Orthodox education cannot necessarily prevent a Jewish man from intermarrying. Jewish education aside, it remains to be seen whether the long-term effects of social media, JDate in particular, will decrease the overall rate of Jewish intermarriage or influence the rate at which men or women intermarry. Certainly any tools that enable Jews to meet each other increase the chances of them falling in love, but none ensures this outcome any more than a weather prediction guarantees sunshine.[80]

As of yet, no systematic quantitative study exists focusing solely on marital statistics and personal dynamics between Jewish men and Asian women. However, the 2011 *Forward* headline subtitle "New Study

Suggests That Asian-Jewish Families May Be Likely to Raise Jewish Children" is very telling. Sociologists Noah Leavitt and Helen Kim interviewed thirty-seven Asian-Jewish couples in New York City, Philadelphia, and California, ranging from Reform to Orthodox affiliation. Their qualitative study found that all of the couples were "raising children with some element of Judaism" and that less than three were incorporating another religion in addition to Judaism.[81] Although suggestive rather than conclusive, Leavitt and Kim's findings are pioneering because of their focus on religion; previous scholarship on intermarriage and Asian Americans concentrated on racial and ethnic differences between partners. Most significant, from my perspective, is the gender element in their study that reinforces the findings in both of my books on intermarriage. According to Leavitt and Kim, "Most male participants commented that raising children in a Jewish household is a priority for their Jewish wives" and that some Asian women contemplate how converting to Judaism will contribute to a common religion because they regard their children as Jewish.[82] Kim reflected on her personal experience: "It's easy for me to deliver the Jewish stuff as a parent [to our son] because . . . part of me always felt culturally Jewish, and to some extent drawn to Judaism as a religion."[83] Feeling culturally Jewish may reflect the commonalties between Jewish and Asian cultures, such as emphases on academic achievement and honoring one's parents. Her comment about Judaism's appeal is not atypical among non-Jewish women who marry Jewish men.

The phenomenon of Jewish-Asian couples raising Jewish children exists regardless of whether the wife is Chinese, Japanese, Korean, or Thai. While the excerpt from Yale Law School professor and author Amy Chua's book *Battle Hymn of the Tiger Mother* reprinted in the *Wall Street Journal* focused on "Why Chinese Mothers Are Superior," the parenting backstory is that she and her Jewish husband are raising Jewish children.[84] Chua, who was raised Catholic by a Protestant father and a Buddhist mother, asserted long before her parenting memoir was published that while her children are fluent in Chinese, they are Jewish.[85] Chua's husband, Jed Rubenfeld, may play a less dominant role in parenting than his Asian wife, but the children's religious identity stems from him. Although they may share parenting responsibilities, the fact that Rubenfeld took himself out of the memoir left Chua as the parent-in-chief, much to the chagrin of some Jewish mothers who castigated her in the ethnic press.[86] Scholars Leavitt and Kim, who is Korean American, did not find "tiger moms" like Amy Chua (who enforces a policy consisting of no play dates, no sleepovers, no television, hours of daily music practice, and demanding academic excellence). Reflecting on her own upbringing, however, Kim admitted that cultural transmission to children is a possibility.[87] Perhaps though, as the above examples illustrate, marrying someone who is ethnically different adds flavor to the intercultural relationship without diminishing the potency of Jewish religiosity.

Capitalizing on the idea that mixing cultures produces a tasty hybrid, entrepreneurs Eddie Scher and Heidi Chien launched their own line of bottled goods. "What do you name a sauce produced by a Chinese girl and a Jewish boy? Soy Vay, of course!"[88] Scher and Chien began making these all-natural, kosher sauces, marinades, and dressings in 1982. The Soy Vay website makes clear that their products are certified kosher by the Orthodox Union. The name "Soy Vay" is printed in both Hebrew-stylized letters and Chinese characters on the bottles. Scher explained in a *San Diego Jewish Press* article, "She was 'soy'; I was 'vay.'" Part of the success of their product lines relies on the fact that the expression "oy vay" has become well known outside the Jewish world. Quipped a reporter, "'Oy vay' is a grimace, but 'Soy Vay' definitely is worth smiling about."[89] On Christmas, the singular day of the year when nothing else is open, Jews have sought out Chinese restaurants. Now, thanks to Soy Vay, they can enjoy Asian cuisine with a Jewish twist without even leaving their own kitchens. Jewish-Asian couples inspire non-culinary hybrids, too. Ethan and Miho Segal's *nengajo* (Japanese-style new year's card) included photos from their daughter Naomi's bat mitzvah at a synagogue and the Japanese characters for "Happy New Year 2013!"[90] When Josh and Jamie Narva got married, her Japanese mother created Stars of David using 1,001 blue and silver folded origami cranes for wedding gifts, and she also wore a traditional kimono to the Jewish wedding. The children from this marriage are receiving formal Jewish education and Japanese language instruction.[91]

Marrying an Asian woman does not lessen a Jewish man's Jewishness; rather it creates a cultural hybrid. Paul Golin, associate executive director of the Jewish Outreach Institute, who is married to a Japanese woman, explained in a *Huffington Post* editorial that exploring another culture "has in no way diminished my own identity; in fact, it's strengthened it because I've had to reciprocate by serving as 'tour guide' into Jewish life for my Japanese wife."[92] "Jewpanese" is the word Golin coined to describe his wedding and his identity as a couple with his wife, Yurika, and his children's identities.[93] Rejecting other labels, Golin claims they are not "interfaith"; "there is only one faith represented in our holiday celebrations and in our home: Judaism. Our wedding was a Jewish wedding, with 'intercultural' aspects."[94] Regarding his children, Golin emphasizes, "Their religion will be 100 percent Jewish and their culture will be half Jewish, half Japanese ... and 100 percent American!"[95] Answering the oft-cited question posed by in-marriage advocates, "Will his grandchildren be Jewish?" Golin suggests that it will depend on whether the Jewish community has successfully attracted, welcomed, and retained Jews of diverse cultural heritages. In his usual satirical style, comic artist Eli Valley took to town the sociologists who contend that intermarriage spells the demise of the Jewish people. In one frame of the strip "Bucky Shvitz: Sociologist for Hire," Valley illustrates Paul and Yurika on the cover of a pseudo publication, "The Japanese Menace," with the text insinuating that the sociologist specializing in intermarriage fixed the numbers so that the children of the Jewish-Japanese couple would commit suicide in the womb.[96] Clearly, Jewish men like Golin and Valley dispute the idea that out marriage inhibits Jewish continuity.

Even without the benefit of a full-scale historical account of Jewish-Asian marriages, one can easily see that a dramatic shift occurred between the end of World War II and the present day. Japanese war brides then, Asian women "abandoned" their race by marrying Jewish "white men." In the years after the Second World War, American servicemen entered Japan as conquerors to find an impoverished people and some Japanese women who sought greater autonomy than they would have found in a traditional Japanese marriage. According to historian Paul Spickard, "Despite intense opposition from the Japanese populace and the American military, thousands of couples married."[97] Nat Lehrman's 1957 marriage to Kazuko Miyajima, whom he met while serving in Japan during peacetime, was unconventional according to American and Jewish social norms. Japanese people were still viewed as "murderous kamikazes who bombed Pearl Harbor," according to one scholar, and Lehrman's mother threatened to kill herself when she first learned of the interracial couple's plans to wed.[98] Less than sixty-five years after the war ended, Asian Americans were dealing with continuity issues not entirely dissimilar from the American Jewish community's concerns. In "No More Jewish Husbands," an American woman of Chinese parentage, whose three sisters married Jewish men, wrote, "Now the pressure from my parents for me to marry a Chinese guy is too much."[99] Fear of cultural assimilation cuts across Asian groups. Helen Kim's parents repeatedly told her, "You are not to date or marry anyone who isn't Korean."[100] However in more recent years, resistance to intermarriage from Asian family members seems to have diminished, according to Kim and Leavitt's study.[101] Illustrating the cultural shift, novelist Gish Gen captured the change over time in her fictional portrayal of one Asian group when they became "the new Jews" in her 1996 book *Mona in the Promised Land*. In the story, teenage Mona's Chinese immigrant parents move to Scarsdale, New York, and she not only falls in love with a Jewish boy but also considers converting to Judaism.[102] It appears that Jewish mah jong and Chinese mah jong, to raise a humorous point made by author Amy Tan in *The Joy Luck Club*, may not be so different after all.[103]

OVERVIEW

This book looks at two age cohorts of men: those born between 1922 and 1945, and baby boomers born between 1946 and 1964. I argue that Jewish men, like most American men, were socially encouraged to achieve professional success first and foremost, to become good providers for their wives and children. This pressure, combined with a Jewish cultural emphasis on educational aptitude and family solidarity, influenced the belief that Jewish men make good husbands. Childhood experiences influenced marital choices and perspectives as fathers. The life experiences of men who intermarried between 1991 and 2008 illustrate that becoming a father reawakened men's Jewish identities in cultural ways, yet their involvement in the Jewish community and their children's upbringing remained hampered by gendered family dynamics and ongoing pressures to be the primary breadwinners. Revealing the actual women behind "shiksappeal" turns the readers' attention to the Christian wives the Jewish men married and dismantles the myth that so-called shiksas lured men away from their religion and family of origin. American Jewish culture has long condoned Jewish men "practicing" on Christian girls, with the understanding that they would not actually marry them.[104] One need look no farther than White House senior advisor Rahm Emanuel's quip to President Bill Clinton after the Monica Lewinsky scandal: "You got it backwards. You messed around with a Jewish girl and now you're paying a goyish lawyer. You should have messed around with a goyishe girl and gotten a Jewish lawyer."[105] Studying the "other woman," rather than merely reiterating outmoded and pejorative comments about her, provides a fuller understanding of the gendered meaning of intermarriage. With the exception of direct quotes that use the word "gentile," I refer to these women as Christians. Although "gentile" means "non-Jewish," it is primarily used by Jews talking about non-Jews and, however inadvertent, can be offensive to people of other faith backgrounds.[106] An analysis of intermarried Jewish celebrities and representations of Jewish intermarriage in popular culture grapples with the extent to which life influences art. Examining the gendered patterns of fictional portrayals over time illustrates how these depictions increasingly prioritized interfaith romances between Jewish men and Christian women. Finally, I explain how men's involvement in Jewish parenting and the Jewish community needs to be considered in their fuller contexts, which include interactions with members of Jewish leadership and the ongoing American reality of men spending more hours at work away from their families than do women.

Marrying Out: Jewish Men, Intermarriage, and Fatherhood is my second book on intermarriage, and it differs from my earlier published work in at least three major ways. It is a study of intermarried Jewish men in the latter decades of the twentieth century and the first decade of the twenty-first. In this volume I strive to get at the meaning of intermarriage and fatherhood for Jewish men. Hence, there is less content about intermarriage history in general and about religious community-generated literature. My first book *Still Jewish: A History of Women and Intermarriage in America,* readily available, focused on intermarried Jewish women across more than a century, referenced the biblical period, and cited advice manuals.[107] Yet I draw some comparisons between intermarried Jewish men and women in the concluding chapter to emphasize why studying *both* sexes is critical to developing a full picture of Jewish intermarriage and parenting.

While *Marrying Out* may be seen as a companion book, it aims to complicate the picture, not complete it. Although intermarried Jewish women became Jewish matriarchs when they had children, they did so less in relation to their Christian spouses and more on terms of their own. In contrast, intermarried Jewish men's experiences as husbands and fathers were directly influenced by their relationships with their wives and traditional conceptions of gender roles in American families. While becoming a parent exerted a similar impact on the Jewish identities of intermarried Jewish women and men, their experiences differed. Traditional gender roles challenge intermarried men raising Jewish children. By and large, men continue to be the primary income earners, while women continue to be the information gatherers and social organizers and, as such, maintain greater influence over their children's ethnic and religious upbringing. Hence, the presence of men at places where Jewish identity is nurtured (at home, the community center, the school, the synagogue) is more limited. Unless contemporary society creates gender balance, the upside of being an intermarried Jewish woman will continue to be the downside of being an intermarried Jewish man.

1

Professional Men

Immersed in a society that converted them from humans into machines, they learned how to make money but not how to make love.

—Rabbi Shmuley Boteach

The life of one man speaks volumes about Jewish men and intermarriage in mid-twentieth-century American culture. Morris Aker was born in Detroit in 1922, grew up in a mostly Jewish neighborhood, and attended the Conservative synagogue B'nai Moshe. His parents spoke Yiddish at home, the social climate was Jewish, and he assumed he would marry someone Jewish: "It was implicit." Morris attended Wayne State University and then moved to Ann Arbor to pursue doctoral studies at a more prestigious university. He met a fellow graduate student from Carrollton, Ohio, in 1951, and their acquaintance soon became intimate; while he was enjoying their sexual relationship, she insisted that if they were going to be "together," it necessitated getting married. This was, after all, the 1950s and sexual liberation had not yet come into vogue. Marriage was not on his mind; Morris was focused on making an intellectual contribution. "I was looking forward to a great life," he reminisced, including "having a sense of importance in the stream of things such as being a university professor." Morris did not mince words when it came to male privilege: "Being a man is a special opportunity. Being a man is terrific; it's like being a Jew. And if I were a Jewish woman, I don't know whether I would feel the same way." His commitment to monogamy prevailed and he eventually agreed to get married in 1953. His future wife's mother teased her daughter: "Well, if you are going to marry a Jew, why don't you marry a rich one?" Morris's character, his potential as a good partner, and his altruistic inclination to make an honest woman of his romantic conspirator were not at issue; financial comfort and social status were. That he became a faculty member created a positive valance for the woman's parents. Whether to get married was negotiable for Morris, whereas raising children as Jews was not. Fathering Jewish offspring was an inherent part of his identity. To conceive otherwise was unfathomable: "It was very important to me"; otherwise, Morris observed, "I don't believe I would have gone along with our getting married."[1]

This chapter focuses on research findings based on two age cohorts, men born between 1922 and 1945 and baby boomers (men who were born between 1946 and 1964), consisting of an analysis of twenty-seven of the fifty-four oral histories in the larger project. While I conducted the interviews in Ann Arbor, the men hail from all over the United States and Israel. They are of Ashkenazi descent; their affiliations at birth included Reform, Conservative, and Orthodox; their intermarriages occurred between 1953 and 1989.[2] While each man's story could constitute a book of its own, my task is to offer a comprehensive analysis of the set of interviews within their historical contexts.

Four patterns are evident. First, the belief that Jewish men make good husbands was a symptom of American culture that associated masculinity with earning power. Second, American Jewish men's childhood experiences influenced their choice of marriage partners and how their intermarried lives evolved. Third they maintained and in some cases enhanced their Jewish identities, despite marrying "out," by shifting to a more accepting branch of Judaism. Fourth, while many men expressed indifference about whether their wife converted, most were adamant about raising Jewish children.[3]

Before I launch into the men's experiences, it is worthwhile to establish the background context of Jewish intermarriage.[4] Marrying "out" became increasingly conceivable as the twentieth century progressed, though not necessarily more acceptable within Jewish circles. The increasing visibility and, to some degree, acceptability of intermarriage in American society between 1930 and 1960 made it more plausible to defy the cultural imperative of religious endogamy. Marriage between Jews and Christians was relatively uncommon in the United States, as it was in the first three decades of the century. However, the number of cross-faith marriages was growing in America. The estimated Jewish intermarriage rate was 3 percent between 1931 and 1940, which doubled to roughly 6 percent between 1951 and 1960.[5] The American culture of intermarriage changed markedly between 1930 and 1960. As marriages between Catholics and Protestants became more widespread, it eased the way for Jewish men to marry "out." In 1931, a minister sermonized, "It is best . . . for Americans to marry Americans, and Presbyterians Presbyterians, and Christians Christians, and Jews Jews."[6] By the late 1950s, such rhetoric appeared outmoded in the mainstream press, when intermarriage was a commonly discussed topic. For example, a *New York Times* author stated in 1957, "For some years it has seemed to many Americans narrow-minded, intolerant, almost un-American to raise objections to marriage on the basis of 'creed.'"[7] A new abundance of social science studies as well as lay and advice literature contributed to making intermarriage seem more common in American society at large, albeit still undesirable to organized religion and many parents. Jewish communities remained vigilantly opposed to interfaith unions despite the growing pervasiveness of the intermarriage topic. Thus, although Jewish men who married non-Jews did so in an American society that slowly became somewhat more tolerant of intermarriage, most Jews continued to consider their actions as malevolent. However, American Jews composed a disproportionate number of the whites who married blacks in the late 1940s, albeit still a small number overall. Despite bans on interracial marriage, Jews who were involved in radical politics, including the Communist and Socialist parties, were more likely to meet prospective black spouses. Moreover, uncertainty about their own racial status as "white" may have made some Jews more inclined to consider crossing the color line.[8]

Intermarriage between Jews and non-Jews became a common phenomenon to an unprecedented degree within the larger social context of the increased rate of marriages across lines defined by European ethnic ancestry in mainstream American society.[9] Although surveys were criticized for their design and data collection or for how Jews were identified and who may have been missed, they did highlight an unmistakable rise in intermarriage over time.[10] A 1990 national survey of the Jewish population found that 52 percent of born Jews had intermarried from 1985 through 1990, a significant jump from the 32 percent rate seen in the years 1966–1972.[11] Another national survey in 2001 found that 47 percent of Jews (who were born and remained Jews) intermarried from 1996 through 2001, up from 43 percent between 1991 and 1995. Applying the broad definition "born Jews" (those born to at least one Jewish parent but not necessarily raised as Jewish), this same study yielded rates of 54 percent and 53 percent respectively for the same time periods.[12] Two studies of the Boston Jewish community, however, found lower overall rates, as they had in 1965 and 1975, but again also found significant increases in the rate of intermarriage the more recently the marriage had occurred: 29 percent of the spouses of Jewish adults who married for the first time from 1981 through 1985 were not Jewish, compared to 10 percent twenty years earlier; this increased to 34 percent from 1991 through 1995.[13] These findings confirmed that American Jews were steadily becoming as exogamous as other ethnic groups.

The marriage patterns of the seven largest European ancestry groups likewise showed a marked increase in intermarriage among most white ethnic Americans born after 1950 compared to those born in 1920 or before. The percent of spouses not from the same ancestry group changed for the major ancestry groups as follows: Polish (from 47.8 to 82.3); Scots (from 74.2 to 85.2); Italian (from 40.7 to 75.0); French (from 78.9 to 77.4); Irish (from 53.7 to 60.0); German (from 50.9 to 49.7); and English (from 37.6 to 44.1). These numbers reflected that the influence of ethno-religious origins on marriages between whites had declined significantly by the end of the twentieth century.[14] Analysis of 1980 census data allowed researchers to create the first comprehensive national portrait of ethnic and racial intermarriage in America, with a representative sample of 226,000 of the 43.8 million American married couples in which both spouses were native-born. Dr. Richard D. Alba, then director of the Center for Social and Demographic analysis at the State University of New York at Albany, elaborated in a September 1986 paper that Jewish-Jewish marriages in the United States were "well below the in-marriage tendencies of eastern and central European groups and about on a par with those of the British and Irish, two of the weakest."[15] Hence, non-immigrant-generation Jews were considered along with other white ethnics from Western Europe to intermarry extensively. The increase in Jewish-Christian marriages was paralleled by increases in other forms of interreligious marriages; for example, approximately half of Catholics married non-Catholics, mainly Protestants.[16]

GOOD HUSBANDS

The belief that Jewish men make good husbands derives from interpretations of Jewish marriage law, cultural stereotypes about their upbringing, and a contemporary emphasis on professional success. Rabbi Jeffrey K. Salkin explains a low standard, or in his words, "why Jewish husbands are such a prize," with a piece of ancient text: "because it is not the way of Jews to strike their wives" (*Shulchan Aruch, Even HaEzer*, 154:3). This legalese contributed to folk wisdom that Jewish men do not commit domestic violence, making them appealing marriage partners.[17] Reports about wife beating in modern North America and Israel are greeted with "Jews don't do that."[18] Jewish men are also the beneficiaries of a long history of maligning Jewish mothers for being overprotective and domineering, nurturers par excellence.[19] "Generations of Jewish moms have taught their sons to love, honor, and, above all, *obey* the whims of their women" may be a joke, but it suggests that Jewish "mama's boys" grew up to be doting husbands who do *not* have blue-collar jobs.[20] Jewish men's financial success, fueled by the determination of earlier immigrant generations to make it in America, often depended on Jewish men pursuing advanced degrees or otherwise excelling in business. The humorous *Jewish American Prince Handbook* has this quip on its cover: "Med School, Law School or B-School: The Great Debate."[21] Jewish men's achievements in the public arena, which were overrepresented relative to the size of the Jewish population, encouraged the Jewish community to prize its husbands and eligible bachelors. Ben Levine, who was born in 1940 and intermarried in 1969, insisted that Jewish men make good husbands because "we're good providers." He knew from an early age that he wanted to go into the medical profession.[22] Another explanation for why Jewish men make good husbands was loyalty to family and home. Novelist Philip Roth fictionalized the Jewish husband's appeal to non-Jewish women as "a regular domestic Messiah!" who does not drink, gamble, or cheat on his wife; he's "a Jewish boy just dying in his every cell to be Good, Responsible & Dutiful to a family of his own."[23] The Judaization of American culture signaled that "Eros itself turns, or seems to for a little while, Jewish; as the mythical erotic dream-girls of us all yearn for Jewish intellectuals and learn to make matzo-balls," wrote literary critic Leslie A. Fiedler.[24] The theory that Jewish men make good husbands became known outside of the Jewish community over time, and there are now Christian women specifically seeking Jewish partners on JDate.[25] Although the idea that Jewish men make appealing husbands is spreading, it has yet to fully become common lore.

The Protestant work ethic socialized American Jewish men to be the major breadwinners who provide for their family yet also generated some ambivalence. The nineteenth-century Industrial Revolution removed men from laboring alongside their wives and children and left a legacy of association of masculinity with earned income. Although the Great Depression may have shaken the concept that a man was what he made, because so many men were out of work for prolonged periods of time, the economic prosperity following World War II and men's renewed financial successes suggest that men's role as primary earner in the mid-twentieth century was more similar to the nineteenth-century model than not.[26] Calling for a restoration of traditional patriarchal family structure, Barnard sociologist Willard Waller wrote, "Women must bear and rear children; husbands must support them."[27] A paycheck symbolized success as a man and contributed to the social construction of masculinity throughout the 1950s and 1960s. The need to work, according to psychiatrist Robert E. Gould in his article "Measuring Masculinity by the Size of the Paycheck," extends beyond any real need and even the prestige of a respected position. Even men who earned sufficient money to support themselves and their families were unsure of their masculinity, Gould contended, "Quite simply because money is—and always was—a pretty insecure peg on which to hang a masculine image."[28] Decreasing religious traditionalism among American Jews contributed to their adaptation of the Jewish father's historical role as the link between the family and the Jewish community. This role was reinterpreted and manifested itself in a man's dedication to work and commitment to instill the values of achievement in his children, rather than in text study and worship.[29] This disassociation between religion and men's identities spawned an American Jewish masculine mystique. Jewish upward mobility in the postwar years generated widespread ambivalence among rabbis, writers, intellectuals, and laypeople in the 1950s and early 1960s. "The pressure to become a prosperous breadwinner, they contended, had turned Jewish men into soulless moneymakers, stripped of their idealism, their intellectual curiosity, their bravery, and even their authentic Jewish identity," according to historian Rachel Kranson. Despite however much commentators valorized Jewish men who chose meaningful careers over lucrative ones, and tough Israeli soldiers for their heroism and physical strength, most American Jewish men chose the path of professional degrees and earning potential that guaranteed their place in the American middle class.[30]

Success for Jewish men meant in the *professions:* doctor, lawyer, businessman, professor. Most of the forty-one men in my study had advanced degrees, with a large number of MDs, JDs, and PhDs among them, an artifact of professionalization among Jews and the university community I chose to study. Long-time editor of *Commentary* magazine Norman Podhoretz wrote in his 1967 book *Making It* about his mother's expectations: "My mother wanted nothing so much as for me to be a success, to be respected and admired." But when he became a writer and an editor, she commented, "I should have made him for a dentist." According to Podhoretz, his mother's words illustrated her accurate perception that "whereas Jewish sons who grow up to be successes in certain occupations usually remain fixed in an accessible cultural ethos, sons who grow up into literary success are transformed almost beyond recognition and distanced beyond a mother's reach."[31] Talk show host Larry King, who never went to college and is currently married to a Mormon woman, remembers the vision he had of his deceased mother when he gave the commencement address at Columbia University Medical School and received an honorary degree: she looked down, rubbed her eyes, looked again and said, "He's a *doctor!*"[32] Hence Jewish men in America faced the dual challenge of earning their bread in a manner that was valued by their model ethnic minority group. If they did not have sufficient education or did not aspire to join the medical, legal, business, or academic ranks, some Jewish men experienced a sense of not being "man enough." Kirk Edwards, who was born in 1946 and intermarried in 1969, remarked upon how one's manhood in the 1960s was intimately linked to profession: "Now there are probably a lot more options available to what it means to be a man than there was then . . . certainly there's much more equality of the sexes than there was forty years ago. So that means there's options open to men that weren't open, or at least seemed strange then. It's no longer strange to see, say, a male nurse or male teacher. Back in the '60s those were professions that were predominantly for women."[33] Although his comment speaks to the sexism that influenced all American men, in their quest for achievement Jewish men seem to have had even fewer acceptable options, partly constricted by employment discrimination.

The American labor force changed a lot between 1950 and 1980; however, the social expectation that men would continue to be the primary breadwinners remained nearly constant, as did the reality of wage disparity between the sexes. After their work in the war industries, employers encouraged women to be content with their domestic responsibilities and men with work outside the home. Postwar, the percentage of women in the professions actually slipped backward, and with the baby boom, middle-class family size increased from approximately two children to four, which further enforced domesticity for women and providing for men. The men who married and became fathers in the 1950s and 1960s were part of a low-birthrate generation who upon reaching maturity had little difficulty finding jobs. All of these factors contributed to increasing pressure on men as breadwinners and reinforcing the traditional family configuration of father in the office and mother in the home.[34] Although the pressure men felt was no doubt real, the idea that these family dynamics reinforced past patterns was a distortion; as historian Stephanie Coontz has argued, "the 'traditional' family of the 1950s was a qualitatively new phenomenon."[35] The focus on finding private security within the nuclear family was born out of the mutual reinforcement of cold war era ideology of containment and domestic revivalism.[36] Although women's attitudes about work and career aspirations shifted, giving them some degree of confidence in their own earning ability, their earning power remained dwarfed by men's, thereby relegating them to secondary breadwinner at best.

The strictly husband-provider and dependent-wife model of marriage gradually diminished, but Jewish men continued to shoulder most of the responsibility for feeding their families. A major shift in women's attitudes toward work and family occurred from 1943 to 1971. The proportion of college women who would opt for full-time homemaking and volunteer activities declined dramatically; 62 percent in 1971 indicated that they would definitely go back to work after the birth of a child, compared to 30 percent in 1943.[37] However, women who did not work were less liberal in their attitudes than women who did, and according to one 1976 study, Catholic and Protestant women appeared to be more accepting of women's traditional familial role expectations and responsibilities than Jewish women.[38] By 1960, 30 percent of married women were in the labor force, double the percentage in 1940. By 1970, 40 percent of all American wives and two-thirds of mothers with children under six were working outside the home.[39] However, the man-as-provider model endured. Rabbi Michael Gold wrote in 1988 about the biological and physical emphasis of paternity that did not take Jewish thinking into account, "Fatherhood in modern life entails two major tasks: being a sperm donor and a bread winner."[40] Despite the rise of second-wave feminism, the sexual liberation movement, and the anti–Vietnam War movement of the 1960s, the New Right politics of the 1970s and 1980s that defeated the Equal Rights Amendment revived the domestic ideology as it ushered Ronald Reagan into the White House. The "traditional" family was politically restored, even without a consensus.[41]

Massive inequalities continued to hinder women's economic roles and men's familial ones. The term "dual-career family," invented by 1969, illustrated how American marriage had changed to include a wife and a husband who both took their work and professional needs seriously. This constituted a significant alteration from when a wife's income was supplemental and women subordinated their professional aspirations to that of their husbands.[42] In 1977, more than half of all mothers with school-age children worked outside the home, and more than a third of mothers with children under three years old. Women who entered the employment marketplace gained greater confidence, tasted independence, and were less easy to satisfy.[43] Yet in the 1980s, women earned only 60 percent of men's wages and were mostly confined to feminized job categories. Even for highly educated women, whose jobs increased steadily after 1960, their success lagged behind men's. Women in academic jobs, for example, had far fewer tenured positions, and it remained difficult to climb the academic ladder while taking time off during childbearing years or to take care of aging parents. According to historian Peter Stearns, "Here too was a factor in the absence of full-scale female challenge to men's job hold: women were more likely than men to work part-time, or to select specialties different from men's (pediatrics, family practice, and obstetrics in medicine, for example, all rather low-paying fields, with a much smaller scattering in the higher-paying medical branches)."[44]

MORE THAN SEX

Although fictional portrayals such as the 1972 film *The Heartbreak Kid* (discussed at length in chapter 4) and the novel title *In Search of the Golden Shiksa* would have us believe that men actively sought out non-Jewish women for their physical attractiveness, Jewish men's expressed reasons for dating and marrying non-Jewish women focused on Jewish-Christian population ratios, falling in love, and seeking partners who provided the acceptance or love some had not received during childhood. Fred Stevens was born in 1951 and grew up in Carnie, New Jersey, where there were approximately fifteen Jewish families. He remembered, "I never went out with a Jewish girl. There were only four, so they were like sisters."[45] Seth Roller lived in a small Ohio town where he was the sole Jewish person in his high school graduating class; hence when he was beginning to date in the 1970s, there was no opportunity to socialize with someone Jewish.[46]

Residential proximity, mixed with attitude, education, and employment, generated opportunities for cross-religious romance. Moving from Jewish neighborhoods to the more religiously heterogeneous suburbs increased the ability of Jewish young adults still living under their parents' roofs to befriend larger numbers of non-Jews than in earlier decades. Between 1945 and 1960, the social and economic profile of American

Jews came more closely to resemble the wider American population, with a larger percentage living in the solidly middle-class suburbs and working in the professions.[47] It has been estimated that one out of every three Jews left the big cities for the suburbs between 1945 and 1965. Some Jews clustered together in suburbia, while others ventured to suburbs with few co-religionists.[48] Propinquity to Christians was greater than it had been before 1945 in either case, as a Jewish Daily *Forward* observer wrote of the self-segregation in New York City neighborhoods of the 1920s, when "four-fifths of all the Jews . . . practically have no contact with Gentiles."[49] Historian Elaine Tyler May wrote regarding the move to suburban developments, "Second generation European immigrants moved out of their ethnic neighborhoods in the cities, leaving their kinship networks, along with their outsider status, behind. . . . Jews and Catholics joined Anglo-Saxon Protestants in these all-white communities, even if they could not join their country clubs or social gatherings."[50] De facto segregation did not, however, prevent rising youth and consumer culture from creating opportunities for suburban Jews to meet non-Jews.

While the majority of Jews, Catholics, and Protestants married their own kind, residential proximity between groups increased chances for a Jewish man to meet, fall in love with, and marry a non-Jew.[51] In *Jewish Identity on the Suburban Frontier,* Marshall Sklare observed that twice as many respondents in 1957–1958 spent more time socializing with friends than with family compared to their parents' generation, reflecting the pervasive peer culture of American youth. He hypothesized, "The shift to a group which is self-selected rather than inherited may portend the end of in-group solidarity." The 7 percent who reported that non-Jews constituted an equal number or a majority of their close friends suggest that there was room for enduring interfaith relationships to develop in suburbia.[52] The more young people participated in commercial amusements, school, and other activities outside of the family circle as well as outside the segregated country clubs, the more they selected marriage partners beyond their parents' influence, according to historian Ellen K. Rothman.[53] Suburban propinquity fostered socialization between youth from different religious groups, contributing to the comfort level Jewish men had when they went to college and entered the labor force, where non-Jewish women abounded. The majority of men that I interviewed met their Christian wives either through work or at college.

The men in my study may not have sought out non-Jewish women intentionally, but they did seek women with whom they could have satisfying sexual relationships. Sex, in other words, played an important role in men's thinking about women, regardless of religious or ethnic background. Frank Morton described his reaction to his wife's body: "When she took her clothes off and invited me into her bed, I thought I had died and gone to heaven . . . all other things considered, that was a big part of it."[54] Bert Feldman compared his preference for darker-skinned women to actor Robert DeNiro's attraction to African American women: "I've got 'brown fever.'" His first wife was Puerto Rican. "She turned me on physically. I mean, when you're twenty-two years old that's very important. It is when you're sixty, too."[55] When I asked author Roger Levine about the focus on sex in his semi-autobiographical novel, he responded, "In my opinion, such preoccupation is not unique to Jewish men, but to all men. I think that's just the way it is."[56] The men's statements reflect the lasting influence of the Kinsey Reports, *Sexual Behavior in the Human Male* (1948) and *Sexual Behavior in the Human Female* (1953), two books that changed how Americans discuss sex in public.[57] While some of the men I interviewed were quite vocal about their sexual prowess, none of their wives mentioned the physicality of their dating history or marital relationships. Likewise, none of the intermarried Jewish women in my first book, *Still Jewish: A History of Women and Intermarriage in America,* raised the issue of sexual intimacy. The topic of sexual relations seemed to come up with significant ease for men, whereas women were either wholly reticent to discuss it or focused on other matters. Then again, "getting the boy" (in bed) has never had the social currency that "getting the girl" has had.

A few men reported good relationships with both parents, but many more had bitter things to say about their own Jewish mothers, which likely affected their views of Jewish women and contributed to their choosing women who possessed qualities they believed their mothers lacked. In his book *The Secret Lives of Men: What Men Want You to Know about Love, Sex, and Relationships,* psychologist Christopher Blazina writes, "One of the legacies of the mother wound involves the fantasy that a romantic partner will make up for all the emotional needs left unfulfilled."[58] Jewish men's comments about their mothers illustrate this psychological finding. "She was tolerant, my mother, but she was never loving," Bob Feldmen said. According to Nathan Bloomer, his mother was passive aggressive, inconsistent, selfish, and narcissistic; "I think that's probably why I married a strong, intelligent woman. I think it was a sense of what I missed from my mother."[59] Frank Morton described his mother as being overprotective, afraid, and too dependent on other people. He stated bluntly, "I did not want to marry a woman like my mother."[60] His wife, by comparison, was independent, intelligent, and kind. Morton's negativity toward his mother, including his contention that she risked emasculating him by overdressing him, is reminiscent of author Philip Wylie's vilification of American mothers that he termed "momism."[61] Another man described his mother as very negative, superstitious, and critical, whereas his wife is very positive, non-judgmental, and accepting.[62] Conversely, when a man had positive things to say about his mother, his choice of a mate resembled the maternal figure in his life, albeit a Christian one. Ben Levin stated that he was attracted to his wife because "she was just very similar to my mother . . . a very, very giving person."[63] Hence a negative correlation encouraged a choice who was different from one's mother, while a positive association encouraged one who possessed similar attributes. Although mothers commonly receive more of the blame—especially Jewish mothers!—in reality, relationships with both parents contribute to what men sought or expected from romantic partners.[64]

Jewish men's criticism of their fathers seemed to influence men's choices of wives and how intermarried men behaved as fathers. One of the laments was about paternal absence. The men's experience with absent fathers was, however, a sad norm for married men. Employed fathers living with their children shared an average of two hours of activity together per week, according to one study of two-parent families and paternal absence.[65] Brian Geller was born in 1959, raised in a secular home, and married in 1985. Neither of his parents came to his childhood activities, whereas he wouldn't miss his children's marching band performances or baseball games. The only instance when his father ever said anything to convey that he was proud of Brian was when he earned his second master's degree. "I'm very different from the way my father is," Brian commented, " . . . and some of that's deliberate."[66] His conscious decision to distinguish himself from his father illustrates what men coming of age in the 1960s and 1970s did: they began to question their family role and their commitment to work as their primary focus. Stearns contends, "On some key issues, sons simply decided that their fathers had been wrong." The 1970s ushered in "new fathering," which included spending more time with their children.[67] Felix Phillips was born in the Bronx, raised Orthodox, and attended a yeshiva. He recalled that the only thing he and his father ever did together was go to synagogue. His father disciplined Felix harshly; by today's standards he was physically abused. Regarding the paternal figure, Felix lamented, "So mostly what I remember growing up is just being afraid of him."[68] The fact that his father was a Holocaust survivor makes Felix's experience all the more heart wrenching.

SECOND GENS

For the children of Holocaust survivors, or Second Gens as they are sometimes called, intermarriage added another layer to the secondary psychological trauma. Five of the men who intermarried between 1953 and 1989 had parents who were Holocaust survivors. All talked about how the silence of their parents about the past, whether to protect them or because it was too painful to discuss, made them feel lucky to be alive but also made it hard to truly grapple with what being a Jewish man meant for them personally. Born in 1951 in Minneapolis, Nathan Bloomer grew up with a survivor father who was, in his words, "an authoritarian German." Commenting on being the child of a survivor, Nathan said, "I think it creates a tremendous amount of internal conflict, and it's been the two-edge sword of my life." He was angry to never have met his grandparents; "I feel robbed," he told me.[69] On the one hand, Nathan resisted the pressure to conform to the idea that he should marry someone Jewish; yet not surprisingly, he married a woman whose Lutheran background echoed that of the Righteous Gentiles who saved his father's life.[70] Adult children of survivors, such as Nathan, experienced difficulty in identity formation when the parent of the same sex was emotionally absent. "I haven't got a father," a college-aged child told a mental health clinician in the late 1960s. "The war killed him. He is a weak and frightened man."[71] The dedication of the novel *The Silence of the Parents* reads, "To the 2Gs, the resilient children of severely traumatized parents."[72]

Survivors of the *Shoah* taught their children and grandchildren, "Never again," while American society reinforced the idea that religion was second to nationhood. Civic nationalism, a model of citizenship and national identity, encouraged Jews and other European ethnics to declare their loyal allegiance to the American nation.[73] Nationalism was the religion of choice, and the tie that bound all Americans together was stronger than their differences. The historical debate about the significance of the Holocaust in the American Jewish memory illustrates that despite narratives to the contrary, within the civic culture was a Jewish subculture devoted to memorializing the genocide of European Jewry. According to historian Arthur Hertzberg, the minority status of all Jews encouraged "group amnesia," a preference to look away from the death camps so as not to stand apart from the rest of America.[74] Hertzberg's analysis exemplifies the view held by many twentieth-century historians that from 1945 until the first half of the 1960s discussion about the destruction of European Jewry was extremely limited.[75] In sharp contrast, historian Hasia Diner's award-winning book *We Remember with Reverence and Love: American Jews and the Myth of Silence after the Holocaust, 1945–1962* corrects the apparently erroneous historical record: American Jews were haunted by the persecution of their co-religionists, and rather than experiencing memory impairment or avoidance of the Holocaust as a result of the Cold War, they forged a memorial culture.[76] Citing numerous examples of Holocaust imagery used to describe contemporary events, Diner writes, "While in the 1950s and 1960s American Jews did not place the events of World War II at the top of their public and communal agenda, they did make room for it in communal discourse and political strategy."[77]

Growing up in the shadow of the Holocaust meant that Jewish men (and women) developed a sense of Jewish identity that was strongly associated with human suffering, slaughter, and survival. As James Rubin, former State Department spokesperson in the Clinton Administration, who married Iranian Catholic Christiane Amanpour, described, "My whole life, the Holocaust has colored my understanding of world history. It's been high up on the list of things that I understood from a very young age as the ultimate in evil."[78] Several men in this study had grandparents who were survivors. Even those men who were not the direct descendants of survivors came of age surrounded by pressure not to give Hitler a posthumous victory. The childhood lesson of "them or us" was a pervasive theme for many of the men. Likewise, some of the men's parents held little to no belief in God because of the Holocaust, inculcating their children with the idea that if there were a God, "he wouldn't have let this happen."[79] Some parents were excessively protective of their children, and as a result, some developed what one psychiatrist who treated children of survivors characterized as "a suspiciously hostile attitude to the Gentile world around them."[80] This parental attitude prompted some children of survivors to rebel by dating non-Jewish partners.[81] A preference for a non-Jewish partner could be, in the words of psychologist Aaron Hass, "an endeavor to escape what was perceived to be an oppressive background, and/or an attempt to still fears of vulnerability to another genocidal assault."[82] Although none of the men who participated in my study explicitly stated these objectives, any or all may have subconsciously contributed to their decisions to intermarry. Gary Brodin, who was born in 1966 and married a Catholic, was psychically tortured by his survivor mother's heart wrenching comment, "In this household, Hitler won."[83] The intensity and weight of such comments clearly lodged in men's minds and permeated their experiences.

Baby boom men were contemptuous of Judaism that was characterized as a response to the Holocaust and Christianity. "Do it for the Six Million" and "Bear the torch for those who were torched" was the rhetoric surrounding a child born during the immediate and not-so-immediate postwar period.[84] Kalman Long, born in 1957 outside of Philadelphia, expressed how his Judaism growing up was reactionary, an effort to preserve rather than to practice. That bothered him. "I don't mind carrying some of the baggage because that's my history," he said, "but I'm not responsible for all of it."[85] As an adult, he still struggled with living a Jewish life that was positive in its own right:

I just get the sense that our Judaism is not about us. It's a reaction to those around us. And that bothers me. It bothers me a lot, because I'd like to know what authentic Jewish life is like. And it might be not possible for . . . the generation or two after something like the Holocaust, to understand that. Or it might not be possible in the Diaspora at all. And it might not be possible in Israel. And this might just be authentic Jewish life.

Kalman yearned for the circumstances when, in his words, "it's not about them, it's about *us*."[86] Men who grew up during the 1950s, '60s, and '70s, those who were children of Holocaust survivors as well as those who were not, waged a war of their own trying to determine for themselves what being a Jewish man meant during a time of peace and prosperity in the United States.

JEWISH MIGRATIONS

Men shifted from more traditional to more liberal branches of Judaism and deepened their Jewish identities in the process. Among those men who intermarried between 1953 and 1978, ten out of fourteen changed from their childhood affiliation. In all cases, the shift went from more intensive religious observance to more moderate practices. Their transitions included from Orthodox to Conservative, Orthodox to Reform, Conservative to Reform, and Conservative and Reform to secular. Among the men who intermarried between 1980 and 1989, nine out of twelve made a shift from the denomination of their childhood; their moves were identical to their predecessors—with the exception of one man who was raised secular and became Reform. Altogether, eighteen out of twenty-seven men moved away from their childhood affiliations. Mark Entennman described rebelling against being brought up in an Orthodox synagogue, where "the teaching was not that great or inspiring," his marital negotiation, and his journey through fatherhood to a deeper connection to Jewish life:

I became disillusioned and I'd say for a number of years even through college and medical school I rarely went to synagogue except for the high holidays. . . . I think when we had children—and really the rubber met the road then—and [my wife] said, "If you want to bring them up Jewish you have to step up to the plate and participate." Be an active member of the religion and become involved in a congregation and be responsible for raising them. . . . I agreed. I thought she was right. And you know it's been an interesting journey since then because I've become very, very interested and much more comfortable with religion.[87]

Mark considers himself more Jewish now, after intermarrying in 1982 and becoming a participating member of a Reform temple, than when he was Orthodox. His enhanced identity stems from having a better understanding of Torah, becoming more knowledgeable of Jewish history and culture, being accepted in a community, and raising Jewish children.

Jewish men's slide toward liberal Judaism also illustrates what demographers analyzing the 2000–2001 National Jewish Population Survey have noted about the more Jewishly engaged segment of the Jewish population (4.3 million Jews)—specifically, that "Reform has now become the most popular denominational preference among American Jews." Twice as many Jews were raised Orthodox (20 percent) as are currently Orthodox (10 percent); a third of American Jewish adults reported being raised Conservative (33 percent), which declined to 27 percent who said it was their current denomination; whereas Reform Judaism has gained adherents, with 26 percent of adult Jews raised Reform but 35 percent who currently consider themselves Reform.[88] Reinforcing these findings, the 2013 Pew Research Center's *A Portrait of Jewish Americans* reported identical percentages for Reform and Orthodox Jewish denominational identity, 35 percent and 10 percent respectively, but an even sharper decline to 18 percent for Conservative Jews.[89] That many of the Jewish men in my study left the denomination in which they were raised also reflects the larger American religious picture. According to Pew's 2008 *U.S. Religious Landscape Survey,* more than a quarter (28 percent) of American adults left the religion in which they were raised. Among Protestants, 44 percent of adults either switched affiliations, moved from unaffiliated to affiliated, or ceased connecting to any specific religion. In addition, Reform Judaism is the most affluent of the major American religions; hence as successive generations of Jews became more prosperous, they also gravitated toward the left.[90]

When those interviewed were asked why they joined one congregation over another, the rabbi's response to their intermarriage and the word "welcoming" were repeated over and over again. George Maze, who intermarried in 1987, initially sought out a Conservative congregation, his original affiliation. Unfortunately, as George described, "people were unwelcoming to us. Even people that I knew well and that I thought cared about me and had known me since I was a child were rude to [my wife]." In contrast, at the Reform temple, "people welcomed us"; it was "a really warm community. Very friendly."[91] Another man who went back to the Conservative Judaism of his youth after intermarrying and a brief affiliation with Reform was reassured by the Conservative rabbi telling him that if anyone did or said anything to make his wife feel uncomfortable, the rabbi wanted to know about it.[92] The fact that the rabbi took a personal interest in making sure that this interfaith couple would be genuinely accepted into the congregation carried great weight with this respondent. The men's experiences at synagogues describe a time when the outreach to the intermarried movement was in its infancy; significant strides have been made in the past three decades to create a more inclusive Jewish community.[93] However, the men's stories serve as poignant reminders that being welcoming remains a key component of keeping the doors open to greater Jewish involvement and competence. Sociologists who argue that a lack of Judaic knowledge—not a lack of welcome—keep intermarried people from participating in Jewish life are putting the cart before the horse, as outreach professionals know only too well.[94]

The histories of one Reform temple and two rabbis illustrate the influence a more welcoming approach can have on affiliation with organized religion. Founded in 1966, Temple Beth Emeth in Ann Arbor today has a thriving congregation, religious school, adult education programs, and singing and music programs for every age group and holds both adult and children's services *every* Shabbat (unlike many shuls that have sporadic children's programming). When he was first ordained in 1979, Rabbi Bob Levy would not officiate at interfaith marriages. Some years later, he changed his mind because he believed that refusing to do them was actually "lowering the bar for conversion," as people were converting so that he would officiate.[95] Levy is among an increasing number of Reform rabbis who originally refused and subsequently said, "I do," to intermarriages.[96] Rabbi Keith Stern is another such rabbi, in the Boston area, who does not require conversion of the non-Jewish spouse. His 2006 sermon "Intermarriage: A Reappraisal" eloquently described his

professional journey from ordination in 1984, when he would not per-
form intermarriages, to when he would; "I will do this because I believe
it is the best way to take the reality of intermarriage and still get Jewish
children. This is how we will make Jews."[97] These and other pioneering rabbis prompted the Central Conference of American Rabbis, the
Reform rabbinate, to formally readdress the issue of intermarriage at
their 2010 convention. The CCAR Task Force on the Challenges of Intermarriage for the Reform Rabbi expanded the dialogue beyond the
1973 dichotomous discussion about whether rabbis should officiate to
develop a greater understanding of how intermarriage had changed over
forty years. Among its many discoveries the Task Force identified "vast
changes in the rabbinate and in the makeup of the members of our congregations and communities, as well as a desire on the part of our colleagues not to argue with one another on issues of conscience, but to be
guided by the wisdom we possess, collectively and individually, on how
best to do what we each may choose to do as rabbis."[98] In 1995–1996, Beth
Emeth had 373 dues-paying families. A decade later, in 2005–2006, it had
nearly doubled its membership to 720 families. The recession of 2008
contributed to a decline in membership by 100 families; but by 2013 it
had regained half of those, and membership was more than 670 families.[99] Regardless of the fluctuations, its membership is nearly half the
total affiliated families in the city. Without a doubt, part of the rise in
membership reflects the warm welcome Beth Emeth exudes to interfaith
and in-married couples alike. In Rabbi Levy's words, "The key to being
inclusive is to be so inclusive that you forget you're being inclusive—
the welcome needs to be so welcome that it's not an effort, it's just who
you are."[100] Men who are members of this Reform congregation have
clearly benefited from this rabbi's approach, as one commented, "Everybody loves Rabbi Levy," and "If he wasn't Jewish, he'd be a saint."[101]
Men made similarly glowing remarks about the cantor, Annie Rose. The
transformation occurring in Reform Judaism to better satisfy the needs
of interfaith couples, including rabbis willing to officiate while also setting conditions for doing so, recognizes intermarriage as an opportunity
for generating Jewish engagement.[102] Beth Emeth offers a free one-year
membership to any newlywed couple married by Rabbi Levy or by Assistant Rabbi Delson.[103]

PATRILINEAL DESCENT

How the children of intermarriage were raised and subsequently identify, rather than how married individuals identified, is the crucial issue for long-term Jewish continuity. If approximately half of American Jews intermarry and less than half that do raise Jewish children, the future of Jewry appears to be in jeopardy, and the halachic (Jewish legal) position against intermarriage seems pragmatic. However, if more than half of children of intermarriage are raised as Jewish and later identify as Jews, the picture of retention is brighter. The 1990 and 2000 national estimates were that roughly a third of the children with intermarried parents were being raised Jewish.[104] In 2013, researchers elicited more nuanced responses: among Jews married to non-Jews, 20 percent said they were raising children Jewish by religion, 25 percent partly Jewish by religion, and 16 percent Jewish not by religion or mixed (Jewish by religion, partly Jewish by religion, and/or Jewish but not by religion).[105] Although the parsing of definitions and accompanying ambiguity make a grand total of those raising children Jewish elusive, that only 37 percent of respondents were raising children as "not Jewish" is clear.[106] Defining children's Jewish identity strictly by religion or more broadly influences the extent of one's optimism, as does bearing in mind that many Jews by religion are not particularly religious and most Jews of no religion are proudly Jewish. Furthermore, according to research scientist Theodore Sasson, "the propensity of adults with intermarried parents to identify as Jewish steadily increased [over generations], from 25 percent in the 65-and-older group, to 37 percent in the 50–64 age group, to 39 percent in the 30–49 group, to 59 percent in the 18–29 group."[107] While the exact percentages of children reared as Jews differs between national and communal studies, and there is more to learn about how millennials' identities manifest, a consensus surrounds the intermarried Jewish parent.[108] Extant scholarship contends that more Jewish children are raised by Jewish mothers married to Christian fathers than by Jewish fathers married to Christian mothers.[109] I am not contesting that data. However the majority of Jewish men I interviewed were adamant about their children being raised Jewish. Because the men self-selected to participate, my sample undoubtedly has a disproportionate number of men who raised Jewish children. Nevertheless, it is important to shed light on their stories to understand the meaning of intermarriage for this segment of the intermarried population and what can be learned from it. And, if Gordon is right about academics being ahead of the curve in assimilation, then these choices may point to a different Jewish future. Among the men who intermarried between 1953 and 1978, nine out of fourteen raised Jewish children. Two men raised children with dual religious traditions, two as Christian, and one as Humanist. Among the men who intermarried between 1980 and 1989, ten out of twelve raised Jewish children, one as "nothing," and one had no children from his intermarriage. That more men in either grouping did not raise children as "both" or "neither" is noteworthy, because it suggests that the "double or nothing" concept, that intermarried families practice religious syncretism if anything, does not apply to these men.[110]

What do their personal journeys teach about transmission of Jewish identity? Men's testimonies about fathering Jewish offspring suggest that their investment in how their children would be raised was a particularly Jewish take on American gender during the postwar decades. Fathers' centrality increased during the late 1940s and 1950s by emphasizing their contributions to the personality development and psychological health of their families. However, the same conservative family ideology that sensitized men to their children's needs also reinforced the sex-based division of labor that meant men continued to control political, economic, and social affairs while their wives tended to the home.[111] Although Jewish men, like most American men, still did far less of the actual childcare than did women, some Jewish men who intermarried have at least been "deciders." Recalling his Christian fiancée's promise to raise children in his faith when they married in 1953, Morris said, "It was very important to me" to raise Jewish children; otherwise, he continued, "I don't think I would've married her." Raising children with "no religious orientation" was likewise unacceptable to him.[112] Keith Soller described the conversation he had with his betrothed: "When we got married, I made the point to her that if you don't want to convert, that's up to you, but *all of our children* . . . are going to be Jewish."[113] Fred Stevens, who married an Episcopal woman in 1977, told his betrothed, "Look, if we have children, they have to be Jewish, otherwise the deal is off. I have to get

Eddie Fisher and Elizabeth Taylor kiss after their wedding ceremony in Las Vegas, Nevada (May 12, 1959). *Deutsche Presse Agentur/Landov.*

married in a synagogue. You can do what you want."[114] Television anchor Aaron Brown was not concerned with whether or why his wife Charlotte, raised Presbyterian, converted: "I didn't care at all. I *did* care how we raised our kid; *that* I did care about."[115] The men's comments illustrate a lack of investment in whether their brides chose Judaism for themselves combined with commitment to Jewish continuity through their children.

Despite the men's lackluster comments about whether their wives converted, many of the women decided on their own to become Jews-by-choice. Slightly more than half of these Christian women, fourteen out of twenty-seven, converted. Many of the men I interviewed encouraged me to speak to their present and even former wives, which inspired me to dedicate a chapter in this book to their experiences. Regardless of whether the men wanted their wives to convert to Judaism or not, all expressed feeling positive when they did. "I don't think it's changed our relationship," Brian Geller told me, "but it sure feels complete now. It just feels good. It feels right."[116] Singer Eddie Fisher, who intermarried three times, described in his memoir how he felt when Elizabeth Taylor insisted on becoming a Jew: "I was secretly pleased."[117] Sharing the Jewish identifier contributed to the men in my study being connected to the Jewish community, even if it was their wives, not them, who sang in the temple choir. When a man's wife remained Christian, she could still be "the best Jew in the family," as journalist Steve Roberts described his wife Cokie. When their daughter had to bring *haroset* to a Passover Seder, "she called her Catholic mother for the recipe." Linking Jewish holiday food and being coerced by his Christian wife to attend Rosh Hashanah services with Jewish identity is an attenuated equation, yet her effort made him happy because it demonstrated that she cared about his religion.[118] In cases where a Christian wife did not convert, either before or after marriage, the couple's children would later face questions about their identity.

Identity politics has taken a devastating toll on some intermarried Jewish men who raised Jewish children only to have those children face exclusion from the organized Jewish community. After much debate, the Reform movement made the historic decision to accept patrilineal descent, sharpening the distinctions among Jewish denominations in the process. The resolution adopted in 1983 by the Reform rabbinate presumed Jewish descent regardless of which parent was Jewish and included that the child's Jewish status was "to be established through appropriate and timely public and formal acts of identification with the Jewish faith and people."[119] This followed a lesser-known decision of the Reconstructionist movement in 1968.[120] By making descent egalitarian, the Reform movement essentially declared that the children of all Jewish-Christian marriages were Jewish, provided that the child lived a Jewish life. Conservative and Orthodox Jewish leadership, however, continued to uphold matrilineal descent. For example, Orthodox rabbi J. Simcha Cohen denounced the patrilineal descent decision as an illegal position in 1987: "It is without dispute . . . that the children of gentile mothers and Jewish fathers are categorized as gentiles. They are simply not Jews."[121] The lack of agreement had several important consequences. Most significantly, it created different standards between movements for who is a Jew that continue to affect intermarried Jewish men and their children. Reform rabbi Nadia Siritsky acknowledged both the risk and the potential of intermarriage: "The claim that our survival is in jeopardy is true. By many objective standards, we do not seem to be growing. But, I disagree with [the] assessment of the threat. We are losing Jews, not because of who they choose to marry, but because of how we respond to them. The more restrictive our definition for 'who is a Jew,' the more we will shrink."[122] Although acceptance of patrilineal Jews has increased over time, perhaps as understanding of the decision and the population of children with Jewish fathers grow, the history of insults to men who came of age prior to the decision is long lasting, and the legacy continues to permeate the identities of children of intermarried parents. In *Love in Black and White: A Memoir of Race, Religion, and Romance,* former U.S. Senator William S. Cohen (born in 1940) describes his horror and anger on learning that he would not be permitted to become a bar mitzvah by his rabbi in Bangor, Maine, because Cohen's mother was not Jewish: "I was suspended between two worlds. Every day at public school I proclaimed myself to be Jewish, refusing to recite the Lord's Prayer. Yet in Hebrew School I was treated as a non-Jew." He had spent six years learning Hebrew and looked forward to the rite of passage; Cohen refused to undergo a conversion. He threw his miniature mezuzah necklace into the Penobscot River, declaring to himself, "I no longer had to pursue a prize that had never been mine for the taking. I no longer had to pretend. The Jewish community would not change its rules to accommodate me, and I would not yield to its acceptance."[123]

The term "patrilineal Jew" is offensive; by attaching the word "patrilineal," it defines the identity of someone with a Jewish father as somehow less than a Jew. It is not simply a categorical distinction between matrilineal and non-matrilineal descent. Writing in the *Forward,* author David A. M. Wilensky described his decision to convert to Conservative

Judaism after growing up Reform. He points out that not all patrilineals would do the same: "They are Jews—by my definition anyway—who will never set foot in a Conservative synagogue, because of an anachronistic policy that forces them to question their own legitimacy and brings them great anguish." He calls on the Conservative movement to accept patrilineal descent just as it adopted new positions on female rabbis and gay rights.[124] Members of the Conservative movement acknowledge the potential for hurt feelings yet stand their ground on Jewish law.[125] While the descent controversy focuses on which parent is Jewish, one cannot help but wonder whether the real anxiety is over the fact that only one out of two parents have Jewish genes. Even Jews with a Jewish mother and non-Jewish father have had their identities questioned, especially if they did not look stereotypically Jewish.[126] Groundbreaking research about adult children of intermarriages suggests that which parent is Jewish matters less than previously thought. According to the Jewish Outreach Institute, Jews with only a Jewish father "express similar levels of Jewish engagement, are equally likely to say that being Jewish is important in their lives, and are just as likely to participate in events organized by Jewish institutions" as Jews with only a Jewish mother.[127]

The tenacious idea in the popular mind that Jewishness is "in the blood" makes having a non-Jewish parent a social impediment, an odd reversal of the Nazi definition of who was a Jew, that plays itself out in the stories of mixed-ancestry children and characters. "Halachically (according to Jewish law), there is no such thing as a Half/Life. If your mother is Jewish, you're Jewish. If your mother is not Jewish, you're not Jewish. . . . But in today's secular world, I'm amazed by how many people concern themselves with such distinctions . . . even if they never consider Jewish law at any other time," writes Laurel Snyder, editor of *Half/Life: Jew-ish Tales from Interfaith Homes*.[128] The barriers to full Jewish citizenship extend from American-born children of intermarriage to those born in the former USSR who emigrated here only to find their identity questioned in new ways: "And then there's me. A strange creature, too Americanized for the Russians, too Russian for the Americans ('Where's your accent from?'). A refugee Jew by Russian terms, not technically Jewish by Jewish law. *C'est vraiment dégueulasse* (It is truly disgusting)."[129] Fictional children, too, share the impediments to full inclusion and social worth. Consider Harry Potter, the son of a pure-blood wizard and a Muggle-born witch, in J. K. Rowling's book series. Sure, he was accepted at Hogwarts School of Witchcraft and Wizardry, but some of his classmates never let him forget that he was a "Mudblood."[130] The stigma of having mixed blood persists even if a character claims the more acceptable part of his self. In *Star Trek* (2009), Spock decides to be completely Vulcan yet is bullied and persistently reminded even as an adult of his "disadvantage": having a human mother.[131] The preoccupation with pure lineage and its influence persists in life as it does in fiction.

Since Conservative and Orthodox Jews reject patrilineal descent, intermarried Jewish men have sought acceptance for themselves and their children wherever they could find it, usually among Reform, Reconstructionist, and Humanist Jews. Samuel Isserman shared with me the pain his son experienced when, preparing for his bar mitzvah, he was kicked out of Torah class when the rabbi discovered that his mother wasn't Jewish. The family joined the Jewish Cultural Society in Ann Arbor because, in this Jewish father's words, "you were Jewish if you wanted to be."[132] A past president of the Jewish Community Center, he also encouraged both children to go on Birthright to visit Israel and gave a talk at the *Kol Nidre* service on Yom Kippur. People will go where they and their offspring are counted and valued. His son, determined to prove his Jewish identity beyond question, eventually moved to Israel and underwent an Orthodox conversion, illustrating that there were no obstacles too great for him to overcome in his pursuit of a Jewish status that would be considered legitimate by all Jewish authorities. Patrilineal descent continues to be one of the most divisive issues between Jewish movements and within the organized Jewish community, as a 2012 headline indicated: "30 Years On, Still Dissent on Patrilineal Descent."[133]

The lack of consensus about patrilineal descent in Jewish circles is exacerbated by a lack of awareness in the general public, perpetuated by journalists, and creates fodder for humorists. Naomi Schaefer Riley, former *Wall Street Journal* editor and author of *'Til Faith Do Us Part: How Interfaith Marriage Is Transforming America* (2013), stated matter-of-factly about religious rules, "Children of a Jewish mother are considered Jewish," without mentioning patrilineal descent anywhere in her book.[134] Steve Solomon's one-man comedy based on his life is titled "My

Mother's Italian, My Father's Jewish, & I'm in Therapy!"[135] Comedian
Yisrael Campbell echoes a patrilineal Jew's experience in his autobio-
graphical show "Circumcise Me," as he describes with humor and pain
his journey as the child of Italian and Irish Catholic parents becoming first a Reform, then a Conservative, and finally an Orthodox Jew.
He asks, "Was I Jewish the first time? The second? Or only the third?
Was I always Jewish? Am I still not Jewish?"[136] Jon Fisch, who appeared
on *The Late Show* with David Letterman and on *Last Comic Standing*,
entertained a Jewish audience on Christmas Eve with a joke about encouraging his intermarried brother to raise one child Jewish and one
Catholic: "Then we get to see who wins!"[137] Their children's identities
are no laughing matter for the intermarried Jewish fathers in this study.

The "dissent over descent" contributes to shifting allegiances across
branches of Judaism, but for these intermarried Jewish men it does not
undermine their conviction that any children of theirs are Jewish. Intermarried men who raised Jewish children exemplify a new definition
of Jewish identity that can be described as paternal connection. Their
children are Jewish because they are connected to Jewish fathers who
themselves had Jewish fathers. All but one of the men in this study who
had children came from families with two Jewish parents. The men
maintain their Jewish self-identification and, by association, share it
with their children. Whether the children in turn embrace it, sustain
the connection with the previous generation, and share it with the next
generation will only be determined once sufficient numbers of children
of intermarried Jewish fathers have started families of their own and
scholars have conducted longitudinal studies. Related work has already
begun—for example, *The Jewish Futures Project* by Brandeis University
researchers studying the Taglit-Birthright population, discussed in the
next chapter.[138] However, much more in-depth gender analysis is still
needed to determine the extent to which an Israel experience influences
an adult child of an intermarried man to raise Jewish children—not
just how he views doing so—compared to an adult child of an intermarried woman. For the time being, however, based on my study it
is possible to see an emerging form of Jewish identity stemming from
paternal connection. At once traditional and post-denominational, the
idea that fathers can play a significant role in fostering children's Jew-

ishness deserves further study. This analysis is reinforced by the work of social psychologist Bethamie Horowitz in her report *Connections and Journeys: Assessing Critical Opportunities for Enhancing Jewish Identity.*[139] Like other connections, the father-child bond is a source for inspiring Jewish identity.

The men's narratives illustrate the fluidity of Jewish identity and the impact a single rabbi can have, negative or positive, on their Jewish identities and affiliations.[140] Some Jewish men described their paths from Conservative and Orthodox childhoods to affiliation with a Reform congregation. Deciding who would officiate at an intermarriage sometimes influenced men's Jewish identity. When Fred Stevens asked a Conservative rabbi in 1976 to marry him and his Christian bride, the rabbi refused and also told Fred he couldn't be a member of his congregation. Fred described the impact of this eight-minute conversation: "That was the end of me being a Conservative Jew." While scholars and rabbis debate the relationship between rabbinic wedding officiation and subsequent Jewish engagement—some arguing that there is a positive influence on Jewish involvement and child raising when rabbis officiate, and others admitting a connection while cautioning against causality—my qualitative research suggests that Jewish men are considerably more soured by rabbis who refuse to participate than are Jewish women.[141] "I had been maritally ex-communicated," Edward Cohen wrote in his memoir about growing up Jewish in Mississippi and his rabbi's "rejection" as he described it.[142] To fully understand the relationship between rabbinic officiation and Jewish involvement requires further gender analysis.

Men's Jewish identities could change over their life course, which sometimes surprised them. Morris Aker described his journey from Conservative to Reform Judaism: "It never would have occurred to me that I would be a Reform Jew . . . Reform was a strange thing to me, not fully Jewish." Interviewed a half-century after joining a Reform temple, Morris now believes that Reform Judaism is "fully Jewish" and insists, "I love being a Jew."[143] Another man who grew up Conservative and married in 1963 admitted, "I didn't like the idea that if you're not Orthodox, you're not a Jew."[144] When he moved to Ann Arbor from Chicago, after having intermarried, he tried the Conservative synagogue but did not feel comfortable there and so joined the Reform temple. Regarding his current identity, he stated, "I feel much more Jewish now than when I was Conservative."[145] His reflection illustrates the arbitrariness of denominational distinctions with regard to intensity of identification.

REAL JEWISH MEN

The American men in my sample became "more Jewish"—not along denominational lines but according to self-definition—due to personal relationships with a rabbi and Christian wives who made them "step up to the plate" after the men gave ultimatums that their children be raised Jewish. Disaffection for organized religion prompted moves for some men from Orthodox and Conservative Judaism to Reform Judaism, which offered a Jewish nest for men who were turned off by *halacha* and more traditional rabbis. Reform (and Reconstructionist) Judaism, it seems, changed with the times so as to keep more Jews in the fold— even if they married outside the tribe. Intermarried men also determined their own children's identities. "We see him as Jewish," one father commented about his and his wife's view of their son.[146] George Maze described how extended family members did not consider his children Jewish, and as a result they would not be given aliyot or allowed on the bimah at their cousin's bar mitzvah. Given that his children became b'nai mitzvah and self-identify as Jewish, he contends, "They're as Jewish as the next Jew!"[147] Intermarried men's sense of Jewish continuity is personal; it is *they* as parents—not any rabbi, denomination, or movement—who authorize the Jewishness of their children. Yet they also want communal and familial validation. Hence, from this view, personal choice by a parent trumps the controversial issue of descent. Birth as a Jew matters less than parental decision to raise a child as a Jew.

While intermarried Jewish men may help broaden the concept of continuity, traditional gender behaviors that continue to influence American family life are strong enforcers of marital dynamics in Ann Arbor and, I suspect, elsewhere. Although some of the men were able to craft careers that allowed for flexible schedules so they could be more involved with their children's daily lives, and seemed happier as a result, the male breadwinner ethic continued to prevail. When asked how they envisioned their role as a man, a husband, a father, many men responded with the words "to provide." Additional characteristics included "hard work-ing," "financially successful," "family oriented," "committed to helping others," and setting a "good example." Men who intermarried in the mid 1970s and 1980s used the term "partnership" and "two-career" marriage when describing their roles as husbands, a change from their predeces-sors who intermarried in the 1950s and 1960s. However, the majority of men in both age cohorts still identified being the provider as their primary defining role. Even those men who strove to share domestic tasks equally often admitted that their wives still did more around the house and spent more time with their children, while they spent more hours working outside of their home.

The changing meaning of fatherhood influenced Jewish men's expe-riences, yet fell short of creating a paradigm shift in the way society val-ues men for their earning power and women for their nurturing abilities. There are more dual-career couples today than a half-century ago, and the concept of equal parenting has begun to take root.[148] However, more traditional gender behaviors continue to influence family life, includ-ing men's available time for parenting and women's earning capacity.[149] Those Jewish men who married in the last quarter of the twentieth cen-tury wanted to be different kinds of parents than their fathers were, re-sisting the corporate ladder to devote more time to their children. When Frank Stevens was growing up in the 1960s, "mothers were parents and fathers worked." He was a good high school football player, but his father only attended a couple of games. Frank was determined to spend more time with his children, to be there for them. His son was a soccer player; Frank went to every game and many of the practices.[150] His commitment illustrates a change in American families; since 1965 fathers have nearly tripled their time with children; yet mothers still spend about twice as much time with their children as fathers do.[151] While the reemergence of what historians dub "new fatherhood" of the 1970s and 1980s helped men legitimize spending more time with their families, it unfortunately did not fully reconstruct gender relations to create equity in domestic or paid labor.[152]

In the next chapter, my focus turns to the men who intermarried between 1990 and 2008, when my research began. This cohort shares some similarities with its predecessor but also illustrates a new era in

Jewish husbandry and fatherhood, with an emphasis on *tikkun olam* (repair of the world). The most recently intermarried men exemplify the ways in which it is possible to be manly *menschen*. The first decade of the new millennium ushered in cries in the Jewish community about a "boy crisis," which some scholars argue is actually part of a longer historical trajectory of concern.[153] Are Jewish men truly dropping out of organized Jewish life as contemporary commentators have lamented, or are they exhibiting their connections to Judaism, community, and peoplehood in as yet unpredicted ways? Intermarried Jewish men may, in fact, offer new insights about the extent to which some Jewish men are drawing closer to understanding how gender equity in the workplace and in the home is a goal well worth achieving in America.

2

Sex and Money

Being the richest man in the cemetery doesn't matter
to me . . . Going to bed at night saying we've done
something wonderful . . . that's what matters to me.

—Steve Jobs

Studying the experience and meaning of intermarriage requires a longitudinal approach, investigating behaviors and attitudes over a prolonged period of time, with eyes also on the recent past. Focusing on
the life experiences of Jewish men who intermarried between 1991 and
2008, this chapter analyzes the remaining fourteen of the total forty-one
oral histories of men (the thirteen interviews with women born Christian are analyzed in the next chapter). While some of the patterns from
the earlier age cohorts continued to be evident, three new themes also
arose from the interviews with men who married during the more contemporary time period. First, many men experienced a reawakening
of their Jewish identities when they became fathers that they expressed
in terms of *gemilut hasadim* (acts of kindness) and *tikkun olam* (repair
of the world) rather than in strictly religious terms. Second, a persistent
antagonism toward what some men saw as a formidable hierarchy within
the Jewish community distanced them from becoming more involved
in organized Jewish life. Lastly, despite the men's and women's movements of the preceding decades, intermarried men's Jewish lives were
hampered by traditional family dynamics and the American imperative

to make money. Their identities as Jewish men and fathers were likewise influenced by social constraints on their gender roles.

During the 1980s and 1990s, a high degree of disaffiliation permeated American society, enabling men of Jewish heritage to marry women of other faith backgrounds in the following years.[1] The decrease in religious identification and observance among many Americans muted the differences between young Christian women and Jewish men. The proportion of adult Americans among a nationally representative sample who indicated membership in a religious institution declined from 61 percent in the early 1970s and early 1990s to 54 percent in 2001, while the number who did not subscribe to any religious identification more than doubled between 1990 and 2001.[2] The rise of the "nones," the growth in number of unaffiliated Americans, continued into the new millennium, illustrating the long-term effects of this shift in the religious landscape. In 2007, the number of unaffiliated U.S. adults was just over 15 percent, which rose to slightly less than 20 percent by 2012.[3] With one in five American adults claiming no religious affiliation and increasing numbers of Jews who identified by non-religious criteria, it was all the more likely that Jewish men could find compatibility with non-Jewish women.[4] People met and fell in love unimpeded by stark distinctions between their beliefs and practices. Escalating national divorce rates simultaneously suggested that marriage was a gamble regardless of whether one married within one's own religious group. Paradoxically, as the Jewish men in my sample married and became fathers, they also began to navigate their personal and communal ties to Jewish religion and culture. Increasingly and as their narratives illustrate, the end of the twentieth century and the beginning of the twenty-first continued the shift begun in the 1960s and 1970s by most Jewish men, who identified more strongly with their Jewish heritage; fatherhood partnered with intermarriage fostered an increased sense of the importance of their cultural and religious heritage, combined with greater commitment to its endurance.

While intermarriage across ethnic and religious lines became the norm in American society at large, Jewish communal concern over the marked increase of marriages between Jews and non-Jews meant that Jewish men (and women) who intermarried were considerably more visible defectors from the group than had been the case earlier in the twentieth century. As the intermarriage rates for each gender converged—Jewish women, who had been thought to intermarry less frequently than Jewish men, became just as likely to do so—intermarriage appeared to be a serious liability to Jewish continuity. The 2000–2001 National Jewish Population Survey found that, overall, the intermarriage rates among men and among women within the same age bracket were quite similar: 33 percent and 29 percent, respectively.[5] Although the concern about Jewish women intermarrying may have been mitigated by matrilineal descent, the children of those unions counting as Jews across Jewish denominations and movements, Jewish men did not have the same social insurance across the board, with only two out of four of the major branches of Judaism accepting patrilineal descent. Thus, rising popularity of intermarriage in the United States did not correlate with increased Jewish communal acceptance.

Being the "only Jew" growing up continued to influence Jewish men's dating patterns before they eventually married Christian women, as did integration in non-Jewish circles. Larry Rush remembered what it was like being one of less than a handful of Jews in Rutland, Vermont: "There were only four Jewish kids my age in the whole town: Hillary, David, Ronnie, and me. That was it." The only positive of living in such a tiny Jewish community was not having to share his bar mitzvah day with another person as his son had to do in Ann Arbor, where his Hebrew school class had fifty students in it.[6] Born and raised in New York City, Charles Revkin always thought he would marry someone Jewish, and his parents stressed how important they thought it was to do so. He agreed that having more in common with a prospective spouse could make marriage easier and was sympathetic to the idea that intermarriage might contribute to Jewish discontinuity; however, he dated mostly Catholic women who were not very religious and eventually married one of them. Charles held his parents and social integration between Jews and Christians, in part, responsible for this marital choice: "If they really thought that I should only marry someone Jewish, then they shouldn't have enrolled me in public school and sent me to Harvard and other places where most people are not Jewish."[7] His statement suggests that he does not believe Jews can integrate in American society *without* intermarrying.

Cover illustration for the Feburary 15, 1993 issue of the New Yorker by
Art Spiegelman, graphic artist and author of Maus. Spiegelman married
Françoise Mouly in 1977; she converted to Judaism in the 1980s.
Art Spiegelman/The Wylie Agency LLC.

Sexual satisfaction motivated men to intermarry in the last decade of the twentieth century and first decade of the twenty-first, as it had their predecessors.[8] They inherited the *Playboy* legacy of the 1960s, when magazine marketers told American men that heterosexual pleasure was theirs to pursue, coming of age during a post-sexual-revolution era; intercourse replaced petting, and widely available contraception made premarital sex convenient behavior.[9] When Gary Brodin was dating, physical attraction and whether he "hit it off in bed" with a woman was far more relevant than whether she was Jewish or not. He admitted he was "thinking with the wrong head" when he decided to marry his (former) wife in 1991.[10] Allan Benjamin explained that he remained single until he was forty in part because "a lot of decisions were made based on easy sexual gratification." He admitted, "I would date anyone who would let me take her top off. Religion had nothing to do with it. If they were Jewish, great. If they were Catholic, fine. If they were Protestant, that was okay, too." When Allan met the woman who would eventually become his wife, he thought she was "stunning" and fondly remembered, "She was wearing a thong."[11] Greg Marin intended to marry someone Jewish but had sexual intercourse with multiple Christian women. His mind-set at the time was, "They were just relationships. They're not Jewish. I'm not going to marry them."[12] Greg conceded that it was "emotionally wrong," because the Christian women might have thought there was the possibility of marriage. Little did he realize then that in 2005 he would, in fact, marry one of them. Morton Langfeld was involved in a sexual romance and initially against the relationship going forward because the woman was not Jewish. He described, "Love or lust, or a combination, gets you over those things."[13] Hence sexual attraction and compatibility in the 1990s and 2000s were important variables for Jewish men.

Jewish identity sometimes meant *not* doing what other American men were doing. One man described, "I'm Jewish, so I don't drink that much."[14] Going to sports bars and drinking never appealed to him or felt like something he needed to do. Gary Brodin described being a Jewish man as atypical because he is communicative and expresses his feelings. He joked that he was absent from school when they handed out the "goy rules" to boys.[15] While Charles Revkin conceded that it sounded chau-

vinistic, he thought that men focused on more concrete and less feelings-
oriented things, such as business and politics, compared to women, who
cared more about who said what to whom about whose child. However,
when it came to Jewish men in particular, he claimed, "I don't think
Jewish men are necessarily fitting the American masculine concept very
well" because there were "fewer beer drinkers, especially with a baseball cap turned backwards," and fewer athletes. Jewish fathers, Charles
believed, had "more intimate families" and were "more able to express
emotion . . . and have very close and warm verbal as well as physical relationships with their kids" than the average non-Jewish man.[16] These Jewish men associated Christian men with alcoholic beverages and athlet-
ics, suggesting that the combination was not part of their Jewish ethnic
repertoire. Although some Jewish men chose reading books over playing
sports, physical strength remained important. Glenn Aker remembered
his reaction when someone suggested substituting a light bulb for the
customary breaking of the glass at his wedding: "What kind of a weakling can't break a glass? We don't need a light bulb. I'm sure there was a
glass—I wouldn't accept a light bulb." Hence, while these Jewish men
perceived their identity as distinct from other American men, they still
clung to the post 1960s-era version of Jewish manhood as strong in body
as well as in mind.

Jewish men also still linked their identity to being a provider. Larry
Rush described manhood as "taking responsibility for the loved ones
in your life" and commented that there were lots of expectations about
what a husband and father were supposed to do: "Although it's kind
of sexist to say, I think a part of what men do is help make sure that
their families are well provided for."[17] One man, who did not actually
have children of his own, speculated about why, in his opinion, mothers were more focused on making sure that their children receive a
Jewish background than fathers: "If he's a Jewish man, he's just going
about his business—we're just going about our business, just making
the money, making the living, providing as best we can. . . . I really don't
think we give it much thought. We're being the dutiful dad and the
dutiful husband, and going out there and working and bringing home
what we're supposed to bring home."[18] The respondents' comments, like
their intermarried predecessors, reflect sociologist Chaim Waxman's

contention that the reinterpreted role of the less observant Jewish father manifested itself in the father's commitment to his work and to instilling the importance of success in his children, which persisted late in twentieth century and beyond.[19]

MORE JEWISH

The meaning of being Jewish deepened for this cohort of intermarried men after marrying a woman born Christian and becoming fathers, as it had for some of the men who intermarried earlier in the twentieth century. It may be said that men may experience a reawakening of their Jewish identity when they marry, regardless of whether they intermarry or in-marry, due to greater communal opportunities. The Jewish community gears far more of its programming toward family units than to single Jewish men or women. Moreover, once Jews have children, they are more likely to join synagogues.[20] Likewise, Jews may become "more Jewish" as they age, consistent with American religious demographic patterns. According to the *U.S. Religious Landscape Survey* conducted by the Pew Forum on Religion & Public Life, older adults are more likely (69 percent of adults sixty-five and older) than younger adults (45 percent of adults under age thirty) to say religion is very important to them. This pattern persists across many religions, especially among Catholics and Protestants, but not among Mormons, Jews, or Muslims, where there is no generation gap. "Within these groups," states the 2008 Pew report, "those who are younger are about as likely as those who are older to say religion is very important to them."[21] Hence it is more likely that intermarriage influenced a deepening of men's Jewish identities in relation to their Christian-born spouses and through becoming fathers, rather than merely aging. For Charles Revkin, being Jewish meant being part of a community, and he acknowledged that it became more important as his life unfolded. "It was a combination of circumstances," Charles explained, "where I married someone non-Jewish and then . . . I knew I wanted to raise my kids Jewish. I know mothers tend to play an important role in that. Here we were not going to have a Jewish mother, so it's almost like an overreaction to make sure it gets done."[22] Hence assuming a proactive role regarding the children's Jewish upbringing became a significant component of Jewish identity for intermarried fathers. The shift could be striking: Allan Benjamin preferred to "pass" as a member of the majority during his college years than join a Jewish fraternity, but after intermarrying and becoming a father, he accompanied his children to Tot Shabbat and listened to Jewish CDs. He reflected, "As the kids grow, I'm becoming more open, more Jewish. I'm now somehow a board member of the Jewish Community Center here. Seven years ago, I'd be looking at you like, 'Where is the JCC in Ann Arbor?'"[23] The influence of intermarriage on these Jewish men illustrates the comment by the Jewish protagonist's Christian wife in Ludwig Lewisohn's novel *The Island Within:* "You didn't know you were going to resurrect the Jew in you."[24]

The majority of men who intermarried during the last decade of the twentieth century and the first decade of the new millennium were equally adamant as their intermarried predecessors that their children be raised Jewish whether or not their wives converted to Judaism. Eleven out of fourteen of the men who intermarried in the 1990s and 2000s had children; eight of those fathers raised their children to identify as Jews, one as Christian, one as both Jewish and Christian, and lastly one as "neither." Larry Rush, who was born in 1958 and married in 1991 a woman brought up Fundamentalist Christian, described how he and his wife determined that any future children would be Jewish: "Because it was important to me and not important to her." Charles Revkin reminisced that during each relationship he had with a Christian woman before getting married, it was always clear that if they ever got married they would have a Jewish family. He recalled, "I'm not sure that I ever presented it as a line in the sand. I probably just presented it as something that's important to me." Fortunately, his wife-to-be recognized this fact and within three weeks of dating volunteered that she would be happy to have a Jewish family if their relationship culminated in marriage. As this respondent intuited, however, when a Christian woman agreed to raise Jewish children, she may not have made such an offer based on a full understanding of what that entailed . . . and what it did not. Only after marrying such an accommodating woman did he learn that "I don't think she knew 80 percent of what she was talking about."[25] Years later, when the couple had children, she had the realization that Santa Claus was not going to visit their house. Jewish men could also find ways to overcome any disappointments related to the "December Dilemma." One father opined in *Moment* magazine, "Instead of making our kids 'feel Jewish' by requiring them to glumly sit out the biggest holiday extravaganza of the year—or, worse, taking part in it—let us relearn the wisdom of the rabbis and reinvent our own midwinter holiday. Let us have presents . . . and latkes with caviar . . . and yes, blue and white house lights."[26] It is questionable how many children actually like fish eggs, but presents and sparkly lights go a long way. Jewish comedian Jon Stewart (born Jonathan Stuart Leibowitz), who married Tracey McShane in 2000, made a similar argument in his April 9, 2012, "Faith/Off" on the *Daily Show,* suggesting that Jews invent a character called Passover Pete to compete with the Easter Bunny. "As a father of mixed-faith children, who are exposed to both Christian and Jewish holidays," Stewart confides to the audience, "I can't help but feel that we Jews are getting our asses kicked out here!" Although one might question Stewart's suggestions, which are after all satirical, he nails the continuity issue when he speaks directly to Members of the Tribe: "The key is the children, people; that's what Christians have figured out. You get the children, you win."[27]

Although most of the men placed little significance on whether their wives converted, one respondent wished he had insisted his girlfriend become Jewish before they wed, for the children's sake. He could have insisted, he realized, but "I didn't have those kind of freaking *cajones.* Even if she did [convert], it wouldn't be of her own volition. And that's what I would want. I don't want anybody doing things for me. For the kids you can do things, but not for me."[28] His comment illustrates a common phenomenon among intermarried Jewish men regarding conversion; they did not want responsibility for their wife's decision. They viewed conversion to Judaism as personal or private, whereas children involved heritage, the whole family and extended community. Men's feelings about whether their wives converted mirrored their feelings about whether the women adopted the men's surnames. While men who intermarried between 1953 and the early 1970s labeled themselves as "traditionalists" and assumed that their wives would take their names, men who intermarried from the mid-1970s on were far more liberal in their attitudes. They often encouraged their wives to keep their own names or to hyphenate. The emphasis, like with conversion, was that it was "up to her." Even when a wife did adopt her husband's surname, his reaction was, "It was nice ... because it symbolized a union between us. However the issue wasn't important."[29] Men's attitudes changed over time from "In my day it was automatic" for a woman to take a man's name, to "It made little difference to me ... because I believed women should have the choice."[30] Whether the men had Jewish-sounding surnames, which some did and liked, they did not try to compel their wives to take them. More significant than their wives' decisions about conversion and surname was finding a house of worship where the men's children would be counted as members.

Intermarried Jewish men who chose to affiliate with a congregation chose one where they were assured that their children's identity would not be questioned. Although he grew up attending a Conservative synagogue, Larry Rush did not mince words when describing why he chose Reform Temple Beth Emeth (TBE) over Conservative Beth Israel: "I felt it was more accepting of interfaith couples and more accepting of [his son] having a non-Jewish mother."[31] Larry was determined to protect his son from hearing, "Well, you know, if your mother's not Jewish, you're not really Jewish," which he thought he might at the Conservative synagogue. Asked why he joined the Reform congregation, Walter Chatham responded, "Because I had a kid and needed to connect." He affiliated where no one questioned his Jewishness or that of his child: "Nobody asked. Nobody cares. I mean it's Temple Beth Emeth. Who knows who is what? It really doesn't matter there."[32] Walter interpreted the lack of attention to whether someone has one Jewish parent or two as an appealing form of openness and inclusion. His perspective may have had to do with him being a child of intermarriage.[33] Beth Israel Congregation, a synagogue with modern brick architecture and an intimate sanctuary, did not attract these men, but it did make an effort to be inclusive when it included the words "Interfaith couples welcome" in its full-page advertisement in the publication *Jewish Life in Washtenaw County 2008–2009*. It is of course easier to welcome "interfaith couples" than "interfaith families" including children.

There was a strong relationship between definitions of Jewishness based on bloodlines during the Holocaust and how some men thought about their children's identities and associated vulnerabilities. Men either proactively declared their children to be Jewish because of the way that they were raised and educated or, in a less positive vein, according to ascription. Although *halacha* might not consider the child of a Jewish man and an unconverted Jewish woman to be Jewish, antisemites did, Jewish fathers contended. One man who accepted matrilineal descent still asserted, "Hitler proved that that doesn't matter."[34] Another man told his daughter, "You're Jewish enough for Hitler."[35] The reference seemed laced with concern that a father could not protect his child from antisemitism any more than African American men could protect their families from slavery during the antebellum era. Roland Warren, former president of the National Fatherhood Initiative, blogged about his experience visiting the U.S. Holocaust Memorial Museum in Washington, D.C. Considering history through the fatherhood lens he wrote, "As I viewed the many pictures of fathers, often taken just moments before they and their families were murdered, I could not help considering how horrible it must have been for them. It is the essence of good fathering to protect, but these dads could not."[36] Not all men made the connection between Jewish identity and antisemitism. Allan Benjamin, for example, discounted the descent controversy altogether, insisting that a child born to a Jewish male–Christian female pairing was equally Jewish as a child born to a Jewish female–Christian male couple. Yet his connection between the Holocaust and his children was profound; he named his son after a righteous Swede known for saving thousands of Jews during the Nazi occupation.[37]

TIKKUN OLAM POST–BAR MITZVAH

Men who became less religiously observant during their adult lives contended that being Jewish meant for them actively pursuing social justice and practicing *tikkun olam* (repair of the world). Regarding this concept, one man asserted, "I think that's an important part of being Jewish . . . living a just life and doing your part to make the world a better place."[38] Bruce Davidson, who was born in 1952 and married in 1995, credited his mother for always emphasizing that Judaism "taught you to do good for the rewards here; it's not because of something you're going to get later."

Ari Weinzweig, co-founder of Zingerman's Community of Businesses.
Photo by Peter Smith.

He was raised with a very strong belief in the rights of free speech and
free association. His mother had worked for Adlai Stevenson, the liberal
governor of Illinois, presidential hopeful, and ambassador to the United
Nations, and she idolized Democratic president Franklin Delano Roosevelt. He further elaborated, "I was raised with a very strong belief in
equality," thanks in part to his parents being leaders in the integration
efforts during the civil rights movement of the 1960s. Hence this man

veered away from the Orthodox observance of his childhood and affiliated with the Conservative synagogue, which accommodated his drift-
ing, sometimes toward Reform Judaism and other times toward Orthodoxy. Felix Garrison, who described himself as "non-religious Jewish,"
related to the "social progress type of Judaism, the part that's involved
in civil rights." [39] Hence, while some men admitted to having issues with
authority and problems with organized religion in general, many sup-
ported the idea that Jews' responsibility was not just for themselves but
also for other people. Ari Weinzweig is co-founder with Paul Saginaw
of Zingerman's Community of Businesses in Ann Arbor, recognized by
Inc. magazine as the "coolest small company in America," which "has
its roots in Jewish food" and its wings in building the local community.
Zingerman's guiding principles state, "It is our chosen responsibility to
make substantial and significant contributions in order to strengthen the
health, social, educational and cultural fabric of this community." Acting on that commitment, they founded Food Gatherers, an independent
nonprofit food rescue program and food bank. [40] Pursuit of social justice
helps explain why many Jewish men sign up to participate in Mitzvah
Day projects; it appeals to their desire to do good without imposing too
much on their limited discretionary time. Men's commitment to social
justice was tied to their Jewish identity.

Most men I interviewed became b'nai mitzvah. However, lack of af-
finity for the rabbi involved and uncertainties about the meaning of Jewish manhood meant the coming-of-age experience had little positive
influence on their emerging adult Jewish identity. Glenn Aker, who intermarried in 1998, became a bar mitzvah at a Reform temple in Massachusetts in the late 1970s. His comment reflects a void of personal involvement in the process: "My recollection is a bar mitzvah is something
that happens to you." [41] The rabbi told him what to do and he did it, Glenn
recounted. Allan Benjamin, who was raised Conservative, recalled being a "troublemaker" and memorizing his Torah portion rather than
actually learning what it meant. At his 1970s bar mitzvah, he moved the
yad (pointer) back and forth "so that it kind of looked like I knew what
I was doing, but I couldn't read Hebrew." The rabbi was well respected
by the board but according to Allan the synagogue had "lost an entire
generation, my generation," because the rabbi did not open up to the

children; rather "he didn't want children in the main sanctuary, didn't want noise, and his sermons were an hour and a half long."[42] The rabbi made the dispiriting impression that Judaism was for adults only. Greg Marin described how his parents had to convince the rabbi to let him wear a *tallis* (prayer shawl), which was not the custom at his temple, and said, "I remember not believing in any of the religious part of it."[43] "All I had to do was recite the weird-sounding words without the inconvenience of knowing what I was talking about," wrote humorist Dan Zevin about his bar mitzvah. "It was downhill from there. One day I ate a ham sandwich, the next I married a shiksa."[44] Hence, just at a time when these young men could be beginning their journey deeper into Judaism, they experienced instead a distancing that inhibited their relationship with religion. Their experiences are common in a society in which wealth rivals "erudition as a marker of manhood," according to historian Mark Oppenheimer. The bar mitzvah is "a ritual that honors a boy's encounter with Torah and his ascent to religious maturity" that "flourishes in a country where Jews do not take religious maturity very seriously."[45] Moreover, organized Judaism during the twentieth century was not yet equipped to help males explore the meaning of a specifically male Jewish identity. As folklorist Simon Bronner has argued, after World War II "the bar mitzvah gained importance . . . in what increasingly became seen as the most important phase of modern life and for a group that felt most in conflict in its definition of masculinity." According to Bronner, the ceremony involved the boy negotiating his relationship to his father, declaring "I am a man," while the party afterward demarcated him from the feminine (mother) by allowing connections to normative masculine culture through decorations dedicated to sports, recreation, and music.[46] Moreover, the increasing popularity of lavish parties, complete with deejays, professional dancers, and decorations costing thousands of dollars overshadowed the significance of the ceremony.[47] Men's struggles to separate from their fathers included unresolved and mixed feelings about their relationships with them and could cause what psychologist Samuel Osherman described as "the kosher rebellion," which had lasting influences on men's masculinity. When Osherson stopped observing the Jewish rules of not mixing milk and meat and not eating forbidden food such as shellfish and pork, he saw his father's dilemma; keeping kosher was a way for his father's generation of men to show love symbolically for their own fathers, because they were disallowed the opportunity to express love verbally and emotionally.[48]

Jewish men who celebrated their b'nai mitzvah during the 1970s and 1980s and intermarried in the 1990s and 2000s illustrate current Jewish communal concern about some boys essentially dropping out of Jewish life after this milestone. The issue even generated its own joke:

> A rabbi has mice in his synagogue and asks advice from a colleague on how to get rid of them. The second rabbi tells him he has a foolproof system. Every time he finds a mouse, he makes it a tiny *kippa* and tallit and gives it a bar mitzvah. After the ceremony, the mouse never comes back to shul.[49]

Scholars disagreed about the extent to which male participation had declined but agreed that men and women behaved in different ways. In 2000, social scientists Barry A. Kosmin and Ariela Keysar studied Conservative Jewish youth four years post–b'nai mitzvah and concluded, "The report card on the class of 5755 at the end of the their high school years is quite positive from the perspective of Jewish continuity."[50] Len Saxe, director of the Cohen Center for Modern Jewish Studies at Brandeis University, was less optimistic: "In the metaphor of physical fitness, our respondents experienced Jewish education like intermittent exercise—they felt the pain of getting into shape, but never the athlete's pleasure of accomplishment."[51] According to a 2007 study, 47 percent of Jewish boys viewed becoming a bar mitzvah as their graduation from Jewish supplemental education, compared to 34 percent of Jewish girls.[52] By the twelfth grade, only 17 percent of boys participated in Jewish education, a third less than girls, according to a three-year study.[53] According to other studies, post–b'nai mitzvah boys felt more pressure than girls to disengage from religious activities to make way for weekend sports and social plans, while post–b'not mitzvah girls attributed more significance to Jewish identity and were more likely to volunteer in the Jewish community.[54] Whether the glass was perceived as half full or half empty, the consensus among Jewish educators was that more could be and should be done to reach out across denominations to Jewish youth in America.

The disaffection for Judaism many intermarried men experienced as adolescents is the focus of efforts to re-engage Jewish males, indicating the issue extends beyond this group of study participants. In 2007, two rabbis collaborated on *The Men's Seder*, initiated by the Men of Reform Judaism (formerly the North American Federation of Temple Brotherhoods), a project to give men of all ages an opportunity to gather together to "explore and celebrate what it means to be a contemporary Jewish man."[55] It mirrors the earlier efforts of feminism's consciousness-raising groups. Similarly, the Conservative Federation of Jewish Men's Clubs listened to men's voices with a mission to involve Jewish men in Jewish life.[56] Moving Traditions, founded in 2004 by Sally Gottesman, was created to help both genders by better engaging them in Judaism in ways that lead to greater parity of men and women. One of its research campaigns, "The Campaign for Jewish Boys," sought to help the Jewish community to reverse the trend of preteen and teenage boys leaving Jewish life by better meeting adolescent boys' needs. The resulting project, *Where Have All the Young Men Gone?*, was geared toward defining and promoting models to the Jewish community that would "attract and inspire the interest of teenage boys, and in the process build their Jewish identities."[57] Dismantling the stereotype that Jewish men do not drink, some efforts to attract them specifically include alcoholic beverages. As part of its Men's Initiative, Mayyim Hayyim held an event called "Men, Mikveh and Malt" in April 2013, which combined tasting fine scotch and whiskey with expert sommeliers and stand-up comedy.[58] A temple brotherhood's event, "Tequila and Cigars," likewise promoted an association between Jewish engagement and alcohol.[59] The long-term success and influence of projects such as these on intermarried Jewish men depends on sustained and creative efforts to make Judaism accessible to men who work full-time outside of the rabbinate and Jewish life.

Catering to intermarried men's needs involves assessing the ways Jewish men became disenfranchised from organized religion and finding new ways to empower them. Those scholars and religious activists who clamored about a "feminization of Judaism" were missing the most important point about gender equity as far as Jewish men are concerned. As sociologist Sylvia Barack Fishman described in 2008, "The problem is patrilineal descent—not matrilineal ascent."[60] The decline in male participation is not because of women's increasing role in the rabbinate or the synagogue social hall, but because Jewish life has not yet adapted to men's changing needs. According to Doug Barden, former executive director of the Men of Reform Judaism, "We need to reverse the disaffiliation of men without setting the egalitarian clock back 30 years."[61] The goal was not to ordain fewer female rabbis, but rather to create opportunities for adult men to gather together for social and spiritual activities.[62] While the labor market evolved to allow women in, there has not been a mass exodus of men from it, because the marketplace continues to fulfill their expectations in the form of salaries and benefits. The currency is less tangible, however, when it comes to Jewish life. According to Rabbi Charles Simon, executive director of the Federation of Jewish Men's Clubs:

> For thirty plus years synagogues created engaging serious adult b'nai mitzvah programs; however, they never considered the implications of dual-career parenting and its possible impact on male involvement. Important initiatives to address women's health concerns were created but similar think tanks or lobbies to consider whether or not similar activities should be created for men failed to emerge. If male involvement in synagogue life has diminished it is not because men don't wish to compete with women; it's because their needs and the means to address those needs have been ignored or forgotten.

Simon urges a new strategy to address gender imbalance, one that reformulates synagogue life so that it includes the necessary ingredients to engage men. Those ingredients include (1) feeling satisfied that something has been gained or learned; (2) feeling that their "volunteer time" is appreciated, not wasted; (3) challenges to rise to an occasion; (4) the presence of camaraderie; and (5) an environment that balances seriousness of purpose with fun.[63] The focus of the Federation of Jewish Men's Club's Keruv Initiative is on generating more inclusivity for intermarried Jews and their families.[64] All of these innovations illustrate the extent to which men were, ironically, left out of the equation when Judaism first became egalitarian during the second-wave feminist movement of the 1960s and 1970s. Designing programs exclusively for men is *de rigueur*, as it once was for women; "having the opportunity to express concerns and personal experiences is intimidating and, quite frankly, new. Creating a comfortable and 'safe' space is critical."[65] Creating safe spaces enables intermarried men to reclaim Judaism for themselves and provides opportunities to discuss Jewish fatherhood with rabbis. Conversely, lack of such opportunities inhibits intermarried men's ability to raise Jewish children as effectively as do intermarried women.

New experiences with rabbis during adulthood could push Jewish men farther away or, in the best cases, draw them closer to Judaism. When Allan Benjamin and his Christian wife explored joining the Conservative or the Reform congregation, their experiences influenced their decisions. They went to a Friday night service at the Reform temple and witnessed a small child fall off his chair, followed by loud crying. Allan, anticipating the wrath of the rabbi of his youth, expected the child to be ordered out of the sanctuary. Instead, to his utter amazement, Rabbi Bob Levy stopped the service, and before anyone else could react, he picked up and soothed the child. His actions had a profound effect on Allan, who thought, "Oh, Lord. Wow. This is what it's really supposed to be like. This is where I want to be."[66] The couple had found their spiritual home and never made it to the Conservative synagogue.

How a rabbi responded to a request to officiate at an interfaith marriage ceremony continued to influence men's relationships with Judaism between 1980 and 2008, as it had in the previous decades.[67] When Glenn Aker sought his rabbi's involvement in his wedding, her response made clear that the temple would welcome them as an interfaith family in order to attract the children to Judaism but that she could not officiate because it would not be a Jewish wedding. She drew a distinction between Jewish ritual and Jewish peoplehood. From the rabbi's perspective, the refusal to officiate stems from a traditional definition of a Jewish marriage ceremony as between two Jews and sanctified with the words "according to the laws of Moses and Israel." The "laws of Moses" refers to the Torah, and "Israel" to Jewish peoplehood. The rabbi's position declares that one can intermarry and remain Jewish but one cannot intermarry Jewishly. Once a couple intermarries, however, the rabbi would keep open the doors to Judaism for the intermarried couple and their offspring, inviting them to join the Jewish people. Glenn did not appreciate the rabbinic tightrope walk, "And to me that was a moment where I said, 'I've not been sure about this for a long time, and now I'm done. I'm finished with you, Reform Judaism. You have turned your back on me in a way that is such an affront.'" Glenn interpreted the rabbi's refusal as an insult to his Jewish integrity: "You are below the Reform Jews. You are down here—you're interfaith."[68] Although his rabbi attempted to be inclusive, Glenn viewed the refusal to officiate as a rejection. Jewish leaders have begun to better understand, in the words of one rabbi, the impact of telling someone, "I love you, I want to welcome you into the Jewish community, but I am not able to officiate": the words "I am not able" are heard as "I am rejecting you," even when that was not the intended message.[69] Jewish men, more than Jewish women (based on my previous research), could be alienated from Judaism on having just one negative experience. This may be because white males in American society are not accustomed to being told "no" or denied what they want. When men feel rejected by a rabbi, they experience an assault to their male egos and Jewish identities, sometimes causing them to react with disdain and aggression, essentially quitting Judaism, as Glenn did. It is an exceptional intermarried man who moves past this fateful interaction and becomes a change agent. Edmund Case, CEO of InterfaithFamily, remembers firsthand how hurtful a rabbi's insensitive remark can feel, even more than three decades later. Rather than turn away, however, he worked tirelessly to encourage Jewish communities to be welcoming and interfaith couples to make Jewish choices. "I wanted people like my children to be involved in Jewish life and community. That was my mission," he reflected.[70] Case spearheaded the creation of a free online Jewish clergy officiation referral service that assists interfaith couples to find a rabbi or cantor to officiate or co-officiate at their wedding and other life-cycle events.[71] While interfaith couples can now more easily locate a Jewish clergy member than they could in the past, some rabbis and would-be rabbis are facing another conflict of opinion within their profession: whether rabbinical schools should admit, graduate, or ordain Jewish students who are engaged, married, or partnered to a non-Jew.[72]

JEWISH HIERARCHY

Men's sensitivity about intolerance toward different models of Jewishness influenced how they felt about their identities. Raised in Conservative Judaism, Larry Rush attended Yeshiva University's Einstein Medical School in New York City, an Orthodox institution. He felt that while his co-religionists tolerated Christians' ignorance about Judaism, they were less forgiving when it came to non-Orthodox Jews: "I felt looked down upon because I wasn't Jewish enough. You know, it's not the Christian's fault they don't know better; I should know better. Why wasn't I Orthodox?"[73] Such normative expectations are based, in part, on the premise that Jews who are part of the same community will behave similarly, when in truth there is a wide range of knowledge and practices, even at the same school. Glenn Aker delineated what he described as levels of Jewishness depending on the extent to which someone observed *halacha* and ritual behavior, a Jew-o-meter: first, "there are the magical people who live in New York City, they wear black hats, and they don't get out of bed without saying the prayer. . . . Then there's the lesser Orthodox who follow most of the rules, but they somehow manage to live among us. And then there's the Conservatives, who follow just enough rules to claim that they are better than the Reform Jews, who are Jewish Lite. And then there's the crazy Reconstructionists, who only exist so that the Reform Jews have someone to hate."[74] Glenn pointed out that despite all being Jewish to one degree or another, there was a lack of respect across the "levels." His description illustrates the antagonisms between branches of Judaism and the competition for authenticity among its adherents. Journalism professor Samuel G. Freedman describes the factiousness between Jews as "the struggle for the soul of American Jewry," a civil war that "pits secularist against believer, denomination against denomination, gender against gender, liberal against conservative, traditionalist against modernist even within each branch."[75] The criticism Rabbi Asher Lopatin received from ultra-Orthodox groups after his installation as president of Yeshivat Chovevei Torah, a liberal Orthodox rabbinical school where the first female "rabba" was ordained by former president Rabbi Avi Weiss, illustrates Freedman's multifaceted point.[76] The contest over who is a "real Jew" has a particular male bent. Glenn described the struggle between Conservative Jews, who insisted that his brother wear a yarmulke at the synagogue, and Reform Jews who objected to this pressure: "These guys think this is what you should do, and clearly the other guys have this sense of 'How dare they tell us what to do all the time!'"[77] Inherent in being an American Jewish man, it seems, was a certain belligerence about being told what to do or how to do it when it came to Judaism. Personal autonomy is critically important to someone descended from a formerly persecuted minority who came to America seeking religious freedom and protection. Moreover, men whose ethnicity exists independent of religion want to determine for themselves what being Jewish means. The tension between "unity" according to America's Orthodox Jews, acceptance of the Torah and all 613 *mitzvot* (commandments), and "pluralism" invoked by non-Orthodox Jews is all the more contentious for intermarried Jewish men.[78]

Jewish men's testimonies highlight the ways in which different Jewish movements exhibited antagonism toward each other and their respective adherents rather than acceptance and inclusion, driving men away in the process. Kalman Long described the tension he felt as a Reform Jew talking to the Conservative Jew teaching his children Torah; when he asked what time they should arrive at the temple, he was told, "We don't have a temple. It's a synagogue." Traditionally, Conservative congregations used the word "synagogue" in deference to the Temple in Jerusalem that was destroyed in 70 CE. The Reform movement founded the first "temple" in nineteenth-century Germany, intentionally alluding to the restoration of the ancient Temple.[79] Both refer to a Jewish congregation and over time came to be used interchangeably; hence the distinction made in this manner was insulting. Then, Kalman described, the Conservative Jew was invited to his Orthodox godson's bar mitzvah. He was asked what kind of hospitality he would like and responded that he has Shabbat dinner with his aging mother and would drive to the Detroit synagogue Saturday morning. He was appalled when he was disinvited from the bar mitzvah. The norm in Orthodox communities under the authority of their rabbis is that anyone attending a *simcha* (joyous event) would keep Shabbat in the same manner as the community, including not driving from sundown on Friday to sundown on Saturday. Kalman, however, perceived it as ironic: on the one hand, the man admonished him for not being "religious enough" by calling a synagogue a temple, and then the admonisher was not "religious enough" for the rabbi who said that if he drove on Shabbat he would taint the bar mitzvah. The scenario illustrates that the differences between Jewish unity and Jewish pluralism can be divisive depending on one's perspective. Kalman concluded, "What the hell? Is that how we're going to treat each other? Is it any of your business what my practice is? It shouldn't be. And as long as that's going on, that's just going to repel me."[80]

While ideas about American manhood during the late twentieth century and early twenty-first set forth requirements for men to assert their competence in their professions, Jewish men often felt that they were unfairly expected also to possess Judaic knowledge and expertise. There are endless jokes about American men not wanting to stop and ask for directions.[81] The premise behind such humor is that men *should* know where they are going at all times and to disclose otherwise would somehow be unmanly. Indeed the invention of the individual global positioning system (GPS) is a godsend for American men. No longer do they have to drive around in circles to avoid asking for directions; Garmin, TomTom, and various smartphone applications can stealthily get them where they need to go without making them feel inadequate in the slightest. In sharp contrast, there are no such available devices discreetly coaching Jewish men about the Hebrew language or Jewish texts, behavior, or rituals. Walter Chatham felt that his Jewish education was so inadequate that he was not fully Jewish. He described experiencing both anger and tears during services, because Judaism resonates so deeply with him yet is somehow unattainable. Following his divorce from a Christian woman, he began dating but did not seek out co-religionists: "To be honest with you—and I've never shared this with anyone before—I don't think a Jewish girl would marry me . . . 'cause I really don't have the Jewish background." The surname of Chatham contributed to his feelings of Jewish disenfranchisement. When I asked him about it, he retorted, "I might as well have been named Christ!"[82]

Men's Jewish journeys continue to reinforce the theory that identity develops over the life course *and* that these varying pathways are less understood than the more-often considered road from Christian to Jew. While there are abundant books about conversion to Judaism for and by Jews-by-choice, the shelves are nearly devoid of books about Jews (men or women) who leave their childhood denomination, intermarry, and venture in other Jewish directions.[83] Testimonies by intermarried Jewish men in the second half of the twentieth century shed light on this dimension missing from scholarly literature and communal discussions.

Bruce Davidson felt what he described as a lack of appreciation for his journey toward greater observance and involvement in the Jewish community. His explanation for why this might be the case was because his personal experience lacked social currency: converts were treated better than "Jewish seekers," he believed, because their experiences were more easily understood, while the Jew who meandered from his origins or was somehow different was "confused."[84] In recent years, however, the Federation of Jewish Men's Clubs is making great strides toward reaching individuals wherever they may be on the observance spectrum. The World Wide Wrap, for example, is "a way of bringing men of all ages into a warm venue to begin to start to wear *tefillin,* again or for the first time," according to Rabbi Simon.[85] Similarly, outreach programs offered by the Union for Reform Judaism describe their introductory class as being for "interfaith couples, those considering conversion and *Jews looking for adult-level basics*" (emphasis mine).[86] Yet despite these efforts, Jewish men who may be journeying or otherwise do not clearly identify with one denomination or another are somehow "other," marginalized within Jewish circles, whereas the convert is simply in transition.

In addition to the hierarchy and competency issues, some men experience a nagging ambivalence toward Judaism and other Jewish people. While feelings about co-ethnics or co-religionists were related to negative stereotypes about Jews, Jewish men's relationship with Judaism was influenced by their views of organized religion in general. Kevin Stephens insisted, "I still want to identify and I still want my kids to be Jewish," but he disliked aspects of Jewish identity, culture, and people. Recounting numerous negative stereotypes about Jews as loud, overbearing, complaining, self-serving, Kevin denounced, "Well, you're the reason there's antisemitism; you're obnoxious." Kevin admitted that accusing other Jews of being obnoxious involved self-loathing, yet it was also evident that he wanted to remain connected. Ironically, he found a connection with other Jewish men who shared similar sentiments about the Judaism of their youth. "I don't feel like a lone voice in this; these guys I grew up with, I think they feel the same way I do to a large extent. So there's a sense of community in that. And if there wasn't that thing against which we rebel, then there would be no commonality."[87] In a sense, then, it was these men's position on the margins of Jewish life that

actually afforded them a connection to it, albeit by virtue of an antago-
nistic relationship. Like siblings whose rivalry keeps them circling each
other with alternating contempt and love, men's collusion in the fight
both *against* Judaism and other Jews and *for* a seat at the table with their
ethnic or religious brethren meant that they still cherished what they
denounced. It also signified that having a dearth of positive associations
was a kind of Jewish affiliation that united some men.

REINVENTING PATERNITY

Jewish identity for the men in my sample continued to be interwoven
with professional success and the ability to earn a substantial income,
but a new version of paternity was also slowing emerging. Although
American men gained more access to jobs previously considered feminine, such as nurse and teacher, Jewish identity remained glued to careers with the highest prestige, status, and income. When his 1991 intermarriage ended in divorce, Gary Brodin decided to try to meet eligible
Jewish women. His online efforts and his appeal to fellow congregants
to play matchmaker were fruitless. Gary claimed that as soon as people
found out that he was a middle school teacher, the interest light turned
off. "I'm not a doctor, I'm not a lawyer, I'm not a self-made business
man," he explained.[88] One respondent suggested that the only career
choices Jewish boys had were between becoming a doctor or lawyer:
"There's nothing else. I didn't like blood and hospitals, so I went to law
school." For some men, the pressure to be successful extended from
themselves to the subjects of their affection. When Morton Langfeld,
who has an advanced professional degree, introduced his pregnant fiancée to his parents, he felt a certain amount of shame because, in his
words, "I wanted to come home with a doctor or a lawyer, not necessarily
an un-degreed" paraprofessional.[89] Kalman Long, who intermarried in
1998, described with disdain the way that the names of large donors are
publicized regardless that the highest level of *tzedakah* is giving anony-
mously: "It's a social construct, this capitalist one. But if you can get
away from the pecking order and just look at are you in a good place? . . .
Are your needs met? . . . Then it doesn't matter whether you're driving a
small car or a big car, if you're happy."[90] Being happy is a quintessential

American value, but accepting happiness as a sufficient life goal did not come easily to all Jewish men.

Unlike their predecessors who married at somewhat younger ages, many of these men who were born between 1959 and 1980 and married in the 1990s and 2000s were focused on their careers or otherwise did not make marriage and fatherhood a priority earlier in their lives. According to a 2002 study by the National Marriage Project, the median age of first marriage for men had reached twenty-seven, which was the oldest in U.S. history.[91] Although much scholarship and media attention have focused on aging women becoming single mothers by choice, very little has been written about how aging single men view parenting. Not until 2008 did the *New York Times* feature an article with the title "The Bachelor Life Now Includes a Family."[92] The number of single-mothers-by-choice still far exceeds single-fathers-by-surrogacy.[93] Although some American men are contributing to the changing definition of family to include single-parents-by-choice, it appears that Jewish men are fewer among them, given the Jewish preoccupation with the traditional two-parent family. Even same-sex partnerships fulfill that expectation, whereas a Jewish single-father-by-choice would be much more of a cultural anomaly at the present time. Public discourse about religious Jewish single motherhood began in 2007, when a thirty-six-year-old modern Orthodox woman in Israel asked her rabbi, "Am I allowed to bring a child into this world without being married?"[94] Jewish men have yet to petition the rabbinical authorities for an answer, and their less religious counterparts do not seem to be acting on their own initiative to become single-fathers-by-choice, at least not that I have witnessed.

For some men, the desire to be a father was at least as strong as the desire to be a life partner. Such men took to the title "father" and its corresponding role, responsibilities, and relationship more readily than "husband." Morton's wife had a child from a previous relationship, and they subsequently had two together. Around age thirty-five, he had found himself wanting a family; all his friends were married with children. When his then-girlfriend became pregnant, Morton "wanted the babies." He was forty years old and had been married for only four months when interviewed. Reflecting on his roles, he elaborated, "I love the father moniker better than husband. . . . I was always dutiful. I was always faithful and supportive, and I assume I always will be, but the whole wife/ husband thing is still kinda weird for me." The phenomenon of becoming a father has, in some ways, evolved more than becoming a husband, perhaps because fatherhood is an obvious sign of men's virility whereas becoming a husband symbolizes the end of a man's sexual forays. Since the 1980s, men have enjoyed considerably more access to their newborn children; while earlier generations of fathers were relegated to hospital waiting rooms, men who became fathers in the past three decades were more often welcomed into the birthing room and could witness their child's entry into the world.[95] However, little is known about how they navigated their new roles as fathers in relation to their roles as husbands. Men's desire to be fathers, married and single, heterosexual and gay, is a seriously understudied area of their lived experiences.

However much some Jewish men may have welcomed paternity, it is unlikely that their desire would be subordinate to their desire for professional success or, if so, that their family dynamics would enable them to become the primary care providers for their children. Although "stay-at-home" dads have grown in number and popularity, they still represent a small percentage of all American fathers. According to the U.S. Census Bureau, there were 66.3 million fathers in the nation as of June 2005, and of that number, 98,000 was the estimated number of stay-at-home dads. "Mr. Mom" as the government report defines them were married fathers with children under fifteen years of age who remained out of the labor force for more than one year primarily to care for the family while their wives worked outside of the home.[96] In 2009, there were an estimated 67.8 million fathers across the nation and an estimated 158,000 stay-at-home dads.[97] Using the same definition, the number of stay-at-home fathers is dwarfed by the 2009 number of stay-at-home mothers: 5.1 million out of 82.8 million mothers total.[98] Popular culture suggests that more men are turning to full-time fatherhood than may be the actual reality. "I'm tired of bringing home the bacon," lamented a male character on the CBS hit show *The Good Wife*. A former professional turned primary childcare provider, this man pointed to his T-shirt and claimed, "I'm Super Dad."[99] One study respondent claimed, "I'd be a home dad if I could in a minute. I'd love to sit home and clean the house. I'd smoke pot all day. It'd be great." His comment suggests the fantasy that stay-at-home parents can do whatever they wish without repercussions. He admitted that while doing laundry sounded "glorious" in the abstract, "in reality, I doubt I would love it. I'd probably get all freaked out and need to start working . . . out of the house."[100] Although most American men have yet to embrace the concept of being an equal parent, let alone the primary caregiver, change is occurring.

THE NEXT GENERATION

Although providing for one's family continued to measure high on the priority list, fatherhood for men who intermarried in the 1990s and 2000s began to evolve and include other components distinct from their forebears. "Support" was a word used interchangeably for financial backing and emotional sustenance. One respondent, who wanted to "be there" for his daughter, included this list of words to describe his role as father: "love, honor, cherish, respect, guide, nurture, protect."[101] He emphasized being a different kind of father than his father had been. If men chose not to emulate the paternal figure of their childhood, how did they learn to become fathers with other qualities? "Therapy" was this respondent's immediate answer. Likewise, some men who married during these decades chose women different from their own mothers. Walter Chatham described, "If I got hit by lightning, my mother would say, 'Well, that's too bad,' whereas his wife 'would just fall apart.'"[102] When a man had a positive relationship with his father growing up, he strove to reproduce that experience for his own child. Gary Michaels recalled about his father that "he worked a lot and, yet, he had a lot of time to play with me. I still have these great memories of throwing footballs and baseballs . . . around with him." Gary used the words "loving" and "attentive" to describe his role as a father and said that being a role model for his son included "sharing the best of who I am with my family to make their lives as full as possible and our collective life beautiful."[103]

The reality of dual careers and parenting meant hardships for men who wanted to fully co-parent, and yet somehow they managed. Flexible schedules and working from home enabled some men to both be the kind of fathers they wanted to be and earn a living. The combination, however, was difficult. When asked how he managed to balance work and family, one respondent explained, "Well it's hell. Right now, it's the hardest thing I've ever done. We tried to avoid daycare. She [his wife] teaches part-time and I flex my time so I can do childcare when she's teaching, and so I work at night, I work in the morning, I work whenever I get a free moment, and she does, too." Challenging as it was to effectively co-parent and co-earn, this man would not have it any other way. "I have my priorities straight on this one," he concluded. Although still a minority among white-collar workers, this man was part of a growing fatherhood movement that seeks to balance co-parenting with co-breadwinning responsibilities. Modern society is more accepting of men taking care of children and sees their doing so as a valuable strength.[104] When a wife earns more than a husband, who should stay home with a child may be decided by income. However, sometimes the decision comes down to which parent is employed. Eighty-two percent of the job losses during the recession at the end of the first decade of the twenty-first century have befallen men, whereas the proportion of women in the workforce has changed only slightly. While men hold the majority of jobs heaviest hit, such as manufacturing and construction, women populate employment areas such as education and health care, less affected by economic winds. On the negative side, this means American families are finding it harder to support themselves, because of women's lower wages. The positive outcome, should the recession be further prolonged, could be the challenge to traditional gender roles.[105] A parallel may develop between men who were laid off from work due to the early twenty-first-century economic recession and became stay-at-home dads and World War II–era Rosie the Riveter. The question is: will these men return to the office (or, in the case of blue-collar workers, the construction site) when there is an economic recovery, or will they continue to find ways to share the caregiving with their wives?

INTER-DIVORCED

Where there is marriage there also is divorce. Had Jewish men seriously debated the potential outcomes, soaring national divorce rates in the 1980s and 1990s would have suggested to them that in-marriage was no more a guarantee of success than marrying out. The American divorce rate hit its highest point in history in the early 1980s. An increase in divorce had been a long-term trend since the colonial period (1600–1775), but after staying level for two decades following World War II, the divorce rate doubled between the mid-1960s and early 1980s. Although the rate declined modestly in the remaining years of the twentieth century, it was described as "leveling off at a high level." The percentage of all adults who were divorced more than quadrupled from 1960 to 1998. Common wisdom about divorce in America is that one in two marriages fail, which studies confirm. According to the National Marriage Project at Rutgers University, the chance of a marriage entered into in the year 2000 ending in divorce or permanent separation was very high: between 40 and 50 percent.[106]

The larger picture of an overwhelmingly high national rate of divorce was further complicated by sociological reports that intermarriage more often led to divorce than in-marriage, which did not necessarily dissuade Jewish men from marrying a Christian. Research in the 1950s suggested that interfaith couples did not have a higher than usual divorce rate and that it was impossible to generalize about interfaith marriage among Catholics, Protestants, and Jews and marital outcome.[107] Subsequent research, however, demonstrated that when the wife and husband were not of the same Christian denomination, the likelihood of the marriage terminating in divorce was significantly higher.[108] Research published by the North American Jewish Data Bank, which analyzed the marital histories of 6,457 never widowed, Jewish adults from nine cities around the United States between 1982 and 1987, found a divorce rate of 17 percent among those who married co-religionists and a rate of 32 percent among the intermarried. This finding confirmed that Jewish-Christian intermarriages reflected the national picture of high levels of divorce. The co-authors' statement that the "most significant predictor of divorce is intermarriage" seemed fairly damning.[109] However much this data was embraced by advocates of endogamy, it is doubtful given the persistent rates of exogamy that Jewish men gave these reports much notice.

The absence of more recent research casts some doubt on whether that 1989 finding that intermarriage ends in divorce more than intrafaith marriage, now more than two decades old, still applies. Yet some social scientists continue to contend that "divorce is twice as high among mixed marrieds" of any religious combination (including between two Christians) or simply "more divorce among the outmarried."[110] Scholars who believe that intermarriage leads to Jewish discontinuity promote a discourse of discord about intermarriage and marital outcome.[111] The "discord approach" dates back to at least the 1960s, according to Marshall Sklare: "This consisted, essentially, of mental-health arguments which emphasized the point that the marital relationship is fraught with enough difficulties without introducing yet another potential disharmony, such as a mate of a different faith." As Sklare wisely pointed out, there were plenty of *successful* intermarriages and, on the flip side, in-marriages that were failing.[112] Moreover, there is no hard data to support the claim that Jewish intermarriage between 1990 and the present day in America leads to divorce any more frequently than in-marriage. In 2009, scholars reported that the percentage of "ever divorced" among intermarried men (31.4 percent) and women (26.8 percent) was nearly double that of intra-married men (18.7 percent) and women (14.7 percent), respectively. However, according to Harriet Hartman, one of the co-authors, "NJPS [2000–01] didn't ask for date of divorce, so ever divorced could have been before or after the intermarriage."[113] The most recent and conclusive evidence reinforces national findings about high divorce rates but does not make intermarriage the culprit. The jury is still out, in other words. "The real reason why interfaith marriages fail," journalist Josh Mintz commented on *Haaretz.com,* could be why any socially taboo marriage might fail: isolation from family and community. He identified the social anti-intermarriage argument devoid of religious objections as "subtle racism."[114]

Religious differences are the most obvious and easiest culprits to point to for marital dissolutions, but little empirical evidence suggests that they are truly to blame. Purely quantitative analysis does not determine whether it was actually differences in faith that influenced attitudes and behaviors causing marital problems or disharmonious cultural differences. Esther Perel, an interfaith marriage therapist, referring to Jewish-Christian unions wrote, "The difference isn't just between Moses and Christ. You're dealing with issues of money, sex, education, child-rearing practices, food, family relationships, styles of emotional expres-

siveness, issues of autonomy—all of these are culturally embedded."[115]
New scholarship suggests that intra-faith marriage does not promote
happiness any more than does interfaith marriage. Clinical psychologist Janice McDavit-Aron studied 365 Jews and Christians nationwide
and found that, contrary to the majority of literature on the topic, partners in same-faith marriages did not have higher marital satisfaction
than did interfaith marriage partners. The 2009 study also illuminated
the influence strength of faith could have on marital satisfaction; lower
strength of religious affiliation did not translate into higher happiness
levels for interfaith marriages.[116] While author Naomi Schaefer Riley
found a higher frequency of divorce among forty-four Jews in her interfaith marriage survey, Jews were also an exception among the 2,450
Americans included: intermarried Jews reported a higher level of marital
satisfaction than in-married Jews. This finding raises questions about the
cause of divorce if it is not attributable to decreased satisfaction stemming from religious difference.[117] Some scholarship acknowledges that
challenges exist within Jewish relationships due to different denominations and levels of observance, finally dismantling the myth that intrafaith marriages are immune from stress, but it is relatively scarce and
unheralded.[118]

Jewish men in my sample seemed to be influenced more by the dynamics of their individual families of origin than they were by alarming
statistics about intermarriage and marital instability. Glenn Aker was
eight when his Jewish mother died; his father remarried a Methodist
woman. When he was growing up, Glenn's stepmother and her children
went to church, while he and his sister went to synagogue. Although the
memories of his Jewish mother stayed with him, including her admoni-
tion never to kneel if he ever visited a church service, his father's actions
more likely had a greater impact.[119] Similarly, Warren Alt was seven when
his parents divorced, and his father remarried a black woman. Warren
married a Protestant woman, with little to no reservation.[120] The influence of a parent's decision to intermarry, after divorce or the death of a
spouse, on the Jewish men in my sample reflected national demographic
data that Jewish adults who were the children of intermarriages were
three times more likely to marry non-Jews themselves.[121] However, the
effect was specific to Jewish men whose parents *remarried* non-Jews;

only one man came from an intermarried home that was a first marriage, casting doubt that the national finding is universal among adult children of intermarriage. Also, whether adult children of divorced intermarried parents will in-marry remains to be seen.

Although their parents' decisions influenced some of the men's marital choices, it is not inevitable that the men's intermarriages will in turn influence their children to choose non-Jewish partners when they reach adulthood. Simple analyses of data about intermarriage do not take into account the potential influence that Jewish education, religious and cultural, can have on a person's decisions about who they marry later in life. Analyses of several national and local community data sources by Saxe and his colleagues at Brandeis have documented that "Jewish socialization in the form of Jewish education, experience of home ritual, and social networks plays a far more important role than having intermarried parents in determining Jewish identity, behavior, and connections."[122] Participation in Taglit-Birthright Israel—the ten-day education program that has sent more than two hundred fifty thousand young adults from the U.S. since 1999 to Israel—is also associated with increases in the importance placed on marrying a Jew and raising Jewish children, for both the children of in-marrried and intermarried families.[123] As part of a longitudinal study of participants in Birthright, the same research team at Brandeis found that visiting Israel has a strong and long-lasting impact on Jewish identity and marital choices. Non-Orthodox Jews who went on the Birthright program were 51 percent more likely to have a Jewish spouse than non-participants, and 35 percent more likely to believe that raising children as Jews was "very important." More than 75 percent of Birthright participants were married to Jews, while only 50 percent of non-participants were in-married.[124] Education and experiences *prior* to marriage will determine what these marriages look like, not whether Jewish men intermarried. It will be interesting to see whether future research determines the success and failure rates of Birthright participants' intermarriages compared to in-marriages.

Intermarried Jewish men's experiences illustrate that whether a Jewish husband and a Christian wife divorced depended upon factors *unrelated* to religion, disputing the notion that exogamy was the reason for divorce.[125] Of the fifteen men I discuss in this chapter, four had gotten divorced; of these four men, one remarried a non-Jew, and the other three had not remarried at the time of the interview. Jewish men who separated from or divorced non-Jewish women did so for secular reasons, as had the men discussed in the previous chapter. A 1989 study found a much higher rate of intermarriage among remarriages than first marriages. Researchers also reported a large amount of "switching," from in-marriage to out-marriage and from out-marriage to in-marriage, upon remarriage.[126] Men who experienced marital failure one way were more apt to try a different way the next time around. There were exceptions, however. One man who intermarried in 1986, divorced, and intermarried again in 2006 explained that it was his ineffective communication skills about his emotions that contributed most to the deterioration of his marriage. "Feelings? Do I have feelings? Um, am I supposed to talk about them?" he asked during marital counseling. "I'm still not very good at expressing my feelings, but at least I know I've got them, which I didn't before."[127] Men's socialization regarding expressing emotions contributed to the demise of their relationships. When Warren Alt went to a couples' therapist with his then-wife, he could not answer the question "How do you feel?" He described the moment, "I had no fucking vocabulary. I had nothing. . . . Men in general, me in particular, there's no upbringing around how to discuss your feelings."[128] Ultimately his marriage ended in divorce as a result of the lack of a shared vision for life that had nothing to do with religion and everything to do with different goals about putting down roots and starting a family.

If divorce were not complicated enough, it is considerably more so when the child's religious upbringing enters into discussions about custody and parenting. There is currently no uniform national law involving religious upbringing and custody, because the United States Supreme Court has not yet decided a case. Hence, the law varies from state to state, with each state applying one of several legal standards concerning protecting the child from harm and the custodial parent's rights.[129] In addition, the First Amendment of the United States Constitution protecting religious freedom influences courts by forbidding them to take judicial action that shows preference for one religion over another or favoring religion over no religion.[130] There has been an increase in conflicts over religion fueled, according to the chairman of the Custody Committee of the American Bar Association's Section of Family Law, by the rise in intermarriage and conversions to a different religion after divorce.[131] In 2010, perhaps one of the most contentious interfaith divorce cases involving custody and religion made numerous headlines in print and visual media, including "Whose God Wins? For Divorcing Parents, It's Not Clear" (*Newsweek*), "Father Says 'Catholic,' Mother Says 'Jewish'" (*Jewish Advocate*), "For interfaith Couple, A Baptism by Fire" (*Jewish Week*), and "Chicago Father Faces Jail for Bringing Daughter to Church" (*ABC News*), among many others.[132] When Rebecca Shapiro, who was raised Jewish, and Joseph Reyes, who was Catholic, married in 2004, they agreed to build a Jewish home together and raise Jewish children. Their wedding was a very Jewish affair, including a *ketubah* (Jewish marriage contract). After their daughter was born, Reyes converted to Judaism, complete with a ritual circumcision. When they divorced in 2008, three-year-old Ela was caught in the religious crossfire when Reyes had her baptized without Shapiro's consent . . . and invited television news crews to film it.[133] An Illinois judge initially ruled in favor of Shapiro, the primary custodial parent, barring Reyes from taking their daughter to church.[134] After the decision, comedian Jay Andrew Allen poked fun at Reyes's Jewish masculinity. "And what's this nonsense about converting to Judaism 'under pressure'? That's just man-code for 'It was easier to cave to my wife than to grow a pair.'"[135] Apparently, implying that a man was cowered by female authority was not limited to Jews-by-birth. In April 2010, Judge Renee Goldfarb harshly criticized Reyes for making Ela the center of his media plan and not getting a job to help support her, but he also ruled that Reyes could legally take Ela to church during his visitation time despite that she is being raised Jewish.[136] The effect of the ruling, based on "the best interest of the child," was a big change from the original restraining order preventing the father from exposing their daughter to any religion other than Judaism.[137]

Notwithstanding the potential minefields and bad press about inter-divorce, some Jewish men have managed to see their Jewish children through these rough waters with the law on their side. Larry Rush was fortunate that his ex-wife continued to be supportive of raising their son as a Jew after they divorced and brought him to Hebrew school. She had a Christmas tree in her house, but, Larry emphasized, her observance is not about Jesus and she does not take their son to church. Regarding the child's identity, Larry surmised, "He says as far as he's concerned, he's been Jewish since the day he was born. He had a bris. If someone doesn't think he's Jewish, they can take a long walk off a short pier."[138] Interfaith divorces involving custody battles illustrate the difficulties Jewish fathers face trying to raise Jewish children. In 2005, a New Jersey Supreme Court ruled in favor of a Jewish man whose ex-wife sought to take their three children to Catholic education classes. The case took many twists and turns, with lower courts handing down judgments that favored each parent to different degrees. Ultimately, the final decision rested with the primary custodial parent, the father in this case. According to attorney Jerold Bressman, who encourages interfaith clients seeking prenuptial agreements to include instructions on children's religious upbringing, "the parent who gets primary custody is going to win no matter what the prenup says. . . . It's different in a joint custody case; then I think the prenuptial agreement may stand."[139] Prenuptial agreements may seem unnecessary to people without extraordinary wealth or assets, but interfaith and intercultural issues make a solid argument for having this document in hand prior to walking down the aisle. Provided that it does not involve constitutional conflicts, write family law specialists, "a valid prenuptial agreement with religious provisions may be enforced like a secular contract." Although a prenuptial "religious upbringing clause" may not be legally enforceable—ultimately the court will determine what is in the best interests of a child on a case-by-case basis—it does provide evidence regarding the parents' intentions, and laws may always change.[140]

Decisions made pre-marriage about raising children sometimes shifted after a child's actual birth and even more so after divorce, illustrating that it is easier to discuss how a child will be raised in theory than to agree in practice. Regarding the tenuous nature of premarital decisions about religious upbringing, the *Cleveland Jewish News* pondered, "After Divorce: Will the Children Still Be Raised Jewish?"[141] Walter Chatham agreed to raise any prospective children as "both" (his wife was Baptist), a decision he later described as "dumb" and "stupid." Their religious differences were not an issue before they had a child; "I was in love; who cares?" Once his daughter was born, however, he insisted that she was Jewish and refused to celebrate Christmas. Regarding his now ex-wife, he admitted, "She was more supportive of my religion than I was of hers. She still is, I can't deny that." Post-divorce, their daughter attends both a Christian religious school and a Hebrew school. Although the child is effectively being raised in dual religions, there is no way to predict which, if any, she may choose as an adult. Asked whether he thought his daughter would become a bat mitzvah, this respondent answered definitively with the exact date already on the family calendar. That said, this Jewish man continues to deal with some tough emotions: "I don't despise Christianity, but I despise that my daughter is not being raised totally Jewish. I hate it."[142] Men whose wives became Jewish likewise found themselves struggling for control once the marriage dissolved. Revlon chairman Ronald Perelman, who married Patricia Duff, an Episcopalian woman who converted to Judaism, had a difficult time after he and his wife divorced; she had an Easter egg hunt and baked leavened cookies with their daughter Caleigh during Passover.[143] Subsequently, he won custody. Perelman, who is Orthodox, describes their daughter as a "conscientious Jew."[144] These cases and others like them suggest that just as identity formation is a fluid and continuous process, religious upbringing of children is rarely set in stone.

Men's experiences, including their Jewish journeys and evolving identities as fathers, complicate the history of intermarriage in America. They make apparent that interactions with rabbis during young adulthood and when they married inform subsequent relationships with Judaism and involvement in Jewish life. Their desire to determine for themselves how to be Jewish is part of the larger struggle between factions over authenticity in America, while ongoing gender disparity at work and at home contribute to distancing them from equal parenting. Intermarried Jewish men's narratives dismantle the myth that they cease to identify as Jews or raise Jewish children. Rather they make evident that men can and do contribute to Jewish continuity but that more can be done to engage and enfranchise them.

Chapter 3 will turn the lens from Jewish men to the born-Christian women they married and their experiences as wives and mothers. No history of Jewish men, intermarriage, and fatherhood would be complete without these female voices. As many of the men I interviewed told me, "You should talk to my wife." Moreover, studying their wives sheds light on the meaning of intermarriage for Jewish men and on Jewish identity.

3

Shiksappeal

Understanding Jewish intermarriage entails studying both individuals who make up the couple, the born-Jewish member and the born-Christian member. While this chapter looks at born-Christian women, it does so with the intention of answering this question: How do these women's experiences and sentiments inform our understanding of intermarriage and intermarried Jewish men? Thus while their stories merit attention in their own right, my goal is to use their testimonies as evidence in relation to themes raised by or about Jewish men; these include stereotypes about non-Jewish women attracting men away from Judaism, Jews making good husbands, and Jewish men not wanting responsibility for whether their wives became Jews-by-choice. When asked how he could marry his beloved without her first converting to Judaism, comedic actor Mel Brooks (born Melvin Kaminsky) responded, "She doesn't have to convert, she's a star!"[1] The quote in the epigraph pokes fun at the idea that a Jewish mother would rather die than live to see her son intermarry, an abiding Jewish joke.[2] In reality, "my mother was very happy," Brooks insisted. "A star is a big thing, you know, six points is better, but a star!"[3] Bancroft and Brooks were married from 1964 until her death in 2005,

Mel Brooks and Anne Bancroft (1983). *The Kobal Collection/Tony Costa.*

illustrating their strong commitment to each other.[4] The fact that today their adult son Max Brooks identifies as Jewish indicates that Bancroft was apparently less of a deterrent to Jewish continuity than myths about Christian women suggest.[5]

Contemporary communal concerns focus almost entirely on how intermarriage affects Jewish life, with very little consideration of how it changes the lives of Christians who marry into the Jewish world. The more men I interviewed encouraged me to speak to their wives, the more I realized how critical it was to include their voices alongside the men's in this narrative. A Christian woman who falls in love with and marries a Jewish man will never be the same again, nor will her life develop as it would have had she married a co-religionist. Her religion and ethnicity at birth notwithstanding, the so-called shiksa (a term I will discuss below) plays a vital part in the meaning of intermarriage and identity for Jewish men. Consider, for example, this vignette.

A Jewish man is about to go off to college to study accounting in order to manage the books for his father's business. Before he goes, his father tells him, "Listen. I know that we aren't very religious, but promise me one thing. Promise me that you won't marry a shiksa." The son is surprised, given his father's liberal teachings, but sees that his father is serious and so he gives him his word that he won't marry a Christian woman.

A few years into college, he meets a very nice non-Jewish woman and they fall in love. He tells her that he can't marry her because he promised his dad he wouldn't marry a non-Jewish woman. She thinks about this and decides she loves him so much that she'll convert for him. She studies Judaism for a year and becomes a Jew-by-choice. They get married and move back near his parents' house.

A few months later, the father tells the son that he wants to get together that Saturday morning to balance the books. Saturday morning comes, and the son doesn't show up. The father calls the son and gets no answer. Finally, worried about his son, he drives over to his son's house and frantically knocks on the door. The son calmly answers the door and the father is furious! He starts yelling, "Where were you? I've been worried half to death!" The son says, "I'm sorry, but my wife told me that I'm not allowed to use the phone, drive the car, or work on Saturday." His father tells him, "See, I told you not to marry a shiksa!"[6]

This joke illustrates the layers of meanings associated with the word "shiksa": a Jewish man falling in love with a shiksa despite his parent's plea; contrary to assumptions that she threatens Jewish continuity, the possibility that she might actually convert instead; Jewish men's concerns that a woman would convert for them rather than out of her own religious conviction; the phenomenon that sometimes a Jew-by-choice becomes more observant than a born-Jew; and lastly, that she, the so-called shiksa, is actually wearing the religious pants in the family by deciding how Shabbat will be observed, usurping the whole idea of Judaism as a patriarchal religion. Nowhere in the joke, however, do we hear from the shiksa herself. Christine Benvenuto offers an explanation for why we have heard *about* Christian women rather than *from* them in her illuminating book *Shiksa: The Gentile Woman in the Jewish World*: "The very fact that gentile women are so intimately connected to the Jewish family may help to explain the absence of any serious consideration of their history or their present role in Jewish communities. Despite generations of shiksa slurs and cultural caricatures, there has been silence in place of these women's voices and stories, a sense that it's been too risky for them to make themselves heard."[7]

Popular culture has served to reinforce both the idea of the shiksa holding some mysterious allure and the fear that she would ultimately cause the destruction of the Jewish people by turning them away from Jewish religion and culture. The "shiksa," as the non-Jewish woman is sometimes casually called, is usually portrayed in one of two ways: the blond bombshell whom all heterosexual men should supposedly desire, surely reinforced by Marilyn Monroe's 1956 marriage to Arthur Miller, or the Christian vixen who lures Jewish men in particular away from their religion, ethnic heritage, and family.[8] One of the more famous, or infamous, examples appears in Philip Roth's 1969 novel *Portnoy's Complaint*. In that fictional work, character Mary Jean Reed is the blond, voluptuous, lingerie model who is, as one literary scholar described, "the materialization of a pornographic scenario that has obsessed him since adolescence."[9] The lesser-known 1978 novel by B. H. Litwack, *The Last Shiksa*, perpetuated the objectification of Christian women by susceptible Jewish men. Arnie Goff, Litwack's character, wants "skyrocketing, dazzling sex" and meets "Christine, the ultimate shiksa of them all,

"Call me . . . Shiksa" cover illustration of *Moment* (June 2006). *Courtesy of* Moment
magazine. *Original pinup calendar illustration by Billy De Vorss, 1940.*

the most beautiful blond he has ever seen, shimmering with northern
lights. His passion for her was immediate and all consuming."[10] Over
the decades since these renditions, the American shiksa character has
morphed into something that less-than-blond women could embody.

In 1997, the popular sitcom *Seinfeld* portrayed how the alluring Christian woman could contribute to the declining engagement of Jewish males with Jewish organized life post–bar mitzvah, an actual concern among contemporary American Jews. In the "Serenity Now" episode, a rabbi tells Adam Lippman, a Jewish boy preparing for his bar mitzvah, that the event signals his becoming a man. The boy interprets this transition to adulthood as qualification for fulfilling his sexual longings, not greater responsibility in the Jewish community. At least that is what the writers for the show would have American viewers believe. When Christian character Elaine Bennes (played by Julia Louis-Dreyfus) offers her congratulations after the service, the thirteen-year-old embraces her in a French kiss and then, with his hand raised in a fist, exclaims, "I'm a man!" When she tries to convince the thirteen-year-old that despite what the rabbi told him, it actually takes a long time to become a man, he responds, "Well, if I am not a man, then this whole thing was a sham! . . . I renounce my religion! . . . As of this moment, I am no longer Jewish. I quit!" Next thing Elaine knows, the elder Lippman tries to kiss her; he denies that it's because he's Jewish and she isn't, and following in his son's footsteps, he too renounces his religion. She's mystified by their attraction to her. In a subsequent scene, George explains, "Well, sure. They're Jewish, and you're a shiksa."

> Elaine: "What?"
> George: "It means a non-Jewish woman."
> Elaine: "I know what it means, but what does being a shiksa have to do with it?"
> George: "You've got 'shiksappeal.' Jewish men love the idea of meeting a woman that's not like their mother."
> Elaine: "Oh, that's insane."[11]

The plot thickens further, or deteriorates depending on one's perspective, when Elaine seeks advice from a rabbi about how to reduce her "shiksappeal" and he not only explains that rabbis are allowed to date but invites her to Myrtle Beach with him after the High Holidays.[12] If there is a positive outcome of the Seinfeld rendition of the shiksa myth, it is that brunettes have equal appeal as their fair-haired sisters.

Cultural representations of Christian women abound in American history, spawning most recently a sub-genre of "chick lit." Shiksa lit, authored by both Jewish and non-Jewish women, includes such titles as *The Shiksa Syndrome; Boy Vey! The Shiksa's Guide to Dating Jewish Men;* and *Confessions of a Nervous Shiksa.*[13] Little, however, is unveiled in these works about the real women who were born Christian and marry Jewish men.

What is the history behind the word "shiksa" and how is it being used today? Who are the actual "shiksas" and what does marriage to a Jewish man mean to them?

Whether the term "shiksa" is used to denote something derogatory or enviable, or even intended as humorous, it is always loaded and evokes a wide range of responses. The word itself deserves some explanation. The word "shiksa" is the Americanized version of the Yiddish *shikse.* The Yiddish *shikse* is the feminine form of the Yiddish masculine form *shaygets. Shaygets* derives from the Hebrew masculine *shekketz.* The Hebrew word translates literally as something "impure." In biblical times, *shekketz,* or *shekketzim* in the plural, described idols, goddesses, and unkosher food. In contemporary Israel, *shekketz* is not used to refer to someone who is not Jewish, since it is understood to be extremely insulting.[14]

However one spells or pronounces the word, the meaning behind it is complicated. While the word "gentile" may be used in reference to anyone who is not Jewish, the word "shiksa" has multiple connotations. The most neutral meaning is a non-Jewish woman. However, many more meanings have been attributed to the word over time, some complimentary and many others not. As the great Yiddishist Anita Norich commented, "The task of the translator . . . is to convey the difference between a *shikse* and a non-Jewish woman."[15] According to "The Yiddish Handbook: 40 Words You Should Know," *shikse* also connotes "young and beautiful," so referring to a man's Christian wife or girlfriend as a *shiksa* implies that he is primarily attracted to her because she is good looking, and possibly blonde.[16] The most negative literal meanings include "abomination," "unclean," "impure," and "dirty." Somewhere in between is the still value-laden idea of the non-Jewish woman being promiscuous, hence the saying "Shiksas are for practice."[17]

The idea that "shiksas are for practice" may have an ancient origin, but it lives on in contemporary times. Tacit approval of Jewish males' sexual relations with non-Jewish females, allowing greater access to Christian women, is illustrated by a Yiddish saying for Jewish boys: "In

"Why I Only Date Shiksas," written by Adam Mutterperl and drawn by Matthew Shultz. *Courtesy of Adam Mutterperl and* Heeb *magazine.*

the Torah it is written, that you may lie with a Gentile girl, but if the girl does not let you 'have' her, may she be afflicted with Cholera!"[18] The saying is likely a cultural manipulation of biblical text that, while not discussing any ailment, dealt with the treatment of sexually desirable non-Jewish women who are captured in war by the Israelite soldier. It prescribes marriage, intercourse, and conversion to Judaism.[19] The Israelite warrior could take a non-Jewish woman captive. He could bring her home, change her appearance by cutting her hair and discarding her clothes, give her a month to grieve for her parents, and "after that you may come to her and possess her, and she shall be your wife" (Deuteronomy 21:10–14).[20] A non-Jewish woman may not be every Jewish boy's secret fantasy, but she seemed to be some Jewish mothers' nemesis. One of the men in my study recalled being told by his mother that Christian girls did not wear underpants. Her comment intended to dissuade him from pursuing non-Jewish women actually enhanced their appeal to him![21] Comic artist Eli Valley ended his 2010 satirical strip "Vader: Half-Jew" with Hans Solo warning his *Star Wars* comrade Chewbacca, "Remember, ewoks are for practice."[22]

In addition to its literal and figurative meanings, what the word "shiksa" conveys depends on who uses it and the larger context. It is interesting that "shiksa" first appeared in *The Merriam-Webster Dictionary* in 1961, a year that initiated the tripling of the Jewish intermarriage rate in America from 5.9 percent for the period between 1956 and 1960 to 17.4 percent between 1961 and 1965.[23] Whether it is used as a friendly term of endearment or in an explanatory manner fuels much of the difference between its connotations. One of the female participants in my study recalled being called a "shiksa" by the people who worked in a kosher general store in Brookline, Massachusetts, she frequented in the early 1960s. She entered and explained that her boyfriend was Jewish, that she was not, and that she needed to learn what to buy and all about kashrut (Jewish dietary laws). The people were "very kind," imparted lessons about what *parve* meant, and over time shared stories about their Jewish lives. At no point did she feel slighted or that she was being called "the shiksa" in a derogatory way.[24] In Roxanne Pomerantz's mind, "shiksa" was not a particularly derogatory term, but rather one that marked her as different from Jews, that is, without Judaic knowledge or understanding.

But "shiksa" can also be used as an insult. In explanation of why her son was the only child not included under the huppah at an Orthodox relative's wedding, a Christian woman was told, "It's because you're a shiksa!" This usage was hurtful: her child's Jewish identity was questioned because of her status as an outsider.[25]

Given the pervasive use of "shiksa," why is the masculine version of the Hebrew word, *shaygets,* not used as commonly or as frequently? *Shaygets* may have been used more often in Eastern Europe (before World War II), but it is rarely used in America today.[26] Historically, it was long believed that Jewish men intermarried much more frequently than Jewish women. It is impossible to know exactly how many Jewish women intermarried and went undetected because they took their Christian husband's surname and became invisible to researchers. There are historical studies that account for some intermarriage cases of Jewish women in Germany and Imperial Russia, for example, but the record is far from complete.[27] Although demographers now contend that the intermarriage sex ratio is closer to even than not, many people still believe that Jewish men intermarry more often than Jewish women. This would explain, in part, why "shiksa" is used more than *shaygets.* The full explanation, however, is far more complex. The matrilineal descent principle makes non-Jewish women who marry Jewish men seem more "threatening" to Jewish continuity than do non-Jewish men who marry Jewish women. In the case of Jewish women, their children will be Jewish regardless of who they marry. In the case of Jewish men, their children will not be Jewish unless they are formally converted, according to two out of three of the largest movements in Judaism. Hence, shiksas pose real or imagined "danger." The most convincing explanation for why one hears "shiksa" and not *shaygets* is a bit more insidious. According to sociologist Diane Wolf, the actual reason for the persistence of "shiksa" in the American lexicon is "just general misogyny and sexism that allows terms derogatory towards women to be perpetuated much more so than terms that are derogatory towards men."[28] Stereotypes about JAPS—Jewish American Princesses—and Jewish mothers and the near absences of the same about Jewish American Princes and Jewish fathers offer a Jewish parallel that is equally noxious for Jewish women as "shiksa" can be for non-Jewish women. According to journalist Dan Friedman, "Shiksa is the 'N' word of the Jewish community. It is so often used jokingly that one can forget that it is a vile, sexist, racist word. Somehow, perhaps because sexism is still tolerated in a way that racism is not, 'shiksa' is

Tori Avey is the "Shiksa in the Kitchen." Check her out at http://www.theshiksa.com. *Courtesy of Tori Avey.*

more acceptable than the equally despicable 'schvartze' [Yiddish slur for a black person]."[29] Fortunately, the twenty-first century ushered in a new meaning for the word "shiksa."

Savvy entrepreneurs and marketers have created products and even a cooking show that celebrate the Christian woman. There is the "Shiksa Goddess" water bottle and tote bag, T-shirts for women that read simply "shiksa" in pink cursive or in Hebrew, and T-shirts for men that read "I," followed by a Star of David, then "shiksas." (Whether the latter shirt is actually meant to suggest that Jewish men Judaize non-Jewish women or is designed as such because men would rather not wear a shirt with a big heart on it, is difficult to tell.) You can now even download a "Shiksa Goddess" ringtone to your cell phone. Moreover, some Christian women have actually taken ownership of the term, infusing it with positive meaning and promoting its ongoing usage. Tori Avey, a Christian woman who married a Jewish man and became a Jew-by-choice on February 25, 2010, is writing her debut cookbook titled *The Shiksa in the Kitchen*. Blogging about her ongoing self-identification, Tori writes, "I am happy that I was born a Shiksa; it made me who I am today. Judaism is my spiritual path, but I will never forget where I came from."[30] Thus even when a woman becomes Jewish, she may choose to let her background empower her and retain the "shiksa" identifier, illustrating the term's change to something with panache.[31] Hence, the word has experienced a rather radical transformation from an intra-Jewish term, that is, one used between Jews, to one that Jews and Christians alike are using. Illustrating how the once derogatory term has come full circle, *The Shiksa's Guide to Yiddish* by Christy Potter Kass shows how language can be co-opted after falling in love with a Jewish man and his people.[32]

REAL SHIKSAS

When I first began seeking interview subjects, I put an ad in the Ann Arbor monthly community paper, posted flyers in many locales, and sent information to Jewish and Christian newsletters and online lists. One day while I was working in my office at the Frankel Center, my phone rang. I picked up and a male voice said, "I'm calling about the study about Jewish men married to shiksas!" I detected what I thought was a note of humor or perhaps bravado in the caller's voice; apparently he enjoyed using the word "shiksa," his interest was piqued, and he seemed more than a little pleased that he qualified for my study. When I actually interviewed him, I asked him about this opening comment. He explained that there was nothing sinister or denigrating about his using it; although he was aware the term can have some derogatory connotation, to his mind using "shiksa" was pure "hilarity." Several of his Jewish friends intermarried, and they joke about it within their social group. Their manner of using the word, as Jews in relation to other Jews and to non-Jews, illustrates selective deployment of a Jewish language repertoire "to align themselves with some people and distinguish themselves from others," according to sociolinguist Sarah Bunim Benor.[33] I also interviewed the caller's wife. She explained that when they first met, she asked if her being non-Jewish was an issue, and he assured her that he preferred to date shiksas, as he put it. Ironically, their story is similar to the joke at the beginning of this chapter because ultimately the wife was drawn to Judaism and became an observant Jew-by-choice who helped him reengage with Jewish life. That was not her objective, however, for this particular born-Christian woman never set her sights on Jewish men; "I dated men with blue eyes. It had nothing to do with what religious or cultural background they had."[34] Apparently, the intermarried man gave considerable more cultural significance to his marrying a non-Jew than did his wife, who did not seek a Jewish man; she happened to meet and marry one.

Actual "shiksas" are neither like the cultural representations nor like the myths surrounding them, suggesting that popular culture and Jewish folklore have vivid imaginations about intermarriage. Certainly some are physically attractive and some have blonde hair, but many more are their husbands' physical equals rather than stunningly gorgeous, and there are as many brunettes as blondes. Going beneath surface level, many non-Jewish women become Jews-by-choice and actually act as the bridges back to their husbands' inherited faith rather than deterrents to it. Out of the forty-one men I interviewed, nearly half of their wives converted to Judaism. Of the nineteen women who became Jews, seventeen converted via a formal process affiliated with the Reform or Conservative movement; one simply became Jewish at the Jewish Cultural Society, where you are considered Jewish if you want to be; and one considers herself and her family Jewish without any formal ritual. The ability to choose your identity and affiliation was a distinctive character-istic of Jewish life in Ann Arbor among academics, where who you are rather than what you are matters most. The large proportion of women, relatively speaking, who chose Judaism reflects the national finding that two-thirds of Jews-by-choice are females.[35] Yet it also suggests that this academic community was more conducive to conversion than else-where in the country, since less than 20 percent of intermarriages result in conversion nationally.[36] The women's conversion stories are complex, illustrating the various ways in which women came to terms with what becomes the correct choice for themselves and their families.

Although this book primarily focuses on intermarried Jewish men, it is important to understand the other part of the gender equation. In or-der to ascertain what intermarriage meant to women who were not born Jewish and who married Jewish men, I interviewed thirteen of them, between the ages of thirty-two and seventy-five (born between 1935 and 1978), all of whom married between the years 1962 and 2003. For eleven of the thirteen women, it was their first marriage; for one woman, it was her second; and for one, her third. Like the interviews with men included in my study, I conducted all of the interviews with women in Ann Arbor, Michigan. Moreover, the women who participated are the current wives of some of the men. The women's backgrounds include Catholic, several Protestant denominations (Episcopalian, Methodist, Presbyterian, Dis-ciples of Christ, Lutheran), and Unitarian. Ten out of thirteen women were born in the Midwest: Indiana, Iowa, Michigan, Minnesota, Ohio, and Wisconsin. Even among such a small sample as thirteen women, patterns arose that shed light on the meaning of interfaith marriage and gender in America.

OPPOSITES ATTRACT

Although most fictional representations of the shiksa suggest that it is her "otherness" that attracts Jewish men, in reality it is the born-Chris-tian women who are attracted to Jewish men's qualities as the "stranger." Roxanne Pomerantz's husband's good looks first attracted her; his work ethic and passion about his work fascinated her. She added, "I think, as much as anything else . . . he was different. He was the other." Roxanne, raised Episcopalian, was intrigued by his being Israeli-born, his knowledge of the Holocaust, and the fact that he came from "a kind of hardscrabble background."[37] Fran Berman, raised Methodist, grew up in the segregated town of Greensboro, North Carolina. She was fascinated by people's different backgrounds, including her husband's Hungarian Jewish family, which she found interesting rather than worrisome.[38] The decoupling of religion and ethnicity for many white Protestants, a result of the Americanization of immigrant churches, meant that Protestantism became less cultural. Protestantism no longer maintained an ethnic exclusiveness it once had for the older immigrant groups (English, Scotch, Scotch-Irish, German, Dutch, and Scandinavian) once newer immigrants, who were largely non-Protestants, arrived and became the lower classes. Poles, Italians, Greeks, and Slavs ethnically replaced white Anglo-Saxon Protestants in America.[39] By the time these women married Jewish men, their own families were considerably less ethnic, thus their husbands' seemed exotic by comparison. Illustrating a turning of the fictive table, Barbara Bartlett wrote in her 1987 novel *The Shiksa*:

> All over Los Angeles, she'd begun to see them—the women who shared her fixation with Jewish men. They were not recognizable on sight; not all blue-eyed blondes were shiksas, in Katherine's specific definition of the term, and not all shiksas were blue-eyed blond Catholics. But most, she imagined, fitted Jed's description of "neuros." They gravitated to Jewish men, both instinctively and reactively, as a way out of the constricted world they knew; they were addicted to the famed Jewish warmth, humor, and intelligence, as well as to the black side, the side that once made her rail at Jed, "You don't have to be a masochist to love Jewish men, but it helps!"[40]

While the women with Episcopal backgrounds came from families who were better off socioeconomically than their Jewish husbands' families, Catholic women's socioeconomic status resembled their spouses' status.

Women born Christian who had career aspirations beyond social norms for the times were attracted to Jewish men who accepted their ambitions. Born in 1940, Fran Berman came of age when women were not expected to work outside the home, and if one did, it would be as a secretary. She left the South in part because of the restrictive social roles and cultural expectations. Fran liked school, studied hard, and pursued a graduate degree in clinical psychology. Her husband had grown up in Chicago and was very accepting of the kind of female role that interested her. She attributed his openness to coming from an urban background, where there was more diversity and freedom to be who you were rather than to conform to what people expected of you. Similarly, Martha Chelm's professional aspirations had been thwarted when she was growing up, and she yearned to do more than was "recommended." When she graduated with an English degree in the 1960s, her career counselor encouraged her to become a teacher, because "teaching is such a nice thing to fall back on." She remembered telling him, "I sure as heck hope my children don't have teachers who have fallen back on teaching. Teachers should want to teach, and I have never wanted to teach."[41] Martha was eager to shake off the 1950s legacy her friends continued to uphold of making a career out of getting married and having children. After she and her husband bought their first house, they were both employed, so they conquered the housework and gardening together.

Although the theory that Jewish men make good husbands (discussed in chapter 1) was widely known in Jewish circles, Christian women I interviewed usually had not heard of it until after they had selected their spouse or married him, or not at all. Martha Chelm's husband attracted her because he was romantic, smart, and funny. After nearly forty years of marriage, she commented, "He fits the theory; he's a great husband."[42] Holly Pedersen's view of Jewish men included "a lot more focus on family involvement," a sense of security, and education. Roxannne believed that the theory that Jewish men make good husbands was true in the past when they had fewer prospects, because they could not wander and were therefore thought to be more faithful. They were also raised to be careful and accomplished and to not make waves. She defined her description as being dated because "Jews are more like everybody else nowadays than they used to be," that is, when Jews were considered less "white" and antisemitism was higher. It seems quite plausible that the theory that Jewish men make good husbands was one fueled from within the fold, eager to project and perpetuate a positive self-image, one devoid of domestic violence, adultery, and desertion despite evidence to the contrary.[43] Alex Piker had never heard the theory that Jewish men make good husbands but had an interesting explanation for it.

She speculated that it stemmed from a stereotype about sons trying to please their demanding Jewish mothers, so they would try to please their wives.[44] Word has spread about Jewish men making appealing husbands. Christian author Kristina Grish promoted the theory and encouraged "snag a Hebrew honey":

> There's a lot to love about a guy who makes your laughter his priority, who talks about your relationship more than you do, who's wildly intense inside the bedroom and out, who thinks nudging him up the corporate ladder is a sign of affection. Jewish men feed your mind and appetite, and they are the ultimate caretakers without a hint of machismo. They're also generous and thoughtful, thanks to a matriarchal culture that's taught them to appreciate women's strength, candor, humor, and intelligence. And because Jewish men value professional drive, your mom can finally tell neighbors that you're dating a doctor, lawyer, or entrepreneur.[45]

A Christian member of JDate admitted having a "positive bias toward Jewish men." "They tend to be very smart, successful, gentlemanly and less sexist," she opined.[46] Print media also reinforces the idea that Jewish men make good husbands and fathers. A 2012 *People* magazine cover, for example, boasted a photograph of actress Drew Barrymore and Jewish hubby Will Kopelman with his hand gently resting on her apparent baby bump.[47] That Barrymore is removing multiple tattoos so she can be buried in a traditional Jewish cemetery suggests she is genuinely attracted to Judaism, not just her Jewish husband. The actress is vocal about marrying into the Kopelman family and their religion: "I love the Jewish Faith."[48]

Many of the Christian-born women had very limited experience with Jews until getting seriously involved with their husbands. Renee Barnes grew up in Plymouth, Indiana, where there was one Jewish family "and no black families, just to tell you how lily white my town was."[49] She had a couple of dates with a Jewish man in college, but otherwise no romantic experience with Jews until she met her husband during their medical training. Some women had never even met a Jew prior to meeting their husband, let alone dated one. Roxanne Pomerantz came from an affluent white Anglo-Saxon Protestant background. She attended a boarding school, associated with people of her "kind," had a French governess, and toured the world. Roxanne remarked, "I probably had hardly met a Jew before."[50] She had a childhood memory of a female playmate who did not have a Christmas tree whom she thought was poor, who might actually have been Jewish; her husband was her first male Jewish acquaintance.

Although much of Jewish intermarriage scholarship focuses on the *Jewish* family's response to a child intermarrying, scant if any attention is given to the Christian woman and her relationship with her family of origin. The original Jewish mother's lament was Rebekah's to her husband Isaac (Abraham's son) when she expressed concern about their son Jacob: "I am weary of my life because of the Hittite women. If Jacob marries one of the Hittite women such as these, one of the women of the land, what good will my life be to me?" (Genesis 26:46). Rebekah and Isaac's other son, Esau, married several non-Jewish women.[51] Since biblical times, there have been many other permutations of the Jewish mother bursting into tears at the prospect of her son marrying a non-Jewish woman.[52] In the postwar period, Christian parents had their share of woes over Christian daughters marrying Jewish men. Holly Pedersen, raised Catholic, had dated a wide variety of men and delved into Eastern religions before intermarrying. She described the response to her decision to marry a Jewish man as follows: "My parents were just overjoyed that I was marrying somebody who was in the Judeo-Christian tradition." Her family migrated from the yoga community to Temple Beth Emeth, the Reform synagogue, and then to the Jewish Cultural Society. Mentioning God was prohibited from her daughter's bat mitzvah ceremony, which she thought was ridiculous and put her in a very awkward position with her Irish Catholic family of origin, who came and said, "Now you don't believe in God?" In sharp contrast to Holly's parents, Roxanne's parents, direct descendants of the *Mayflower*, were very upset that she was intermarrying. They never told her explicitly that it was because her betrothed was Jewish. "They told me he was from a very different background. He was an immigrant."[53] Although the socioeconomic class difference between the two could not have been greater, this couple was unusual because most Jewish men married women with similar class backgrounds as themselves. Another woman's parents made it clear that they thought she was making a mistake, her father telling her, "You can still change your mind," moments before he walked her down the aisle at her wedding.[54] Her parents' disapproval stemmed from their concern about his Jewish background and having a physical impairment. Renee described her mother's worry about how the pairing would appear to other people. These women were unusual because some were the first women in their family to pursue careers and move away from their hometowns. As a result, their worldviews were broader than their parents' and their ambitions greater.

Christian women faced cultural disparities when they met their Jewish in-laws, experiences that sometimes reflected popular culture's influence on American perceptions of Jews. Roxanne's future mother-in-law initially refused to meet her, saying she would not attend the wedding and was going to sit *shiva*, tear her clothes, and mourn her son as if he were dead. Her husband-to-be assured her that his mother would "come around." By the time she did, he was already in basic training, so Roxanne courageously flew to Florida by herself to meet his family. She took her seat on the sofa as the family members came in the front door; they, however, walked past her and sat down for the meal at the dining room table. She remembers her surprise: "Oh! I'd never been in a house where there hadn't been cocktails before dinner."[55] Her upper-class upbringing did not prepare her for a working-class Jewish family. Neither had her betrothed. (Illustrating the disparate backgrounds was her husband's experience visiting her family: he inadvertently stepped on the buzzer for the maid or butler multiple times.) Alex Pike recalled her future mother-in-law looking her in the eye, standing very close, and telling her in no uncertain terms, "You don't have to convert, but your children will be Jewish."[56] Ultimately Alex did convert—to spite her mother-in-law, she joked. At the time of the conversation though, she felt that a personal boundary had been breached because her husband's mother stood so close to her, disrespecting her accustomed space for conversation. In addition, Alex considered her religious identity her own private business, as was how she and her future husband would raise their children. For Christian-born women, prying into their family's religious life felt invasive. Try telling that to a Jewish mother who considers it her business to ask, "Will my grandchildren be Jewish?" This is a pressing question among Jewish parents of intermarried couples. Hence what Christian women considered out of social bounds, according to their understanding of behavior norms, Jewish in-laws considered ripe for discussion.

Alvy Singer (Woody Allen) appears to Grammy as "a real Jew" in
Annie Hall (1977). *Courtesy of Trevor Gilks/everywoodyallenmovie.com.*

"Does he have a beard?" was the first question Charlotte Steven's
mother asked when Charlotte told her she was dating a Jewish man—
"like she was like all freaked out he was going to look like, you know,
one of those bearded guys and just oh my God, you know?"[57] The visual
connotation is reminiscent of the caricature portrayed by Woody Allen
of the Hasidic Jew in the film *Annie Hall.* Allen appears to be beardless
to everyone except to Grandmother Hall, who, Allen imagines, sees
him through her own lens, complete with beard, side curls, and black
hat. Woody Allen's caricature of the ultimate Jew conveys his own sense
of unease, imagining that he looked like a Hasid in the eyes of someone
he thinks does not like Jews—or at least is uncomfortable around them.
Charlotte's mother's initial reaction stemmed from inexperience with
Jews and ignorance about Jewish diversity; in her mother's mind, like in
Allen's character Grammy Hall's, all Jewish men had beards.

CONVERSION

Women who intermarried later in the postwar period converted to Judaism later in their relationships with Jewish men than did women who intermarried earlier, illustrating the changing relationship between men

and women in general and women's increased assertiveness regarding their identities in particular. Roxanne Pomerantz, Kelly Darnell, and Martha Chelm, who married in 1960, 1962, and 1970 respectively, all converted prior to their wedding dates. A lack of commitment to Christianity facilitated Martha Chelm's decision to convert two weeks before she wed, as well as her view of her husband's religion. "I thought that Judaism was beautiful," she recalled.[58] Helen Carlton and Alex Piker, on the other hand, converted after their 1988 and 2003 nuptials. The legacy of the second-wave feminist movement of the 1960s and 1970s encouraged women of all faith backgrounds who intermarried in the 1980s, 1990s, and 2000s to make their own decisions about, for example, keeping their surnames when they wed. Expectations regarding how wives should accommodate husbands also changed in the latter decades of the twentieth century, influenced by women's increased paid labor outside the home and a decrease in subordination to men's professional aspirations.[59] Women who married in later decades, when American women had more autonomy, often took their time converting to Judaism. Sally Srok Friedes, who wrote about her journey in *The New Jew: An Unexpected Conversion,* describes sitting in the rabbi's office and announcing her decision to convert: "Now, here I am, expecting our second baby, wanting a religion that reflects my beliefs."[60] I was privileged to hear Sharon Bak speak about her conversion in June 2010, long after she married and gave birth to two sons. She began with the question, "After fifteen years of trying out Judaism, you might ask: why take the plunge—both figuratively and literally—and convert to Judaism now?" Her answer: there was no single event, rather a process of experiencing Jewish life over time.[61] The practice of converting shortly before or sometime after children came into the marital equation reflects a sense that marriage truly begins when a child is born (or adopted).[62] A woman's decision to become a Jew-by-choice in response to her role as a mother illuminates the relationship between parenthood and intermarriage. The process of becoming a parent serves as an impetus for Christian women to begin reinventing themselves as Jewish women. No longer are they simply married to Jews; now they are raising Jews, which inspires introspection and a reevaluation of their religious identities.

Judaism held a strong allure for women raised Christian who had begun to question their religion long before meeting their husbands, suggesting that intermarriage was sometimes a tipping point rather than a catalyst. Roxanne wanted to become Jewish to marry the man she loved, because he was a Conservative Jew and insisted that he could not marry someone who was not Jewish. As she also described, "I wasn't crazy about the religion I was in, so this was a very good match for me. The things that I didn't believe in, as a Christian, were things that didn't exist, such as the virgin birth and that Jesus was the Son of God and died on the cross for my sins and all that."[63] Roxanne's rejection of some of the fundamental articles of Christian faith suggests she had already distanced herself from her childhood religion before she met her husband. She liked Judaism, especially that a lot of ritual happened in the home. The reason she gave the rabbi who asked why she wanted to convert was simply because she wanted to marry a Jewish man. In 1960, such a motivation was acceptable to the rabbi, who, ironically, was relieved that she did not claim to have "seen the light." He encouraged her to read about Jewish history and discussed with her what it was like to be Jewish and encounter prejudice, but he did not emphasize learning prayers or attending synagogue. Rabbis today have a very different approach, as discussed below. In 1993, decades after she converted and wed, Roxanne became a bat mitzvah at the Conservative synagogue in Ann Arbor. She explained that after she had long been very active in the Jewish community, "I needed to make the religion mine."[64] Making Judaism her own was accomplished not through ritual at home but through study of text and mastery of Torah and public prayer, illustrating how her ideas about becoming Jewish evolved over time. Sharon Miller wed, for the third time, in 2006. She was raised as a Catholic, as were her first two husbands, but she contended, "I always felt like a misfit in the Catholic religion." Sharon's attempts to voice her ideas about Catholicism had been dismissed; so she kept them secret . . . until she met her Jewish husband. People now try to blame him, but she argued, "My whole entire life I questioned Jesus—I just always felt he was a mortal."[65] Christine Benvenuto wrote about her departure from Christianity long before she wed a Jew: "The Catholicism I inherited from my family was an uneasy fit for me as far back as I can remember.... Within a year of leaving Catholic school, serious doubts had turned into permanent disaffection."[66]

Some women who sought spiritual sustenance grew alienated from Christianity and readily welcomed Judaism into their lives. When Renee Barnes was in college, she was bothered that her Presbyterian background was not more religious. She investigated an evangelical group on campus and then realized that some of the questions she had simply did not have answers. By the time she met her husband, she remembered thinking that it was nice he was Jewish because "I'm kind of done with the Christian way of looking at things." Although they decided to raise Jewish children, her husband identified as an atheist, while Renee clung to the spiritual belief that "there might be a power or energy that unites the world."[67] They lived in Utah for a while, where there was one synagogue for several bordering states. She considered officially converting to Judaism, but there was a requirement that her husband also attend the classes with her; he had no interest in going and refused. "I wasn't happy about that," she recounted. "I would have preferred that we did it." Making conversion a family affair, involving both the born Jew and the prospective Jew, was a significant change from the 1960s, when a Christian woman pursued it alone. Although achieving membership in the Jewish people through formal conversion eluded Renee because of her husband's disinterest in the process, she considered herself Jewish along with her children, who were converted. "I see us all as Jewish," she affirmed.[68] For Renee, Jewish identity was a family identity, *her* family. The status of her Jewish family was not questioned while they lived in Ann Arbor, a far more cosmopolitan city than the one in Utah, and she and her children were welcomed into the Reform temple and both children became *b'nai mitzvah*.

For these women, becoming a Jew-by-choice was not so much a departure from their religion at birth as a return, illustrating that intermarriage could be a way for people to find their spiritual home. Helen Carlton described her experience deciding to become Jewish as an epiphany. Raised attending church weekly, she described her family of origin as committed to the church community. After intermarrying, she attended a Reform synagogue service with her husband when they were living in North Carolina. She recalled thinking, "I'm not anti-religious. They're just saying all the things I believe here." She had already agreed to raise their children as Jews and have a Jewish home, but she began discussing Judaism in depth with her husband and learning more about it to better understand what that actually meant. She and her husband moved to Ann Arbor and joined the Conservative synagogue, his original affiliation as a boy. After years of attending services there, an interaction with an elderly congregant catalyzed her conversion. The older woman asked her, "Why aren't you up there davening . . . leading services?" When she responded, "I can't, I'm not Jewish," the woman asked: "Why not?" During a visit to her hometown shortly after that conversation, she found that she could not take communion nor pray "in Christ's name." That night she told her mother, "Mom, I'm going to convert." One might wonder, how is it that women who were raised as observant Christians can become observant Jews, even encouraging greater involvement by their Jewish husbands? As Helen Carlton explained, converting "was not a rejection of who I was, but a more accurate living out of the way I was raised."[69] Regarding her church-going family of origin, she elaborated, "I think that's why I'm so comfortable as a Jew. Our values are totally the same." She was raised to believe that she was put on earth to make it a better place and to be kind, "and that's what draws me to Judaism."[70] Her experience illustrates how a woman's religiosity could be transferred from one faith to another.

While conversion to Judaism is often conceived of in the twenty-first century as a set period of study culminating in an interview with the *beit din* and submersion in a ritual bath, many women described their conversion as much lengthier and even ongoing processes. As Roxanne described, "You don't become Jewish by dunking yourself in a *mikveh*. It takes a long time." Seven years after she converted and wed, in 1969, Roxanne and her husband traveled to Israel. She "fell in love with Israel." Once she developed a passion for Israel, *that's* what, in her words, "got me hooked on being Jewish."[71] No longer was being Jewish limited to marrying a Jew. It became important for her to find people who shared her feelings about the Jewish state. Her commitment to Israel also further distanced her from her Protestant family of origin, not for religious reasons, but because they simply did not understand her passionate feelings about the country, the language, the history, and the culture of the

Jewish people. For Roxanne, as for others, visiting Israel transformed her experience of being Jewish by connecting her to the Jewish people and spurred her to affirm her Jewish identity.[72]

After converting, women who were Jews-by-choice sometimes held themselves to higher standards than their born-Jewish husbands in their efforts to gain full citizenship, so to speak. Alex Piker had been living a Jewish life for a number of years before she converted. "I kind of felt grumpy that I even needed to make it official because I had felt this way and was doing everything I would be doing after the conversion," she recalled. Once she accepted the interpretation that conversion was simply an official stamp on what she knew already in her heart, she felt better. Yet she considered her formal status as a Jew to be fragile because it was by choice rather than by birth, and she did not want to risk doing anything that might threaten it. When her husband encouraged her to have a Christmas tree if it would make her happy, she refused. Alex explained:

> I have a higher standard to live up to, because I've converted.... When you're born a Jew, nobody can say that you're not and there's not really all that much questioning.... But I think when you're a convert, like I converted in a Reform conversion and there are Jews who don't think I'm Jewish. They don't see me as Jewish.... It invalidates who I see myself as and ... I don't want to create any questions by embracing things that are very much not Jewish like a Christmas tree.

Thus while her born-Jewish husband could continue his practice of eating bacon pizza on a weekly basis, Alex gave up pork and shellfish. "There's this higher standard to uphold; you know, if I'm going to be Jewish, I'm going to be *Jewish*!" Admitting leniency about not mixing meat and milk, Alex commented, "I'm a cafeteria convert, I guess."[73] In reality, Alex is more observant of kashrut than many Jews-by-birth who would not consider giving up pork or shellfish. Her narrative lends support to the oft-quoted idea that Jewish "imports" are often better than "exports." One such "import" to Judaism, Jetskalina H. Phillips, did something no born Jew ever had: forty plus years after her 1964 conversion and intermarriage, she left the bulk of her estate to the Museum of Fine Arts in Boston for the acquisition, study, and display of Judaica and endowed a curatorship in her name.[74] Her generosity and vision demonstrate that

Jews-by-choice can be committed Jews with lasting influence on Jewish life in America.

Christian women who chose Judaism offer fresh perspectives on the interplay between religion and culture, the meaning of intermarriage, and the influence or lack thereof of intermarried Jewish men on their quest for deeper meaning. Sally Srok Friedes was initially frustrated when her husband Michael seemed unnerved by her enthusiasm for Judaism, scoffing at her interest in observing Shabbat by having a Sabbath dinner with the remark, "Next you're going to want to keep kosher!" She reminded herself that it was her spiritual journey, not his. During her speech to the congregation about her conversion, she explained the confusion she experienced meeting countless Jews who knew little about their religion, yet for whom Judaism was important: "How could their faith be so important to them when they didn't know the meaning behind their traditions and holidays?" A sermon by the rabbi explained that both Judaism the heritage and Judaism the religion were valid reasons for being Jewish. Friedes remarked, "And it became clear to me, it was all right that I would not be part of the heritage. My ancestors were not Jewish. But I can certainly embrace Judaism as a religion. . . . I have the best of everything. I get to learn about a religion I have chosen. My husband gets to learn about a heritage he was born into. And our children will understand and live the meaningfulness of both."[75]

Women's relationships with their mothers influenced some women's thought process regarding conversion. By interviewing women born Christian about their experiences with intermarriage, I learned that their relationships with their mothers played a significant role in their decision whether and when to become Jews-by-choice. Helen Carlton recounted, "I told Mama—that, to me, was the absolute barrier. . . . Once I had done that . . . the rest was downhill. I made an appointment with the rabbi to talk to him about . . . starting the process."[76] Long before Martha Chelm met her Jewish husband, she became interested in Judaism; after attending a Hillel service during her freshman year at the University of Michigan, she wrote to her mother, "Mom, I think I'm going to convert." She described her mother as being very open-minded and tolerant; her response to her daughter's announcement was reasonable: "Don't you think you should do some reading first?"[77] Martha agreed,

studied, *then* she converted. Charlotte Stevens was quite active in her
children's Jewish day school community and contemplated becoming
a Jew. However, the actual commitment required by conversion made
her shy away. Charlotte explained, "When my mother is gone, it will be
a *lot* easier for me."[78] Time will tell whether she ever actually converts,
but based on other statements about not being spiritual or having any
significant interest in learning about Judaism, it seems unlikely.

Religious homogeneity in the household also inspired some women
to convert to Judaism. In the process, sometimes they motivated their
husbands to become more involved Jews. Born in 1935 and raised as a
Lutheran, Kelly Darnell had trepidations about raising Jewish children,
which her husband insisted on, simply because she did not know a lot
about Judaism at the time. She had studied various religions, however,
and had a strong conviction in the importance of making a decision for
children rather than letting them decide for themselves. "What drove
me was my commitment to *a* religion . . . and only one religion within a
family. . . ." She continued, "If Judaism was what he wanted, then I would
deal with that."[79] Her acquiescence may illustrate her generation as much
as her commitment to a solitary religion. Married in 1963, Kelly grew up
during a pre-feminist era, when women subordinated their goals and
views to their husband's wishes. Women clearly wanted religious unifor-
mity for their family. As Friedes wrote, "Now I had agreed to raise our
children as Jews, and together Michael and I were about to find out what
that meant. I envisioned sharing a religion and feeling at home in a synagogue, just as my parents shared a religion and felt at home in the church.
Another piece of my vision of what it meant to be a couple was sliding
into place."[80] For Friedes, religion was interchangeable and family based;
she could achieve the same family homogeneity as her Christian parents
had shared by converting to her husband's faith. Women who assumed
responsibility for keeping the faith consistent within their families and
homes reinforced the historically gendered role of American women as
purveyors of domestic religion and "guardians of private morality and
piety."[81] In the nineteenth century, religion was thought to belong to
women by "divine right, a gift of God and nature," which was valued
because it kept women in their "proper sphere," their homes.[82] Illustrating the change over time, Alex Piker remarked on how her process of be-

coming knowledgeable about Judaism in the twenty-first century and learning alongside her children allowed her husband to walk alongside her as she took what she called "baby steps"; "he felt more comfortable joining me on my baby-step journey" than he might have had he married someone Jewish and was expected to know everything.[83] Her observation overlooks that some Jewish-Jewish couples learn equally as much from enrolling in introduction to Judaism classes or attending events at their children's Jewish preschool as do intermarried couples. Yet Alex's Jew-by-choice passport facilitated smooth passage for her husband by lessening the pressure of Jewish competence.

The path to Judaism for their family ultimately did not include some women. Holly Pedersen described her experience during couples' therapy: she wanted to do something religiously related, her husband would not consider raising children Catholic, the therapist suggested "pick one." Holly offered Judaism and her husband "conceded." Ironically, it was she who wanted to continue the tradition and ritual of observing Shabbat on Friday nights. She was the one who said, "Okay, let's light the candles and say the blessings," while her Jewish husband and children grumbled. Holly Pedersen described that during the Gulf War there were bomb threats at the JCC and she wanted to convert to be with her children: she had a "I'm going with them" mentality and rushed to the Reform rabbi's study to announce that she wanted to convert. Rabbi Levy encouraged her to think about it more. She studied, learned some Hebrew, contemplated the two priests and a nun in her family, and ultimately felt a yearning for communion that brought her back to Catholicism some twenty years after leaving the church. She was a reinvigorated Catholic, and yet she continued to raise Jewish children: "That was really hard; but it was easier than me trying to make something work for me that didn't work." Similarly, Lauren Apteker, who was raised Unitarian, did not convert but encouraged her husband to become more involved, and she actively raised Jewish children. She noticed that he became somewhat depressed around the High Holidays and asked, "Honey, why don't we affiliate?" She felt welcome at Temple Beth Emeth, they both liked Rabbi Levy, and there was sufficient Hebrew in the service for her husband, who had been raised Conservative, so they joined. She recalled, "I was very willing to raise the children

Jewish because I thought identifying with something . . . was good for the identity of a child."[84]

Women who celebrated Christmas during their pre-married life missed it even after becoming Jews-by-choice, indicating that conversion did not eliminate the emotional complexities of being intermarried. When Martha Chelm married at nearly twenty-four years of age, she converted and agreed to raise Jewish children. However, she still found the "Christmas season" a difficult time of year. But she was quick to point out that what she missed about Christmas had nothing to do with her faith: "It's not the religious part of it, it's the cultural part. It's the decorating of the house, it's the music."[85] She managed to combine her nostalgia for the Christmas of her youth and her commitment to Jewish life by singing with the University Choral Union, which did *Messiah* every year, and in the Temple Beth Emeth Adult Choir. In Martha's own words, "I sublimate; I collect dreidels and snowmen."[86] After Holly's children were grown, she remarked, "I think I'm done with Christmas trees, so it's not a big loss. It's like Santa Claus." The comparison suggests that the tree was something she outgrew psychologically and emotionally. Renee Barnes commented that she had a Christmas tree for two-dozen years before she intermarried, and that was the hardest thing for her to give up. Although her Jewish husband was adamant about not having a tree in "his house," his mother encouraged him to let his wife have a small one, telling him, "It's just a tree." Her Jewish mother-in-law's support eased the transition from her former life as a Christian to having a Jewish home. Renee admitted, "After a year or two, I didn't care anymore."[87] Along with the tree, however, Renee also gave up celebrating Christmas with her family of origin. They went to her parents' house once or twice but quickly realized that it was not going to work for them as a Jewish family. As a result, her family of origin shifted their main gathering time to Thanksgiving, which made life for Renee considerably easier.

Women's outward appearances influenced how members of the Jewish community and Christians they met reacted to their Jewish identity. These responses to physical appearance remind us that identity is socially constructed rather than essential. If a woman had dark curly hair and was with a Jewish man, some people assumed that she was Jewish even prior to her conversion, whereas someone with features that were not stereo-typically Jewish would be assumed to be Christian. In the decade after her marriage and preceding her conversion, Helen Carlton became increasingly immersed in studying Conservative Judaism and participated actively in the synagogue community with her spouse. Unless someone knew their personal history, fellow congregants thought she was already Jewish because she fit their American expectations for how a Jew looked and acted. In contrast, although Martha Chelm converted prior to marriage, she was told by Jews and non-Jews alike, "Funny, you don't look Jewish!"[88] This infamous comment, historian Susan A. Glenn explains, "worked both as a cautionary tale about the taboos of passing for gentile and as a meditation on the growing importance of Jewish visual connoisseurship to the development and main tenance of an ethnic Jewish identity" in the postwar decades, when intermarriage was increasingly perceived as a threat to Jewish continuity.[89] These reactions to Christian-born Jews-by-choice also uncover prejudice on both sides: Jews against Christians and how they look, and Christians against Jews and how they look. While antisemitism was something with which women were familiar, secondhand at least, some women were surprised to learn that Jewish anti-Christian attitudes existed. Martha Chelm grew up among extended family members who made derogatory remarks about Jews and learned after she intermarried that her husband's Jewish family harbored prejudicial ideas about Christians. The irony was not lost on her: "I never really thought about it happening the other way around," that is, people who were persecuted being prejudicial.[90]

Women's experiences with their husband's extended family members sometimes made clear that some Jews still could not accept intermarriage. When Lauren Apteker's husband introduced her to his aunt and uncle, she knew he was hoping for some kind of blessing. His mother was dead, and so the opinion of extended family held greater meaning than had she still been alive. His aunt, who had never been able to have children of her own, gave Lauren a positive review but told her future husband that by marrying her he would be doing what the Nazis tried to do.[91] Thus the connection between intermarriage and Hitler's "Final Solution" was made to both Christian women and Jewish men. It was not a matter of who married "out" of their religion, whether the Jew or the Christian; the end result, from this lachrymose perspective, was the same: annihilation of the Jewish people.

While some Christian women inadvertently passed for Jews after they intermarried, other women born Christian participated in a form of reverse passing whereby they did not want other members of the Jewish community in which they lived to know that they were not actually Jewish or, if they did convert, that they were not a Jew-by-birth. When Roxanne Pomerantz was stationed with her husband in Châteauroux, France, in 1962, the other Jews on the base thought that they were very religious because they kept kosher. As a result, Roxanne was invited to orchestrate the Passover Seder that her husband led for sixty to seventy Algerian Jews. She did not want to tell anyone that she had never actually been to a Seder, let alone coordinate one, enjoying the fact that they assumed she was already Jewish and preferring instead to quickly learn how. Charlotte Stevens was married in 1994 and was raising two Jewish children when the local Chabad rabbi called and invited her to a class he was teaching for Jewish leaders in the community. She politely declined the invitation, without clarifying that she was not Jewish.[92] Alex Piker became Jewish, yet still found telling people that she had not always been Jewish socially uncomfortable: "I feel like it's a little bit of coming out of the closet to say, 'Oh no, I wasn't born Jewish.'"[93] Her use of the words "coming out of the closet" is analogous to gays and lesbians telling family and friends about their sexual orientation. In both cases, the individual is sharing a genuine part of him- or herself that the community is struggling to fully embrace.

Provided the welcome was sufficiently genuine, women who did not become Jews-by-choice actively participated in their children's Jewish lives. Lauren Apteker considered herself a mix of her Unitarian background and the spirituality she gained from an experience she had with Native American religion before she married. Despite not being Jewish, she commented, "I feel I can attend services at Temple Beth Emeth. My children were bar and bat mitzvahed there. It was a very meaningful experience for me, for our family. I didn't feel in any way like I was a poser or that it was artificial to me. It felt very, very much that it sprang organically from who our family is."[94] Evidently the high level of comfort she experienced at the Reform temple facilitated her involvement in raising Jewish children. Christian women raising Jewish children illustrate a disjuncture between religious identity and gender identity that enabled them to be both non-Jewish women and "Jewish" mothers. Their religious identity was personal, while their gender identity was practiced in a familial manner. Ethnographer Jennifer Thompson, who studied participants in the Mothers Circle, a project of the Jewish Outreach Institute for women of other religious backgrounds raising Jewish children, calls for a rethinking of women's religious leadership. Their "leadership within the family suggests that gender roles are more powerful than religious identification: the non-Jewish woman, not the Jewish man, handles the family's religious life," Thompson writes.[95]

L'DOR V'DOR (FROM GENERATION TO GENERATION)

Women who married Jewish men often had strong feelings about the Holocaust, some of which dated back to their earliest exposures to Judaism or Jewish people. Martha Chelm was one of several women who recalled the impression made by reading *The Diary of Anne Frank* at a young age and then seeing the movie based on the book. Identifying with Anne, she had dreams about Nazis pounding on her door.[96] Holly Pedersen described how she saw the relationship between the destruction of European Jewry and agreeing to raise Jewish children: "Part of my reasoning for choosing Judaism was I felt like I didn't want to be a part of anything that would be dwindling the numbers of Jews after the Holocaust. . . . So, I want my kids to carry it on. . . . And God knows there's enough Irish Catholics out there from my family! *That* won't get lost."[97] These women made intimate connections between their understanding of the decimation of the Jewish population and their personal rationale for raising children in a faith other than the one in which they were raised. Lauren Apteker remarked on the irony of how children born from two Jewish parents are sometimes less observant or Jewishly engaged than children from an intermarriage.[98] Moreover, the bottom line of Jewish identity as she described it was "my kids are Jewish enough to be killed in the Holocaust just as much as" the children of Jewish-Jewish marriages.[99] Some women viewed actual Jewish suffering through a distant lens. Charlotte described how the Holocaust influenced her marriage because of her husband's mind-set that Jews could be in peril again, whereas she grew up looking at the Holocaust as something akin to slavery in the United States that would not reoccur. She felt the emotional weight of inheriting the Holocaust, however, and struggled with the reality that her children would one day feel its enormity, too.[100] These women's determination to stand by their Jewish men and children demonstrates "resistance of the heart"; they stared into the specter of antisemitism like the German women who married Jewish men during the Third Reich.[101]

The legacy of the Holocaust and the whole Jewish immigrant experience made it difficult for women who converted to Judaism to take full cultural ownership of their new identities. Martha Chelm converted prior to marriage and strongly identified with Judaism. Yet, she described, "Sometimes I feel as if I'm not completely part of the Jewish people."[102] Her feelings stemmed from not having ancestors who were driven from their homes and killed or who came to the United States and peddled on the streets. Her background dated to the *Mayflower* voyage and inhibited her ability to believe that she was worthy of the emotional baggage that comes with being Jewish. She aptly described how different the history of Jewish persecution is for Jews-by-choice than for Jews-by-birth: "One of the most important things . . . is the feeling that maybe I don't truly belong because I don't have family that died in the Holocaust."[103] Her sense of exclusion illustrates the depth of her commitment to being Jewish in cultural terms. Although women could adopt Jewish religion, absorbing Jewish culture with all its tradition and history proved more challenging. Alex Piker described how she felt about bringing homemade kugel to potlucks. When people asked her about the noodle dish, she confessed, "I feel sometimes silly . . . like I don't have the right to ownership over this dish because it's not my cultural background, you know, by blood to be bringing this."[104] Evolving food tastes have brought foods associated with Jewish cuisine, such as bagels and hummus, into mainstream American culture. An Indian American boy won a national spelling bee in 2013 after correctly spelling "knaidel," a Yiddish-derived word for a traditional Jewish dumpling.[105] Yet some women who did not grow up eating or making typical Jewish food felt like imposters because it was not part of their gastronomic heritage.

Women who became Jews-by-choice wished that their children would marry Jews or, if their children intermarried, that at least they would raise Jewish grandchildren. Roxanne Pomerantz had three sons, all of whom intermarried, and the two that had children were raising them as Jewish. Like their father, each had a deal with his wife that all children would be raised Jewish. Roxanne's reaction was, "I think it's great. I wish my kids had married Jewish women—but I love my daughters-in-law."[106] Her comment, which seems hypocritical, reflects how profoundly she identified as a Jewish woman; perhaps if her daughters-in-law were also Jews she could connect with them on a deeper level. Although some women thought their children should be free who to wed, regardless of background, and how to raise children as they had, the majority felt that Judaism was sufficiently appealing that they hoped their children would choose it for their grandchildren. Admitting that she did not know what her grown children would ultimately decide, Renee Barnes hoped that they would perpetuate Judaism through the next generation: "Because it's nice . . . I think it's worked well for us. I think it's a religion that has a lot of room for a wide breadth of beliefs."[107] Alex Piker expressed the desire for her children to continue being Jewish regardless of who they eventually marry: "I hope that my kids grow up to be Jewish just because, selfishly, I've found it so enriching and fulfilling and the connection to history is so meaningful to me and I hope they continue that. But I hope they marry whomever makes them happy."[108]

While organized Judaism offered a range of choices for women born Christian and their families, domestic life was often less innovative than they expected. Asked what percentage of the labor, household and childcare, they divided with their spouse, the majority of women allotted themselves significantly more, which only decreased slightly the more recent the marriage. When Kelly Darnell married in 1963, she did not work for wages. "I was home; in those days that was the role of the mother," she described. "He would change diapers but he would leave them in the toilet."[109] Married in 1987, Lauren Apteker observed, "Sadly, I think we're a little more traditional than I thought we would be. Something changed when we had kids." She claimed to do most of the cooking, a lot of the cleaning, and three-quarters of the "kid driving," while he handled the repairs and finances. Lauren thought they had a

80/20 split, with her shouldering the larger portion although she was a full-time teacher.[110] Alex Piker, an attorney by training who married in 2003, was surprised: "We're so traditional, which is *so* not how I intended to be." In her marriage, the couple had a 60/40 split, but the gender breakdown was identical: the husband took care of the cars, repairs, and "outdoor things," and the wife was responsible for childcare, cooking, and cleaning.

CONCLUSION

Consistent with the men's assertions that there is something unique about Ann Arbor, the women's narratives illustrate their belief that this city combines a set of variables that fostered their abilities to be intermarried and participate fully in the Jewish community. When Roxanne first moved to Ann Arbor, someone from Hadassah asked her to do some volunteer work for the organization. When she confessed that she had not been Jewish very long, the response was, "So? Will you help us out?" It was her willingness to get involved that mattered, not the length of her "status" as a Jew. According to Roxanne, being able to donate one's share of money to the community was important, but being a major player in the volunteer circle in Ann Arbor depended not on the size of one's pocketbook as it might have in much larger cities. On a related note, the people she met in Ann Arbor also did not particularly care what kinds of clothes one wore, which appealed to her because she was never very interested in fashion.[111] Fran Berman described Ann Arbor as a city where many people had graduate educations and had children later in life, as she did. She noted, "It's a pretty diverse group in Ann Arbor in terms of people being interracially intermarried as well as religiously." Regarding her experience living there as a Methodist woman married to a Jewish man, she described, "Nobody cares."[112] Perhaps the organized American Jewish community could learn something from the way that Christian-born women experience intermarriage in Ann Arbor. Their stories indicate some of the components necessary to create an atmosphere of inclusion: inviting women to participate in Jewish communal life regardless of their current religious "status," acknowledging their roles as "Jewish mothers" even when they are not

Jewish, and compassion for their struggles to fully accept themselves as Jews if they convert.

Christian-born women's religious journeys, relationships with their mothers, experiences with in-laws and extended family members, husbands' attitudes and behaviors, ideas about the Holocaust, and the extent to which the community welcomed them all influenced how they felt about becoming Jews-by-choice and, therefore, what intermarriage would mean for them and for the Jewish people. The change over time, combined with location, illustrates that Jewish communities vary significantly, and some became increasingly open to accepting the intermarried into the fold, even before they had converted. Kelly Darnell's quest to become Jewish lasted a decade. In 1965, she initially encountered indifference and hypocrisy in several suburbs of Chicago, then had an unsuccessful Orthodox conversion when she refused to promise to keep kosher, and finally converted with the help of a Conservative rabbi in Glenview, Illinois.[113] In contrast, when Alex Piker married in 2003 in Ann Arbor, her experience of inclusion reinforced her positive connection to Jewish identity and community. It was Simchat Torah, she was newly married, pregnant with her first child from that marriage, on the road to conversion, and Rabbi Levy at Temple Beth Emeth handed her the beginning of the Torah scroll to hold. The memory made such a powerful impact that Alex became emotional recounting it: "That just made me feel so included and welcomed in a way that I already felt like I was, you know, doing Jewish and was Jewish. And it was acknowledged by him, the spiritual leader of the congregation, that he saw me that way too."[114] She credited Ann Arbor's acceptance of different kinds of families, Jewish–non-Jewish, two-mother households, and grandparents raising children, combined with the fantastic welcoming attitudes of both the Reform rabbi and the cantor. Traditionally, Christians are not given any honor associated with a Torah because it would contradict the Hebrew prayer Jews recite about God's intentions and Jews' responsibilities: "*asher bahar banu mikol ha'amim venatan lanu et Torato*—who chose us from among all the people by giving us His Torah." A rabbi's decision to share a Torah with an unconverted Christian indicates his liberal approach to Judaism and illustrates a new interpretation of *l'dor v'dor* (from generation to generation) that recognizes non-Jewish parents can be links in the chain of Torah transmission to Jewish children. The participation of non-Jews in Jewish services is a matter of much discussion among Reform and Conservative rabbis and their congregations.[115]

American Christian-born women who marry Jewish men aspire for acceptance and inclusion in the organized Jewish community. Some hold themselves to standards that many American born-Jews and secular Israeli Jews do not. Research about conversionary Jewish households suggests that the women in this study illustrate the common phenomenon of Jews-by-choice learning about Judaism and subsequently keeping Shabbat, participating in *tefillah* (prayer), and engaging in Torah study to an extent beyond many Jews-by-birth.[116] According to at least one interpretation, converts are a "blight upon Israel" (the group of people, not the nation-state) because their deeper commitment and zealousness put Jews-by-birth to shame.[117] Even those women who do not choose to become Jewish demonstrate that it is possible to raise children who are. Christian "Jewish mothers" are one of the ways that intermarried couples are changing American Judaism.[118] The women's influence reinterprets the meaning of patrilineal descent and reshapes the relationship between intermarriage and Jewish continuity. Yet "Jewish mothers" who are Christian, like born-Jewish women who become mothers, also reproduce motherhood in ways that perpetuate traditional gender roles. "Women, as mothers, produce daughters with mothering capacities and the desire to mother. These capacities and needs are built into and grow out of the mother-daughter relationship itself," writes psychoanalyst Nancy J. Chodorow. "By contrast, women as mothers (and men as not-mothers) produce sons whose nurturant capacities and needs have been systematically curtailed and repressed. This prepares men for their less affective later family role, and for primary participation in the impersonal extra-familial world of work and public life."[119]

However, unless the mother formally chooses to become Jewish, the children of Jewish fathers and Christian mothers continue to be vulnerable to social ostracism from within the Jewish community. Women who do not convert often find themselves in the awkward position of having to clarify to fellow congregants that their children *are* Jewish even if they are not. Depending on the congregation, some mothers may be offered honors, such as reciting a prayer or lighting candles on the bimah, that are rescinded once the synagogue leader realizes that the assumption of Jewish identification was misplaced.[120] Illustrating the extent to which the patrilineal descent issue can be accepted within the Reform movement but not universally understood, Holly Pedersen's daughter was told by someone teaching Hebrew school at Temple Beth Emeth, the Reform congregation, "Well, if your mother isn't Jewish, then you're not Jewish." Holly recalls the anger toward people who used matrilineal descent to deny her children's Jewish identity despite all her efforts to raise them as Jews and her personal sacrifices toward that end, including attending mass alone:

> We made this choice as a family. How dare you not recognize that? . . . I think there was a lot of resentment on my part . . . about raising Jewish children and not sort of getting the recognition for how hard it is. I mean this whole thing makes me cry, so I know it is still an issue.[121]

Christian women who defined religious identity as a set of beliefs and personal behaviors stemming from certain convictions, who enrolled children in Jewish religious education and practiced rituals with them at home, struggled to understand why their children's identities were questioned based on descent. The contrast between how they viewed their children as Jews and how some Jews viewed their children was like the difference between social determinists and biological determinists. Jewish identity is complex because it has cultural and genealogical dimensions in addition to religious and personal, whereas Christian identity is purely religious.

The beginning of the twenty-first century showed significantly increased awareness of the Christian woman's contribution to and involvement in the raising of Jewish children. In a move that began to dismantle the myth of the shiksa and its correlating lack of respect, Rabbi Janet Marder introduced a blessing for non-Jewish spouses on Yom Kippur morning 2004 at Congregation Beth Am in Los Altos Hills, California. It included the following words:

> What we want to thank you for today is your decision to cast your lot with the Jewish people by becoming part of this congregation, and the love and support you give to your Jewish partner. Most of all, we want to offer our deepest thanks to those of you who are parents, and who are raising your sons and daughters as

> Jews. . . . We know that some of you have paid a significant price for the generous
> decision you made to raise Jewish children. You have made a painful sacrifice,
> giving up the joy of sharing your own spiritual beliefs and passing your own
> religious traditions down to your kids. I hope your children and your spouse tell
> you often how wonderful you are, and that *their* love and gratitude, and *our* love
> and gratitude will be some compensation, and will bring you joy.[122]

Ordained in 1979 by Hebrew Union College–Jewish Institute of Religion
(HUC-JIR), Marder is a pioneer; among her many accomplishments,
she was the first woman president of the Reform movement's Central
Conference of American Rabbis (2003–2005).[123] Marder's sermon subsequently motivated many other rabbis and Jewish commentators to
honor non-Jewish spouses. As Rabbi Norman Cohen wrote in his Rosh
Hashanah 2010 sermon, "Thanks to my colleague Rabbi Janet Marder
. . . for inspiring me and other colleagues in this matter and composing
this beautiful tribute."[124]

The term "shiksa," as well as what it symbolizes, is more about myth
and myth making than about historical truth. "The most blatant aspect
of the myth of the shiksa," according to family psychologist Edwin H.
Friedman, is that she wants to attract a man away from his ethnic origins
or destroy his family.[125] In his twenty-two years of experience as both a
rabbi and family therapist, Friedman found just the opposite: "It is far
more likely that when Jews and non-Jews marry it will generally be the
non-Jewish partner who is influenced away from his or her origins."[126]
Friedman's use of both the male and female pronouns is significant.
Whether one wishes that the term "shiksa" be shelved in the linguistic archives or thinks that it is a harmless synonym for a non-Jewish
female, there needs to be a different descriptor for Christian women
who married Jewish men in Ann Arbor and other welcoming communities: women of valor. In the Hebrew hymn *Eshet Chayil*, traditional
Jewish husbands honor their wives on Erev Shabbat (Friday evening).
So should the Jewish community honor born-Christian women who
marry Jewish men, and whether they become Jewish themselves or not,
these women of valor do their best to include their husbands on their
journeys, raise Jewish children, perpetuate Judaism, and contribute to
Jewish continuity. "In this vibrant and creative milieu, the time is right
to clear away old clichés and to acknowledge and celebrate a long over-

due aspect of our heritage: some of our Jewish mothers were not born Jewish," Benvenuto advocates.[127]

Women's perceptions of their marriages and families varied considerably, however; even if they converted, the label "interfaith" was difficult to shed completely. Martha Chelm did not consider hers to be an intermarriage; she had formally become a Jew-by-choice, and they led an active Jewish life. Renee Barnes, on the other hand, did continue to consider hers an intermarriage because her family of origin was Christian and her husband's was Jewish: "I can't say we ever talked about God in our house. . . . I think my family probably didn't feel comfortable talking about religion."[128] Combining those two perspectives, Alex Piker felt like the part of her that was intermarried was her family of origin being not Jewish, but "in terms of our core family, we're a Jewish family."[129] Women born Christian who married Jewish men, converted to Judaism, and raised Jewish children had "interfaith families" because their parents and siblings were still Christian. Their efforts to create religious homogeneity were successful but also limited to their nuclear family because religious heterogeneity persisted in their extended family. Conversion created a wholly Jewish family for the formerly interfaith couple, but it did not eliminate interfaith issues from their lives. Whatever their perceived reality, these women's experiences dismantle myths about the long-maligned "other" woman and provide insights into the multi-dimensional meaning of intermarriage that is only visible when one sees it from both sides, born-Christian and born-Jewish.

This chapter complicates the picture of intermarriage by interweaving the "other" women's voices into the historical narrative. Considerably more research needs to be done. Christians who marry Jews deserve a book of their own. Moreover, aside from one book written by a Christian man about his experience marrying a Jewish woman, there are no qualitative works from the perspective of Christian men.[130] Hopefully these pages broaden the understanding of intermarriage beyond born-Jewish perspectives by enabling the reader to see it, and intermarried Jewish men, through the stranger's eyes. Perhaps, although I've used the phrase "Jew-by-choice" to differentiate women not born Jewish from born-Jewish men in this book, the time has come to let go of the words "by choice." As a wise man once said, "If I'm a Jew-by-choice, you're a Jew-by-accident."[131] It would behoove Jews worldwide to accept fully those who join the tribe and let religious convictions finally outweigh genetic predispositions.

The next chapter will consider how shiksappeal influenced and was influenced by representations of intermarriage in popular culture, distorting the actual history of Jewish-Christian marriage in the process. Chapter 4 focuses on intermarried Jewish celebrities, who form a "subcommunity" of their own, along with depictions of interfaith romance and marriage. By comparing history with Hollywood, it will become apparent that art has not only been imitating life but also influencing cultural constructions of love, Jewish men, and intermarriage.

4

Heartbreak Kid

I think the breakthrough in my rediscovering the honor of being a
Jew came before *Schindler's List,* when I married my wife, Kate....
This shiksa goddess has made me a better Jew than my own parents.

—Steven Spielberg

The original version of the film *The Heartbreak Kid* (1972) portrays a Jewish "boy" (Charles Grodin as Lenny Cantrow) marrying a Jewish "girl,"
abandoning her on their honeymoon, and remarrying a non-Jewish woman (Cybill Shepherd as Kelly Corcoran). This depiction of intermarriage
reflected both the escalating divorce rate in America and that divorce
was sometimes followed by intermarriage.[1] It was a comedic tale of the
Jewish man who achieves the ultimate success in America by marrying
the "other." He tells her, "All my life I've wanted to be in a place like this
with a girl like you."[2] Like many other films, *The Heartbreak Kid* gives the
audience an idealized non-Jewish woman. Grodin recalled his concern
at the time of production that the film would be viewed as antisemitic
by Jews, which it was, for his character's bad behavior.[3] However, *The
Heartbreak Kid* also garnered much public appeal and was deemed "an
unequivocal hit" by a *New York Times* reviewer, who compared it to *The
Graduate,* the 1967 Oscar-winning film directed by Mike Nichols.[4] Although the fictional portrayal of love across religious lines suggests a
unidirectional series of events, real-life experiences demonstrate that
romance knows no timing. Grodin's actual marriage experiences are the

The Heartbreak Kid (1972), directed by Elaine May. *Palomar/Kobal Collection.*

reverse of the film; he intermarried first, divorced, and then remarried a Jewish woman.[5]

Like the academic subcommunity in Ann Arbor, intermarried Jewish celebrities compose a kind of subculture. Whether they are performing in New York, producing in Los Angeles, or directing halfway around the world, they are connected by their star status, their fans, and their philanthropy and through national organizations such as SAG-AFTRA, the Screen Actors Guild and American Federation of Television and Radio Artists labor union. Moreover, their fame and wealth foster Jewish self-identification outside the confines of a particular branch of Judaism, generating a new take on Jewish authenticity. The history of Jewish actors, writers, directors, and producers in America melds art and life. They are in the vanguard of Jewish professionalism, showcasing careers without medical, business, or law degrees. Lastly, they operate in social circles where, like Ann Arbor, there is usually a high degree of cosmopolitanism and a laissez-faire approach to religious and family life. Jerry Weintraub, film producer, former chairman and CEO of United Artists, and UNICEF's 2009 Man of the Year honoree, is a perfect example. He is married to Jane Morgan, his Christian wife with whom he has children and grandchildren, yet lives with another woman—Susie Ekins, who converted to Judaism. Born in Brooklyn, raised in the Bronx, Weintraub achieved success by using his *Yiddishe kop* (Jewish brains) and, as he has said, "I never hear the word 'no.' It's called *chutzpah*, and it works."[6] Portrayals of intermarriage in popular culture have suggested that Jewish men falling in love with Christian women is normative behavior. Hence, Jews who marry Jews are nearly invisible on television and the silver screen. The actual histories of the Jewish men who shaped what we know today as Hollywood contribute to our understanding of intermarriage, while the depictions distort their lives and, less frequently, represent them. Portrayals of intermarried Jewish men seem reminiscent of that cited Israelite warrior who could take captive the non-Jewish woman he desired and, after some superficial adjustments, "possess her" as his wife (Deuteronomy 21:10–14).[7] While rabbinic midrash (the interpretation of Jewish texts) subsequently argued that non-Jewish women who married Jewish men were not actually foreign—the women were of Israelite origin or had converted to Judaism prior to their marriages[8]—the same could be said of intermarried Jewish men in contemporary popular culture. Their Jewishness, when evident, is not foreign; rather it endears an audience to the character and the actor who plays him. Understanding the men who created these characters is part of intermarriage history.

Some of the biggest names in what is loosely called "show business" are men who married born-Christian women—for example, Eddie Fisher (1928–2010), singer and 1950s teen idol; William Shatner (1931–), "Captain Kirk" of *Star Trek* fame in the 1960s; and Steven Spielberg (1946–), writer, director, producer extraordinaire whose award-winning box-office blockbusters include *Jaws* (1975), *E. T.* (1983), and *Schindler's List* (1993)—among many, many others.[9] Fisher grew up singing in Orthodox synagogues, Shatner was raised in Conservative Judaism, and Spielberg's family was Orthodox.[10] Fisher recalled in his autobiography, "The only sexual advice my parents ever gave me was stay away from shiksas. So naturally I disregarded it."[11] He intermarried with three actresses: Debbie Reynolds, then Elizabeth Taylor, and finally Connie Stevens. Fisher described how Taylor's interest in Judaism fueled his own: "Even though

Steven Spielberg and Kate Capshaw (2002). *The Kobal Collection/Roger Wong.*

I had been brought up a Jew, it was an education for me; for Elizabeth it was a revelation and she became even more determined to embrace Judaism."[12] Spielberg first married Amy Irving, raised Christian Scientist. He is currently married to Kate Capshaw, raised Protestant. Capshaw's insistence on formally converting before they married in 1991 exerted a deep effect on him: "I've actually said *Schindler's List* went a long way in getting me back into the fold, but it really was the fact that my wife took a profound interest in Judaism." He credits Capshaw with keeping "the Jewish momentum" flowing in his family's life, with handmade challah and ritual observance. Despite many Jews' refusal to celebrate Christmas, the Spielberg family enjoys this holiday because it was a tradition in Capshaw's family of origin and Spielberg always wanted to but did not when he was growing up.[13] Shatner and his fourth wife, Elizabeth Martin, both avid horseback riders, visited Israel together in 2006 related to their involvement in the Jewish National Fund Therapeutic Riding Endowment for Israel.[14] These celebrity men's lives illustrate how, like the experiences of "ordinary" men and women I discussed in the preceding chapters, the meaning of intermarriage and Jewish identity are far more complex than popular culture leads audiences to believe.

Creators of popular representations of intermarriage have constructed Jewish-Christian unions largely as something Jewish men do, not their sisters. In rarely depicting Jewish women who intermarried, books and movies in the second half of the twentieth century suggested to American readers and audiences that few Jewish women leave the fold. This distortion of reality contributes to the ongoing perception that Jewish men intermarry far more than do Jewish women, despite demographic reports that men and women intermarry in approximately the same numbers. According to the 2000–2001 National Jewish Population Survey, the difference in the overall intermarriage rates between men and women is only 4 percent. The gender composition of intermarriage fluctuates with age: while men below the age of thirty-five and above the age of fifty-five are more likely to be intermarried than are women, equal proportions of men and women are intermarried in the thirty-five to fifty-four age group.[15] As one cinema studies scholar wrote, "Unquestionably the image of intermarriage between Jew and Gentile that most

Americans hold is the image of the Jewish man who marries a Gentile woman—the *shiksa*."[16] Hence, Jewish-Christian marriage became men's "business" as American Jews became increasingly at home in America in the twentieth century.

Over the twentieth century numerous novels and films that incorporated interfaith unions normalized intermarriage as part of American culture and society. Thus it is entirely possible that depictions of Jewish-Christian marriage had an impact on American Jewish men who chose to marry non-Jewish women. Sociologist Sylvia Barack Fishman argues that "American Jews today are deeply influenced by the ways in which cultural expressions idealize mixed marriage and promote the ethos that religious syncretism within mixed marriage is normative" and that "literary and dramatic images of Jews affect the social construction of reality."[17] Certainly, the very existence of intermarriage in popular culture reinforces the validity of such unions by demonstrating through fiction that religious and cultural differences do not prevent Jews and non-Jews from falling in love and getting married. Moreover, as historian Joyce Antler argues, due to the dearth of television shows depicting love relationships "between young Jews, both men and women absorb negative messages about each other's attractiveness and appeal."[18] Whether these works actually encouraged Jewish men to intermarry is difficult, if not impossible, to determine. Clearly some Jewish men who married non-Jews did so within a cultural milieu with flourishing productions of interfaith romance.

Although it is impossible to assess the impact a single film, text, or television series has on audiences, we can attempt to understand a fictional work as one of many discourses in a particular point in history and how these changed over time.[19] In addition, when biographical details are available, it is possible to tease out similarities and differences between popular fictional narratives and lived experiences of individuals who created them. In the following pages, I will discuss numerous works of literature and film, with somewhat less attention devoted to intermarriage on television, which is a major focus of a different book.[20] This chapter will demonstrate an intimate relationship between the fabrication of interfaith romance and the actual experiences of its creators and portrayers by exploring linkages with some of the individuals who generated fictions about intermarriage, illustrating a reversal in gender roles and a persistent emphasis on Jewish integration in American culture.[21] The time period begins earlier than in the preceding chapters to contextualize the shifts that predated some of the men's intermarriages.

HISTORY

The notoriety of early twentieth-century intermarriages brought the issue of intermarriage to a new level of cultural consciousness, inspiring theatrical and cinematic productions. Rather than depicting those elite Protestant circles into which these Jews actually married however, writers and film producers reinvented their sagas to appeal to mass audiences.[22] These cultural constructions celebrated the American ideal of choosing whom to love and marry, like those who intermarried in real life. The fact that inter-ethnic romance and marriage film plots reached an apex of popularity in the mid-1920s attests to the increased awareness of intermarriage. According to one source, 50 of the approximately 230 films of Jewish interest made in America between 1900 and 1929 dealt with interfaith romance and intermarriage.[23] The effort to portray the lives of the intermarried in print and film was influenced by the notoriety of those relatively few couples who actually did intermarry during this early time period in film history.[24] Yet issues pertaining to Jewish life had become the substance of mainstream interest and consumption.

The ubiquity of melting-pot marriages in cultural productions during the first three decades of the twentieth century, when few Jewish men or women intermarried, suggests that eliminating cultural distinctions between people through depictions of marriage was a means to a positive end. As immigration laws went into effect in the 1920s, American audiences were reassured that the children of foreigners who were already admitted would indeed *marry into* America. The high proportion of movies depicting interfaith relationships illustrates that American interest in such relationships was rising. Moreover, romanticized "happy endings" for Jewish-Christian pairings that resolved all conflicts, the third-generation offspring who united distraught grandparents, and new business relationships forged between formerly warring factions illustrated intolerance of what kept people separate: their religious and ethnic heritage. As scholar Riv-Ellen Prell observed in *Fighting to Become Americans*, "The fantasy of melting pot marriages simply underlined the fact that 'difference' was as unacceptable in the popular culture of the nation as it was to the lawmakers in Washington, D.C."[25]

Early-twentieth-century film portrayals of intermarriage suggested that love across religious lines would triumph over social prejudice against it, while literary works were considerably less sanguine, particularly after World War II. Although fictional portrayals of intermarriage from 1930 to 1960 depicted familial reactions and a potent relationship between antisemitism and intermarriage, these representations also consistently ignored Jewish women's experiences. The examination of novels and films is particularly useful to show how mass culture reinforced negative perceptions that Jewish women were unappealing wives for Jewish men and demonstrates how popular culture constructed Jewish-Christian marriage as a Jewish-male prerogative, highlighting men's experiences and obscuring Jewish women's in the process. Although portrayals of intermarried Jewish women began to make a comeback with several major motion pictures in the 1970s and 1980s, and television reinforced the reality of women's intermarriage by the end of the century,[26] Jewish male–Christian female pairings continued to dominate in popular culture. Allusions to the conversion to Judaism of the woman who intermarried also contributed to a kind of fictional "replacement" of the born-Jewish women. Although late-twentieth-century representations of Jewish women were more flattering than earlier in the century, religious differences were subordinated to socioeconomic ones, with sparse attention paid to faith or heritage.

SEXUAL ANXIETY

Gendered notions of assimilation fueled the persistent focus in the first two decades of the twentieth century on Jewish woman–Christian man combinations in popular culture. Literary and cinematic theories abound for why the ethnic female dominated popular culture during a time when few Jews married outside the Jewish circle compared to later decades. The preponderance in film of Jewish female–Christian male couples illustrates literary critic Leslie A. Fiedler's persuasive contention that "it is always easier to breach the barriers against intermarriage in the popular mind by permitting the assimilation of the forbidden group through the female rather than through the male."[27] Hence Jews could be assimilated through the fictional marriage of Jewish women with Christian, *real* American, men (emphasis mine). The pairing of white men and ethnic women can also be considered a "symbolic literalization of the American dream, both in terms of success and of love," scholar Mary V. Dearborn argues. "Variously, it suggests an assertion of melting-pot idealism, of the forging of a 'new man,' of Cinderella success, of love 'regardless of race, creed, or color,' of the promise of America itself."[28] The overrepresentation of Jewish women in films about intermarriage is, according to cinema expert David Desser, "a kind of displacement of sexual anxiety about ethnicity on the part of mainstream (white male) America, an anxiety which must be alleviated by sexual conquest and ethnic denial (removal). . . ."[29] Without doubt, depictions of Jewish women served as important bridges between an American society that considered all Jews as alien; the medium of film allowed society to see that Jewish females could become Americans symbolically through intermarriage. This portrayal of the American Jewess was a modern-day "Jessica" who, in Shakespeare's *Merchant of Venice* (1596), forsakes her father Shylock and Jewish culture by marrying Lorenzo: "I shall be saved by my husband; he hath made me a Christian."[30]

Early cinematic representations of intermarriage portray Jewish women as beacons of religious tolerance and free love in a social sea of antisemitism and ethnocentrism. They are progressive romance seekers who defy the laws of their fathers and grandfathers to find happiness. In the 1923 film *None So Blind,* Rachel Abrams (Zena Keefe), the daughter of a Lower East Side pawnbroker, marries a Christian, Russell Mortimer. After her mother dies, Rachel's daughter Ruth (also played by Zena Keefe) is kept close to the Jewish hearth by her grandfather. Despite his matchmaking efforts, Ruth meets and falls in love with a Christian while listening to a woman conducting a Salvation Army prayer in the street encouraging true love to destroy hatred between men and achieve the unity of all people in one family. The New World love is portrayed as religion-blind, and Old World love as prejudiced and outmoded. Love conquers all, the film suggests, including antisemitism and Jewish prejudice against non-Jews.[31] If, as film scholar Tom Gunning notes, the film's message of tolerance for intermarriage is "labeled as a specifically Christian concept," the Jewish woman delivers the message.[32]

Examples abound that, like *None So Blind*, exemplify the melting-pot ideal, including *The Cohens and Kellys: A Story of East Side–West Side New York*. The film is based on the play *Two Blocks Away* by Aaron Hoffman (1925) and aired on the big screen in early 1926.[33] The *New York Times* review observed that the film "appeals to one as a sort of step-child of *Abie's Irish Rose*" and praised the acting as well as the plot, without ever commenting directly on implications of the interreligious romance.[34] Apparently, the comical handling of ethnic and class differences in *The Cohens and Kellys* was more likely a selling point than was the interfaith issue. A *Variety* reviewer enjoyed the film for its humorous side, predicting it would be a sure moneymaker.[35] In fact, *The Cohens and Kellys* was shown to packed audiences who erupted in frequent applause.[36] Even an American film depicting interfaith romance in the European shtetl, such as *Surrender* (1927), portrayed the Jewish woman involved with the Christian (Russian) suitor.[37]

ECLIPSED BY JEWISH MEN

Jewish men who intermarried eclipsed Jewish women on screen in works such as the farce *Abie's Irish Rose*, based on the 1927 novel by Anne Nichols. In this tale, Corporal Abraham Levy of "B" Company meets Rose-Mary Murphy, an entertainer and nurse, while serving overseas in World War I. The action revolves around a series of successful shenanigans designed to win Abie's father's approval of Rose before he finds out she is not Jewish (including her introduction as Rose-Mary "Murpheski").[38] In any event, the birth of twin grandchildren to the couple eventually melts their grandfathers' hearts: prejudices are forgotten and the two men wish each other a "Merry Christmas" and a "*Goot Yonteff*" (good holiday). The resounding message of the syncretistic plot is summed up by Abie's statement "It's a free country—every man to his taste."[39] Another interfaith family is born in Hollywood.

Abie's Irish Rose movie poster advertisement (1928).

While the bulk of early films depicted Jewish women intermarrying, the productions featuring Jewish male characters involved with non-Jewish females have received far more public attention, highlighting an increasing obscurity of Jewish women who intermarried in popular culture. The success of both the stage and the screen versions of *Abie's Irish Rose* and the duration of their runs made evident that Jewish male–Christian female intermarriage was a topic for public consumption and entertainment. The play met with initial success in Los Angeles and San Francisco, debuting on Broadway on May 23, 1922, where it ran more for than twenty-two hundred performances. Running for five years and touring in cities as far from the coasts as Detroit and Kalamazoo, Michigan, it also sparked the first national advertising campaign for a theatrical production. *Abie's Irish Rose* was produced as a silent film in 1928, after which it was shortened and modified with sound. Its success on the stage helped carry the film in 1928; when it was re-released in 1946, it received harsh criticism about what was by then considered to be tasteless humor and ethnic stereotyping. What took the mainstream press nearly twenty years to criticize was articulated by the *Jewish Daily Forward* in 1923: "It is about as stupid a play as has been seen on Broadway in a number of years. A play about the Jews and the Irish which doesn't bear the slightest resemblance to Jewish or Irish life."[40] Criticism of the 1946 remake is significant because it suggests that American audiences had grown more sophisticated as well as accustomed to the image of Jews integrating into American society through intermarriage. It also denotes viewers' diminished comfort level with ethnic profiling, undoubtedly caused by the Holocaust.[41]

At the time of its first production, however, *Abie's Irish Rose* was a popular culture landmark. Depictions involving the marriage between a Jewish man and a Christian woman that were widely attended and discussed signified growing awareness that interfaith unions were a social reality. That intermarriage among Jews became a prominent theme in popular culture illustrates that the mixing of religious and ethnic backgrounds was considered an interesting phenomenon, perhaps even inevitable if not enviable. *Abie's Irish Rose* "set the precedent for casting New World marriages as unions of hope," writes Prell.[42] It also offered a cultural salve by suggesting that Jews could indeed be absorbed into society through intermarriage, perhaps calming nativist fears to some extent. The popularity of intermarriage in films of the 1920s suggests not only that mainstream American viewers were entertained by the notion of one faith marrying another, but that it appealed to them as fictional entertainment. A dominant Protestant culture was soothed by the depiction of two "alien" groups mixing together; any excessive, unappealing Irish or Jewish traits are tempered or improved, ensured by the production's happy ending.[43] The films were not made as "pseudodocumentaries to enlighten audiences" about Jewish life; rather, according to film scholar Lester D. Friedman, they were attempts "to make Americans less nervous about Jews and Jews more conscious of themselves as Americans."[44] *Abie's Irish Rose* also suggested a solution to the question "What will the children be?" Twins are born to the couple, one Jewish, one Christian. This model was replicated more than a half century later in a 1981 television episode of *Little House on the Prairie* when Nellie Oleson unwittingly falls in love with and marries a Jewish man, Isaac Cohen passing as "Percival Dalton," and then gives birth to twins. The familiar culture clash is resolved when the parents decide that the girl will have the surname Dalton and be raised Christian and the Cohen boy will be raised Jewish.[45]

Following closely on Abie's heels, another Jewish man struggles between loyalty to his tradition and his love for a Christian woman in *The Jazz Singer: A Story of Pathos and Laughter* by Samson Raphaelson. Although central to the plot is whether Jakie Rabinowitz will follow five generations to become a cantor, his relationship with Mary Dale is key to his crossing over from traditional Jewish to modern American life as a successful jazz singer.[46]

The Jazz Singer made history, while films that starred Jewish female characters such as *A Child of the Ghetto*, *None So Blind*, and *Surrender*, faded into near oblivion. The original production opened on Broadway at the Fulton Theatre in New York on September 7, 1925, starring George Jessel. The *New York Times* gave the premiere performance a rave review, reporting, "The play is a shrewd and well-planned excursion into the theatre, concerned with a theme of obvious appeal, and assuredly so written that even the slowest of wits can understand it." By at least one account, the early theater audience was predominantly Jewish, and its success baffled some reviewers. The play ran for thirty-eight weeks, which ended only because Jessel signed a contract to star in the film version, a role he never got to fulfill.[47]

The screen version of *The Jazz Singer* left an indelible mark, and it is still considered one of the most significant films in movie history. In October 1927, four Jewish men, who came to be known professionally and corporately as Warner Brothers, produced it as the first talking

Eugenie Besserer and Al Jolson acting as mother and son in *The Jazz Singer* (1927), directed by Alan Crosland. *Warner Bros./The Kobal Collection.*

picture at their theater in New York; it was based on the same story and starred Al Jolson, a Russian-born Hollywood actor. While Harry Warner wanted to make the film for "the sake of racial tolerance," Sam and Jack were more interested in, according to cinema scholar Neal Gabler, "a highly personal dramatization of the conflicts in their own lives and within their own family." Hence, rather than use Jessel, whose previous films cast him as strongly Jewish, Sam and Jack chose Al Jolson, a Jew as assimilated as themselves.[48] The film made what historian Michael Rogin calls "a cinematic revolution" by being the first to lip-synchronize musical performance and dialogue while incorporating words and music into the action of the film. Its massive appeal to diverse audiences helped Warner Brothers achieve top rank in the film industry, gaining control over hundreds of theaters and enormously multiplying their assets. *The Jazz Singer* alone netted $3.5 million, a vast amount at that time. Remakes of the film were produced in 1953 and again in 1980, but the 1927 version remains the most noteworthy.[49]

Made when Jews were not yet considered Caucasian, this film promoted Jewish men as white enough to marry white, non-Jewish women.[50] Many Jews sought to affirm "their place as unqualified whites," writes historian Eric L. Goldstein, "demonstrating a clear social distinction between themselves and America's principal outsiders, African Americans."[51] The advent of sound in *The Jazz Singer* shifted authority from the upper classes to the lower classes because, according to historian Lary May, talking films had the power to change racial and class conventions. Urban audiences sensed for the first time that their story was being told; they felt Jolson, the actor, spoke both for them and to them from the screen. Juxtaposing Jack and Mary's differences, accentuated by their costumes, he appears as a black-faced comedian and she as a golden-haired ballet dancer while he sings the jazz song "Back to My Mammy." Rogin convincingly argues in *White Noise* that minstrelsy serviced the Americanization of immigrants using racial difference to accomplish it. While popular-culture productions, like this one, sanctioned interfaith marriages, they still forbade interracial ones.[52] Jack's mother sits proudly in the audience. He and Mary stroll "hand in hand" backstage. The conflict between his Jewish heritage and his career pursuit and love interest are apparently resolved; Jack can have a Jewish past and an American future, a Jewish mother and a Christian wife. Unlike the original play starring George Jessel, in which the Jewish singer takes his father's place in the synagogue and forsakes the entertainment industry, the film reverses the ending.[53] "Assimilation is achieved via the mask of the most segregated; the blackface that offers Jews mobilization keeps the blacks fixed in place," described Rogin.[54] But the cost of the man's social mobility was his Jewishness.

ANTI-ASSIMILATION OR FREEDOM?

Unlike *The Jazz Singer* and other Hollywood representations I have discussed thus far that suggested tolerance of intermarriage, most literary works incorporated Jewish men leaving the fold, rather than Jewish women, and depicted intermarriage in an anti-assimilationist vein.[55]

Two notable exceptions to the Jewish male protagonist and anti-assimilationist pattern were *Salome of the Tenements* (1923) by Anzia Yezierska and Isaac Rosenfeld's *Passage from Home* (1946).[56] In "Seven Candles," written in 1923 by Fannie Hurst, who incidentally was the highest paid novelist in America by 1940, a second-generation son must choose between his Christian wife and his observant Orthodox mother.[57] Although it was a man who intermarried, Hurst focused most of her story on the animosity between his Jewish mother and his Christian wife, who eventually tries to throw the senior Mrs. Palestine out of the house. The Jewish mother blames her son's intermarriage on the Christian woman's physical allure, illustrating the social phenomenon I discussed in the previous chapter. Speaking to her dead husband, the mother laments, "I tried—I prayed—she got him with her white flesh Julius—blond flesh like he wasn't used to. When a woman gets a boy that way—not even his God, Julius—can hold him back."[58] The son banishes his wife, who pleads with him until he reverses his decision and agrees to put his mother in an institution. But before this comes about, the mother dies suddenly, preventing her from learning that her son sided with the blonde "*schikser*." The Jewish son, laden with guilt and grief, once again reverses his decision, casts out his wife, begs his dead mother's forgiveness, and utters the prayer "Blessed is our God who created us for his glory." The conclusion suggests that the second-generation's goal of personal happiness triumphing over familial obligation and tradition was an empty wish; to intermarry was a grave mistake. Hurst's 1926 novel *Appassionata,* in which the Jewish girl "preferred the love of religion" to that of a Christian, likewise suggested to readers that intermarriage was to be avoided.[59]

Ludwig Lewisohn (1883–1955) similarly discouraged Jewish readers from intermarrying in his 1928 novel *The Island Within,* which simultaneously illustrated a double standard between Jewish women and Jewish men. Protagonist Arthur Levy is an educated Jewish man who intermarries with a working woman when he learns she is pregnant, but discovers that what he really wants is a traditional Jewish wife. The Christian wife is cold, heartless, and a bad mother and opines that her Jewish husband is not truly an American.[60] He knows "how happy he would have been ... if his wife could have assumed the part of a Jewish daughter." Arthur rejects the idea of companionate marriage; criticizes his non-Jewish wife, who keeps her name and continues to work; and idealizes Jewish women. Fiedler suggests that Lewisohn vilified the *shikse* as the "false Aphrodite" who caused a loss of Jewish identity, and praised Jewish women as "the true Eros": "Have they not remained at the heart of the tradition the Jewish intellectual has temporarily abandoned, waiting to bestow on him when he returns the warm fulfillment he has vainly sought in strangers?"[61] Literary scholar Joshua Lambert makes the astute observation about author Myron Kaufmann, who wrote *Remember Me to God* (1957), that equally applies to Lewisohn: for these authors, "intermarriage is a justification for exploring the feelings, frustrations, and philosophies of American Jews about their Jewishness."[62] Kaufmann, however, was unlike his fellow male novelists and the character he created: he dated only Jewish girls.[63]

The rebirth of the Jewishness in Lewisohn's protagonist foretold the author's own spiritual journey from assimilation to observant Jew and Zionist, an illustration of the not uncommon close relationship between fantasy and fact.[64] Lewisohn, a German immigrant, wrote, lectured, and edited extensively. Born in Berlin in 1882, he moved with his family to South Carolina and began a religious quest for inclusion and meaning. Struggling to fit into Christian America, Lewisohn became involved in Catholicism and Methodism, writing his way through one identity after another before returning to his mother's tradition. According to his biographer, "She alone offered the comfort he had hoped to find in some eternal and immutable source, and the possibility of finding a way to once again accept his Jewishness that was such an integral part of his being."[65] He became one of the thirteen original faculty members at Brandeis University.[66] In a contemporary review, Rabbi Stephen S. Wise described *The Island Within* as "the belated answer to Zangwill's *Melting Pot*," in which an American Jew discovers how to belong to himself rather than be possessed by others.[67] Lewisohn intermarried.

When Lewisohn fell in love with a Christian woman named Edna Manley, after his first failed marriage and another disastrous relationship, he asked her to convert to Judaism before their 1940 nuptials.[68] His desire for doing so seems to have been both personal and professional. In a 1938 letter addressed "Beloved," Lewisohn makes a request regarding

the rearing of his son and their future home together: "So soon as Jim-
mie is old enough and sits at the table with us we will usher in and out
the sabbath and, if you don't mind, abstain in our house from the forbidden foods—swine and shellfish [*sic*]."[69] However, Lewisohn's plea to the
rabbi who would eventually convert Manley suggests that, as urgently as
he wanted the rabbi to "consecrate her to me by the laws of Moses and
Israel," he nonetheless would marry Manley even if she did not convert.
Lewisohn threatened, "You would not want us, you would not want *me*
to be forced to be married by a magistrate!"[70] The same Rabbi Wise who
spoke glowingly of Lewisohn's 1928 novel urged Rabbi Bernstein to help
Lewisohn, in a letter dated November 29, 1939:

> L. has a right to be in love with this woman if he must be. Such things cannot
> be dictated by law or precedent, but he has no right to make a laughing stock
> of himself and a scandal of his relation to the causes to which he professes to
> give his devotion. He will be finished for us Zionistically. We will have to drop
> him. He will get no hearing on the American platform and you know how Jews
> will feel about his marrying for the third time, or for the second and a half time,
> a non-Jewess.[71]

By having his beloved Christian convert, thereby marrying "in," Lewisohn could maintain his personal political status as a religionist and
anti-assimilationist.

MARRYING "UP"

Portrayals of Jewish men as appealing husbands paired with Christian
females indicated a new genre of novels and films, reflecting society's
increasing tolerance of interfaith marriages and Jewish men's upward
mobility. It had become reasonable by the end of the 1920s to illustrate
such unions to the American reading and viewing public. Various Hollywood producers, themselves Jewish, male, and intermarried, probably
fictionalized their lives in the films they produced. It is likely that both
the star Al Jolson and the producer Sam Warner validated their own intermarriage choices through *The Jazz Singer*. In fact, the film is thought
to be a collective biography of these men, and undoubtedly others, who
created Hollywood.[72] Harry Warner, the more conservative of the brothers, disliked Sam's wife Lina Basquette (born Lena Baskette), who was

Jack Warner with Bette Davis and Joan Crawford (1962).
Warner Bros./The Kobal Collection.

a Ziegfield Follies dancer when they met, whereas Jack did not find fault
with Sam's intermarriage.[73] Upon Sam's premature death, Harry wran-
gled legal guardianship of Sam's daughter from her mother because he
did not think her fit to be a parent and he could not stand the idea of his
brother's child being raised as a Christian.[74] That four men, whose parents left a Polish shtetl to escape pogroms against Jews, could achieve the
level of social and financial success that they did speaks to their abilities
to translate their own life stories into movie material.[75]

   Successful Jewish men in Hollywood replaced their Jewish wives
with Christian women. Jack Warner's first marriage was to a co-religionist, Irma Solomon, of German background from an old San Francisco
Jewish family and hence so dissimilar from his Eastern European immigrant parents that they called her a shiksa.[76] While married to Irma, Jack
used the excuse of going alone to his parents' for Shabbat dinner in order
to visit one of his numerous mistresses after the meal. He fell in love with

Harry Cohn with Rita Hayworth and Anita Louise (1946).
Columbia Pictures/The Kobal Collection.

Ann Page Alvarado, a Catholic, and before his divorce with Irma was final he was already planning his marriage to Ann. Jack postponed the wedding for a year and a half, however, out of deference to his family.[77] When Jack married Ann in 1935, none of the other Warner brothers or their families attended.[78] Notwithstanding the family's aversion to his marriage, a rabbi officiated at Jack's wedding, a concession to his late father's memory, and also at his funeral many years later; the latter was held at Wilshire Boulevard Temple where Jack had been a member for fifty years, never attending services.[79]

The life and work of Harry Cohn, who built Columbia Pictures, illustrates the second-generation American man's climb to the top of a particular industry far from his Jewish origins. Born on July 23, 1891 to his Russian-born, Sabbath-observing mother Bella in an apartment on East 199th Street in Manhattan, Harry moved as far as one could from his origins and stay in the United States.[80] Once he became president of Columbia and owned his own studio in California, Harry divorced his Jewish first wife and in 1941 remarried a Christian woman.[81] Their son, John, was "as devout a Roman Catholic" as his mother, according to one biographer.[82] Avoiding movies with religious themes for most of his career, Harry planned to produce a biblical epic, *Joseph and His Brothers*, casting Rita Hayworth as Potiphar's wife, the female lead. If Harry was subconsciously working through issues related to his own estrangement from his brother Jack, he did not complete the process; *Joseph* was never made.[83] When Harry Cohn died in February 1958, his funeral was not conducted by a rabbi but held on a Columbia soundstage and included the Catholic song "Our Father." According to his biographer, "there was nothing about the service to suggest that the deceased had been born a Jew."[84] Joan Perry Cohn, his second wife, claimed that Harry uttered the name of Christ when he suffered a heart attack. She had his corpse baptized so that they could be reunited in heaven according to her beliefs.[85]

Popular culture depictions of intermarriage changed dramatically between 1930 and 1960. Where earlier representations illustrated interfaith relationships between members of two low-status ethnic groups, literature and film in the 1930s, '40s, and '50s focused more attention on Jews marrying higher-status Christians. Stories of lower-class Jewish-Catholic marriages did not altogether disappear, but changes in the ethno-religious composition of many fictional couples suggested that Jews could marry into the upper social echelons of Protestant America. Rather than the Jewish Nannie Cohen wedding the Catholic Terrence Kelly, fictional unions now included the Jewish Marc Reiser marrying the Protestant Erica Drake, who was "born on top," in the 1944 novel *Earth and High Heaven*.[86] However, social success of intermarried Jews was limited to men in popular culture.

Jewish male–Christian female representations in literature highlighted the enigmatic and sensual appeal of the "other." Frederic Cople Jaher's aptly titled article "The Quest for the Ultimate Shiksa" notes that in Jewish American novels, Jewish men appealed to Christian women as "mysterious outsiders, domestic messiahs, and modern heroes or anti-heroes," while Jewish men saw Christian women as "exotic sirens, *femmes fatales*, humble servants, Christian saints, victims, and American goddesses." This phenomenon actually predated the 1930s—Elizabeth tells Arthur Levy, "I love your Jewish darkness and ardor," in *The Island Within* (1928)[87]—but it proliferated thereafter. The Christian female in Gwethalyn Graham's *Earth and High Heaven* describes her Jewish beau as having "such perfection of line and form in the molding of his body that he seemed unreal in the dimly lit room, like a figure out of Greece two thousand years before."[88] The Christian Tillie Marmon considers the Jewish Jo Boshere exciting in Ben Hecht's *A Jew in Love* (1931) because his "Jewishness had become for her an exotic mask, mysterious and oriental."[89] Tillie's fair complexion and blonde hair epitomized Anglo-Saxon looks and winning her, the authors of *The Jewish Woman in America* suggest, "symbolized, for him, the ultimate triumph of the Jew in American society."[90]

Reversing the cinematic trend of the first two decades and continuing the literary one, cultural depictions of interfaith romance in the 1930s, 1940s, and 1950s illustrated that Jewish men increasingly sought non-Jewish women.[91] For the most part, novels and movies portrayed Jewish-Christian pairings that reflected social scientist Robert K. Merton's 1941 theory of intermarriage, which he called hypogamy. Merton proposed that there was a hierarchy of status among American ethnic groups and a compensatory system of intermarriages, such that upwardly mobile lower-caste men (handsome, talented, rich, or well educated) traded these assets in a marriage for the higher-caste status of women who lacked beauty, talent, wealth, or intellect.[92] For example, Bette Davis starred as Fanny Trellis, the much sought-after bachelorette in the 1944 film *Mrs. Skeffington*. She eventually snared the fabulously wealthy and Jewish Job Skeffington. Fanny was both beautiful and from an elite family, but she was also bankrupt. Job's lack of social status and his "rags to riches" background were compensated for by his extreme wealth.[93] Marrying a socially unacceptable Jew whom she did not love was wrong, the film suggests, but it also supports the contradictory suggestion that accepting his financial rescue was acceptable.[94] The characters in Jerome Weidman's 1958 novel *The Enemy Camp* similarly fit Merton's hypogamy model. Jewish George Hurst grew up poor on the Lower East Side, while Mary, a pretty Christian, grew up wealthy on Philadelphia's Main Line.[95]

Jewish men's mothers and mother figures were ubiquitous in post-war intermarriage fiction. Popular culture depictions emphasized Jewish parents' strong reactions to their children's interfaith romances, painting the role of the mother with extreme strokes. While Irving Davidowsky's Orthodox father in Sholem Asch's 1946 novel *East River* accepts his Catholic daughter-in-law and grandchild into his home, Irving's mother advises him, "It's only justice that you should get rid of the *shikse* and marry the [Jewish] girl who was destined for you."[96] In Norman Katkov's best-selling 1948 novel *Eagle at My Eyes,* the Jewish mother rejects her son's Christian woman and insists that he marry within the Jewish faith. The *New York Times* commented, "It is hard to believe that Joe's mother could turn out to be so implacable in her point of view."[97] That her un-relenting objection surprised the reviewer suggests the extent to which intermarriage had become more acceptable outside of Jewish circles. A subsequent reviewer summed up, "Jewish families are uncompromising about marriage with Gentiles."[98]

Like the Ann Arbor men's complaints about their mothers, the Jewish mother in fiction about intermarriage was similarly the product of an American culture influenced by Philip Wylie's book *Generation of Vipers* (1942), accusing women of weakening the nation through their treatment of their sons.[99] While both sets of parents opposed their children's intermarriage in the 1950 novel *Footsteps on the Stair,* by Myron Brinig, it was the Jewish mother who was characterized as a "neurotic racist."[100] Aunt Tessie, George's adopted aunt in Weidman's *The Enemy Camp,* instructs him against mixing with Christians: "It was from her he had learned that the world was divided into Jews and shkutzim. It was she who had taught him to which world he belonged, and which world he must fear." It was also Aunt Tessie who, after she raised him as her own, proclaims George as being dead when he intermarries.[101] These images of Jewish mothers combined stereotypes that vilified the Jewish woman as vessels of Jewish tradition, and therefore obstacles to Jewish men's full Americanization: she suffocated her children with food, demanded their total loyalty, and manipulated them.[102] Perhaps the most notorious of novels to decry the mother-son relationship was Philip Roth's 1967 *Portnoy's Complaint,* in which Alexander Portnoy opines, "What I'm saying, Doctor, is that I don't seem to stick my dick up these girls, as

much as I stick it up their backgrounds—as though through fucking I
will discover America. *Conquer* America—maybe that's more like it."[103]
Conquering America while maintaining a Jewish identity was not accomplished as easily as Roth's protagonist surmised.[104]

MID-CENTURY AND BEYOND

Although writers suggested that Jewish men could intermarry, they
also depicted an increased degree of tension over maintenance of Jewish identity. The shift toward an approach that mirrored social tensions
indicated an increased presence and significance of intermarriage in
American society. In the 1920s, humor and farce dominated cross-eth-
nic romances, such as *The Cohens and Kellys* (1926) and *Abie's Irish Rose*
(1928). Although mid-twentieth-century portrayals included humor, the
Second World War had a sobering influence on fiction. The topic of intermarriage increasingly appeared alongside such serious subject matter as
antisemitism and the historical threat to Jewish continuity, as in Sholem
Asch's aforementioned novel *East River* (1946). When Mary, a Christian
woman, betrays her Jewish husband by baptizing their son and claims
that she did not know he cared about his religion because she never saw
him practice it, Irving responds, "Maybe we Jews don't practice religion
the way you Catholics do—but we don't change our religion as quickly
as others. A Jew would rather die a thousand times, he would let himself be burned at the stake, rather than deny his religion!"[105] The dialogue
echoes postwar consciousness.

The film *Gentleman's Agreement,* based on the 1947 novel by Laura
Z. Hobson, exposed the ugliness of antisemitism while simultaneously
confirming the viability of Jews—or at least Jewish men—marrying
Christians.[106] Gregory Peck starred as journalist Phil Green, who was
assigned to write a series about antisemitism for *Smith's Weekly* magazine. The film's title referred to the unspoken complicity of the "nice
people" in society who let slide jokes and damning stories about Jews,
never bothering to object to the injustice of those who refused to sell
to, rent to, or employ Jews. Phil's adoption of a faux Jewish identity enabled the viewer to understand some of the issues faced by an interfaith
couple during the late 1940s. His temporary assumed "Jewish" identity

poses problems between him and his Christian girlfriend Kathy Lacey
(Dorothy McGuire). She reacts with perceptible alarm about the mere
prospect of his actually being Jewish. He registers her reaction: "She
wanted him to not be Jewish. She knew he was not, knew that if he
were, he'd never have concealed it. But she wanted to hear him say so
right out."[107] Phil and Kathy's amorous relationship experiences several
blows as he learns what it feels like to be a Jew and to suffer the indigni-
ties of discrimination, and how she, unwittingly at first, continues to
criticize those who were actively antisemitic while passively accepting
their actions.

   Gentleman's Agreement suggested to Christians that intermarriage
with Jews was not outlandish. While impossible to gauge its ultimate
impact on audience behavior, the film suggested that Jewishness was
only a label, not a racial trait; Jew and Christian were interchangeable.[108]
If Gregory Peck, a favorite Christian actor, could play the part of a Jew
who experiences antisemitic treatment, surely a Jew must be no different
from anyone else.[109] *Gentleman's Agreement* was considered "daring and
progressive in its day."[110] The *Hollywood Reporter* called it "the most spell-
binding story ever put on celluloid."[111] *Gentleman's Agreement* shocked
audiences and taught them about antisemitism as no film had done
prior.[112] It also marked a significant change in postwar Hollywood, one
with a profound implication. According to the *New York Times,* "Such
aspects of antisemitism as professional bias against Jews, discrimination
by swanky hotels and even the calling of ugly names have been frankly
and clearly demonstrated for the inhuman failings that they are and the
peril of a normal and happy union being wrecked on the ragged edges
of prejudice is affectively raised [*sic*]."[113] Given such positive attention,
Christian and Jewish viewers, male and female, may have considered
intermarriage more conceivable after seeing *Gentleman's Agreement*; certainly one of the morals of the tale was that interfaith romance could suc-
ceed if people were willing and able to overlook differences of religion
and ethnicity.

   The fascination with interfaith romance and intermarriage that began at the start of the century nearly disappeared in films during the
1950s and 1960s. Despite its growing incidence in American society,
especially among Catholics and Protestants, intermarriage as an issue

seemed to nearly evaporate during the fifties, a period in which many
Jews were blacklisted in front of the camera and behind it.[114] Films that
were produced continued the trend begun by *Gentleman's Agreement*
of depicting antisemitism just beneath the surface of genteel society.
Like their predecessor, four films that were produced depicted Jewish
men engaged in relationships with non-Jewish women. Noah Ackerman
(Montgomery Cliff) in *The Young Lions* (1958, based on the 1948 novel)
is portrayed as an appealing Jewish man. He is eventually accepted by
a Christian woman and her eighth-generation American father, who
"never knew a Jew before."[115] In *Home before Dark* (1958), Jacob Diamond (Efrem Zimbalist, Jr.) becomes the married Christian woman's
confidant; she leaves her husband and Jacob rejects the antisemitism
of his colleagues, and the pair escapes to Boston together, although they
do not to marry.[116] Though meager in number, these examples did show
a change in how interfaith romance was beginning to be represented.
Films of the 1940s showed the Jewish male as seeking the Christian female to concretize his Americanization, such as in *Mrs. Skeffington,* or
the Christian woman accepting the "Jewish" man once she realizes he
is not so different, as in *Gentleman's Agreement*. In contrast, depictions
of the Jewish male in the 1950s showed him as sensitive rather than aggressive, and the Christian woman being attracted to him precisely because he is emotionally different from her co-religionists.[117] *The Benny
Goodman Story* (1956) starred Steve Allen as Benny Goodman, the son
of poor Jewish immigrants who becomes America's favorite clarinet-
ist and the "King of Swing," and Donna Reed as Alice Hammond, a
"high society girl." The film, based on Goodman's actual life, depicts
the Jewish man as showing his love through his music; he asks Alice to
marry him by playing his clarinet. Although this film initially depicts
his mother as standing in cupid's way—"Because you don't mix caviar
with bagels, that's why"—his mother is also the person who eventually
brings Benny and Alice together when she realizes that her son's happiness is at stake.[118] The next decade saw Jewish men's appeal rise to an
unprecedented level.

No film, before or since, has challenged audiences to consider Jewish men in such a physically and intellectually appealing manner as *Exodus* (1960). The powerful production about the establishment of Israel

Ari (Paul Newman) and Kitty (Eva Marie Saint) with his family in *Exodus* (1960), directed by Otto Preminger. *United Artists/The Kobal Collection.*

starred actor Paul Newman as the enigmatic character Ari Ben Canaan, the strong commander of the Israeli underground, who falls in love with an American Presbyterian, Kitty. He tells her, "I just wanted you to know that I'm a Jew. This is my country." She argues that there are no differences between people, while he insists, "People *are* different. They have a right to be different!" The meal they have with his family and the apparent cultural distinctions between them and Kitty under-score Ari's point. In the end, they overcome their differences when Kitty insists on accompanying Ari to relocate the Jewish children of Gan Dafna to safety and he agrees.[119] Although the interfaith romance is a minor theme in this Academy Award winner, it suggested that one could be committed to the Jewish nation *and* fall in love with Eva Marie Saint![120] Ari was the consummate sabra, the native-born Israeli who, like the prickly pear cactus from whence the word came, is tough on the outside yet soft-hearted on the inside.[121] While Newman, in one scene bare-chested and wearing a Star of David necklace, presented the vision of a heroic Jew, Saint simultaneously represented non-Jewish women who developed compassion for the Jewish struggle and fall in love with the new Jew, the Israeli man.[122] Victories of Israeli soldiers, on and off the screen, proved to Jewish and non-Jewish onlookers that "Jews have the guts to stand up and fight—that the Jew is a man, not just a merchant."[123]

Jewish-Christian intermarriage became more apparent in popular culture in the early 1970s, with three major motion pictures and a highly controversial television show that highlighted interfaith romance as a central plot. However, with the exception of Fiddler on the Roof, religion was not a major theme in any of the productions and was, in fact, clearly downplayed.[124] Fiddler "promotes the advancement of daughters as one modern way to be Jewish" at a loss to their old-world father, "with a regrettable but necessary cost to Jewish traditions and the Jewish masculinity that had long been privileged by traditional Judaism," according to scholar Lori Lefkovitz.[125] Minnie and Moskowitz (1971), starring Gena Rowlands as Minnie Moore and Seymour Cassel as Seymour Moskowitz, is a hilarious portrayal of two lovers with seemingly nothing in common who decide to get married days after first meeting. Seymour is a parking attendant with a drooping mustache and a long ponytail who likes to go square dancing. Minnie works at an art museum and loves ballet. Her acquaintances go to Seymour's dance hall to see how the "other half" lives for kicks; Seymour is the other half. The only mention of religious differences occurs during a brief phone conversation between Seymour and Minnie's mother. The audience hears only his side answering imaginable questions regarding his background: "Seymour Moskowitz." "Jewish, right." "Religious? Not terribly." This dialogue combined with the minister who officiates at the wedding seems to reassure the audience that while Seymour might be Jewish, his Jewishness will not be problematic.[126] Yet contemporary criticism (which was mostly complimentary, with thirteen positive reviews and only one negative) highlighted the interfaith aspect. Critic Vincent Canby noted that the "Jewish prince in hippie disguise" won the hand of the "very beautiful, mixed-up, middle-class gentile princess."[127]

The aforementioned *The Heartbreak Kid* (1972) is one of the first films to illustrate a shift away from an assimilationist orientation, while continuing to glorify interfaith romance, to a more critical perspective on intermarriage. Loss of Jewish identity and connections in the 1920s, 1930s, and 1940s films were portrayed as a positive step toward assimilation into the American mainstream. By the 1970s, the meaning of intermarriage and the status of Jews in American society had changed, no longer requiring disassociation from Jewishness and the Jewish group. During the early twentieth century, when silent films and the first sound films were produced, Jewish social achievement was often coupled with intermarriage and escape from the influences of immigrant culture. By mid-century, however, success could be achieved without necessitating loss of Jewish identity through intermarriage.[128] The creators of *The Heartbreak Kid* make clear to their viewers that while Len may have captured his dream girl, he has also, unfortunately, given up everyone and everything else dear to him, including his heritage. Len's wedding to Kelly lacks the celebratory mood of his first Jewish marriage, and he finds himself utterly alone at the reception.[129] Actor Charles Grodin opined in his autobiography that the underlying message in the film is not about leaving one's wife for a beautiful blonde, rather: "Be careful of what you want—you may get it," or possibly "Look at yourself for your problems."[130] Like the earlier Warner brothers and *The Jazz Singer*, one can speculate that Neil Simon and Bruce Jay Friedman, who wrote the screenplay and the story upon which it was based respectively, used their own varied marriage experiences as fodder for *The Heartbreak Kid*.

Three films were produced during a pivotal time in film history and contributed to the industry's success. While both *Minnie and Moskowitz* and *The Heartbreak Kid* were romantic comedies starring Jewish men that had relatively happy endings, *The Way We Were* (1973), starring Barbra Streisand as Katie Morosky and Robert Redford as Hubbell Gardiner, depicted the disastrous effects that differing politics could have on a couple's intermarriage. The creation of more films with ethnic themes, such as Francis Ford Coppola's *The Godfather* (1972), were part of a larger rebirth of American popular entertainment. Some film critics later called the revolution in film production, marketing, and distribution a "Hollywood Renaissance" and Hollywood's single authentic

"Golden Age."[131] The fact that multiple films in the 1970s depicted Jew-ish-Christian couples illustrates the extent to which the intermarriage theme had become imbedded in American popular culture.

While all the films I have discussed thus far depicted intermar-riages, *Annie Hall* (1977) most clearly illustrated stereotypical differ-ences between a Jew and a Christian and their families. Although Alvy Singer and Annie Hall, played by Woody Allen and Diane Keaton, do not actually marry in the movie, the *New York Times* described it as "essentially, Woody's 'Scenes From a Marriage,' though there is no marriage."[132] Indeed, it was this film, more than any other, that men I interviewed mentioned, specifically referring to the "oil and water" qualities, the vast differences between their Jewish families and their Christian wives' families, depicted in the movie. The two characters unite a "real Jew" from Brooklyn with a "real American," a WASP from Wisconsin. When Annie tells Alvy her tie was a gift from her Grammy, he asks her, "What did you do, grow up in a Norman Rockwell painting? My Grammy never gave gifts. She was too busy getting raped by Cos-sacks."[133] Perhaps the most memorable scene juxtaposing an interfaith couple's families is when Alvy goes with Annie to meet her family at Easter. The film is shot as a split scene (with one half depicting his family as loud and raucous and the other showing hers as genteel, refined, and eating ham), suggesting that no matter how intense their attractions and how compatible their respective neuroticisms, ultimately the different individuals would be unable to meld together.

Like Alvy, Woody Allen fell in love with non-Jewish women, first Mia Farrow and then Soon-Yi Previn, a South Korean woman whom Mia had adopted as a child. One observer commented, "To separate the man from the artist is to deny one of the deepest truths and richest pleasures about Woody Allen's work. He managed to infuse both—comedy and drama with his worldview, his philosophical questions, and his real-life romances."[134] Some observers may criticize Allen's choice in women, including those who believe that his affair with Farrow's adopted daughter constituted incest, while others may credit Allen with being the most entertaining writer, director, and actor to grace the screen. Allen, who in 2012 attributed his Jewish identity mostly to antisemitism—"Today I feel Jewish mainly when people attack me because of my being Jewish"—claims that his family will likely visit Israel someday. He attributes their future trip to his wife's curiosity and urging that their adopted daughters "see and understand their father's Jewish culture."[135] Like wives of non-celebrity men who encourage synagogue attendance or lighting Shabbat candles, Allen's wife is the driving force behind going to Israel. Previn has other people besides Allen on her side. The Woody Allen Israel Project, an Internet fund-raising campaign launched by the *Jewish Journal* of Los Angeles to enable Allen to make a film in Israel, might facilitate a trip. Israeli newspaper *Haaretz* reported that President Shimon Peres and Jerusalem mayor Nir Barkat discussed the idea with Allen; shooting a film in Israel is "certainly a possibility," according to his representatives. Where he films is "strictly economics," Allen told the *Wall Street Journal;* he goes to whatever country is willing to pay for the production, an $18 million venture. "As far as I know, Allen himself has never been to Israel," writes *Jewish Journal* editor Rob Eshman. "For a man who has done much to define the image of Jews in our time, this needs repair."[136] If Allen's family does go, hopefully they will have a tour guide experienced in explicating differences between American Jews and sabras.

The television show *Bridget Loves Bernie,* starring David Birney and Meredith Baxter, caused the most controversy when it first aired September 16, 1972. The sitcom featured the intermarriage of Bernie Steinberg, a struggling young Jewish writer supplementing his income working as a taxi driver whose parents ran a Lower East Side delicatessen, and Bridget Fitzgerald, an elementary school teacher and the daughter of wealthy Irish Catholics. Their different backgrounds and their families' reactions to their marriage and attempts to reconcile for the sake of the couple provided the plot material.[137] The half-hour comedy hit a sensitive nerve in Jewish organizations. Soon CBS found itself embroiled in accusations that it condoned intermarriage. Corporate advertisers were threatened with national boycotts unless they ceased commercial sponsorship.[138] "*Bridget Loves Bernie* Attacked by Jewish Groups" headlined the *New York Times* on February 7, 1973. Many organizations objected that the program treated intermarriage in a positive light, including the Synagogue Council of America, the Commission on Interfaith Activities of the Union of American Hebrew Congregations, and the

David Birney and Meredith Baxter in *Bridget Loves Bernie* (1972).
CBS Television Network.

Rabbinical Council of America. Rabbi Balfour Brickner, director of the
Commission on Interfaith Activities, complained, "The program treats
intermarriage, one of the gravest problems facing Jews today, not only
as an existent phenomenon but one that should be totally accepted."[139]

The strong reactions about the show, and the ultimately successful effort to get it off the air after only eight months, illustrated the extent to which intermarriage was *the* hot-button issue for American Jewish communal leaders. The controversy surrounding *Bridget Loves Bernie* illustrated what historian Michael Staub calls "the crisis of Jewish liberalism." While Jewish leaders were profoundly uncomfortable with advocating censorship, they believed that CBS's portrayal of intermarriage and stereotypes of Jews exhibited "shocking insensitivity to the religious beliefs of six million Americans" and warranted opposition.[140] In contrast, Betty Zoss, a writer, castigated the actions of her fellow Jews to ban the show as downright shameful. She wrote in a March 1973 article in *Sh'ma*, "If the survival of the Jews depends on Jewish censorship of a program about the devotion of Jew to non-Jew, then us Jews will neither survive nor deserve to."[141] Another *Sh'ma* writer argued that America's blessings and ideals required taking the term "freedom" to heart. Moreover he asked, "Do we have the right to determine that which is directed at the entire country?"[142] David Doyle, an Irish Catholic cast member who played Bridget's father on the show, speculated that the theme of Irish Catholic and Jewish incommensurability was problematic in a different way. Married to a Jewish woman and raising their daughter as a Jew, he asserted that through intermarriage "you begin to clear up ignorances about other religions and you identify with the other person, too." "Its premise," writes anthropologist Jack Kugelmass about the show, "walked a very murky line between transgressive comedy . . . and social realism."[143] The cancellation of *Bridget Loves Bernie* made network television history; it was the fifth most popular show and the highest-rated series ever to be canceled.[144] The show and associated uproar were far from the actors' actual lives, which would be more accurately depicted with a show titled "Baxter Loved Birney But Now She Loves Nancy." Birney and Baxter's backgrounds were more similar than not (they were both Christian); they wed after meeting on the show, divorced, and Baxter subsequently came out as a lesbian.[145]

While Jewish leaders fought with CBS, at the personal level *Bridget Loves Bernie* introduced American television viewers to a Jewish man paired with a beautiful Christian woman. This 1972 portrayal of intermarriage initiated the reproduction on prime-time television of a Jewish

Paul and Jamie Buchman (Paul Reiser and Helen Hunt) in *Mad about You*
(1992–1999). *ABC-TV/The Kobal Collection/Michael Tighe.*

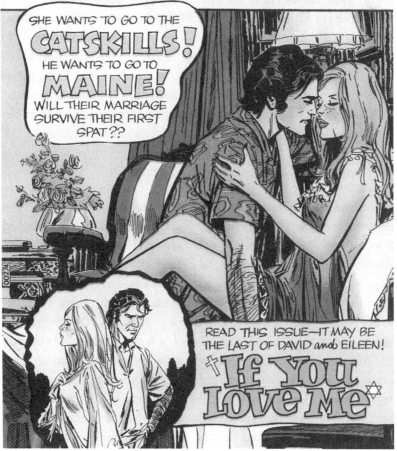

"Just Married" comic series by Charlton Comics featured Jewish David and Irish Catholic Eileen. *Charlton Press Inc.* © *1973.*

man's romantic involvement with a Christian woman that continued with *thirtysomething* in 1987, *Northern Exposure* in 1990, and *Mad about You* in 1992.[146] Television critic David Zurawik argues in his book *The Jews of Prime Time* that Christian female identity on network television "established the non-Jewish woman as superior to her Jewish counterpart."[147] This, Zurawik writes, "in the language of prime time television makes her the feminine ideal of the series."[148] Historian Joyce Antler estimates that while the Jewish intermarriage rate was roughly 50 percent in the 1990s, on television it was at least 95 percent.[149] Illustrating the adaptability of popular culture, Jewish-Christian romance also surfaced in the form of comic books. Published by Charlton Comics from 1973 to 1974, the nine-part series "Just Married" focused on "Jewish David" and "Irish Eileen." As author Eli Valley asks, tongue in cheek, "What better venue to wrestle with issues of cross-cultural conflict than in the pages of America's romance comics?"[150] Hence, Bridget was reborn as Eileen and Birney as David, another rendition of the same theme.

KEEPING THE FAITH?

Even though many Jews married within Judaism, including celebrity men, the overwhelming majority of films in the 1980s and 1990s linked Jews with non-Jews rather than with co-religionists, continuing the idealization of interfaith romance and reflecting increasing intermarriage rates. A hugely popular romantic comedy, *When Harry Met Sally* (1989), paired actors Billy Crystal (Jewish) and Meg Ryan (Catholic). Screenwriter Nora Ephron recounted, "Harry was originally conceived, in my mind anyway, as a Christian and Sally as a Jew. . . . When Billy Crystal and Meg Ryan got involved, that was obviously not going to work, so everyone's last names were changed."[151] Although religion is not explicit in the film, the intercultural element is apparent in the characters' behavior, and through the representation of food in the famous deli scene when Sally, the "eponymous Gentile," fakes an orgasm to prove her point to Harry, who is "overtly Jewish."[152] Offscreen, Crystal remains happily married to the same Jewish woman for more than four decades.[153] While not equal in number to interfaith depictions, there are portrayals of Jewish-Jewish marriage, such as in the 1992 film *A Stranger among Us*. Emily

Billy Crystal and Meg Ryan in *When Harry Met Sally* (1989), directed by Rob Reiner. *Castle Rock/Nelson/Columbia/The Kobal Collection.*

Eden (Melanie Griffith) is a self-referenced "untouchable *shikse,*" a profane New York City police detective who has to meld into the Brooklyn Hasidic community to catch a murderer and ends up falling in love with the chief rabbi's son and spiritual heir, Ariel (Eric Thal). For his part, Ariel's curiosity about the forbidden fruit leads him to kiss Emily, but he ultimately weds his *basherte* (soul mate) in an arranged marriage.[154] This film also gives greater acknowledgment of the religious identity of the Jewish partner, illustrating the shift away from the melting-pot model of films and toward a pluralistic one, which in this case determined the outcome of the interfaith relationship.[155]

Television gave a nod to Jewish in-marriage before retreating to more familiar territory. Ten years after *A Stranger among Us,* in November 2002, television portrayed the Jewish-Jewish wedding of Grace Adler (Debra Messing) to Leo (Harry Connick, Jr.) in the sitcom *Will and Grace.*[156] That was the first time in prime-time history that a Jewish protagonist married another Jew on a sitcom. According to a *Nation* reporter, "More than upholding an age-old tradition that would make parents *kvell*, they communicated to Middle America that a Jewish main character does not need a gentile foil to validate his or her presence on television."[157] Whatever Grace marrying Leo may have communicated, Jewish-Jewish pairs have yet to become popular in film, and they are certainly still far from the norm in television programming. A 2009 episode of the wildly imaginative show *Glee* uses dark humor when romance is kindled between two Jews, echoing the comments some Jewish men heard when they intermarried. While watching *Schindler's List*—on Simchat Torah, eating sweet-and-sour pork—Noah Puckerman's mother (played by Gina Hecht) says to him, "You're as bad as them [Nazis]. Why can't you date a nice Jewish girl?" "Puck" (Mark Salling) then briefly pursues Jewish Rachel Berry (Lea Michele) for the sake of Jewish continuity, serenading her by singing Neil Diamond's song "Sweet Caroline." The teenage romance is fleeting, however, and when they break up, both Jewish characters return to their non-Jewish love interests.[158] Netflix's summer 2013 hit *Orange Is the New Black* with Jewish Larry Bloom (Jason Biggs) and Piper Chapman (Taylor Schilling), his "'felonious former lesbian WASP shiska' girlfriend," suggests to television viewers that Jewish gentlemen still prefer non-Jewish blonds.[159]

Larry David, the co-creator of the hugely successful situational comedy *Seinfeld* and creator of HBO's *Curb Your Enthusiasm*, starring himself, is a living example of the way in which popular culture obfuscates the actual experiences of Jewish men and simultaneously glamorizes intermarriage to American audiences. In real life he was married to fellow Jew Laurie Lennard from 1993 to 2007.[160] However David's wife on *Curb Your Enthusiasm*, the semi-improvised, fictionalized version of his life, is explicitly not Jewish. Hence, it appears that David needs the stereotypical blonde-haired, perky-nosed Christian woman to prove that he has truly made it as a Jewish man in America by forgoing his co-religionist counterpart in favor of the "other" woman.[161] Given that Jewish women have a history of being maligned in popular culture, it is not surprising that the Jewish wife on the show is portrayed as, in the words of one observer, "frumpy and frizzy and a loudmouth."[162] Only after David's divorce did art imitate life with the episode showing his on-screen wife threatening to leave him after she called from a flight she thought was

Larry David and Cheryl Hines in *Curb Your Enthusiasm* (2000–).
HBO/The Kobal Collection.

going to crash and he told her to call back so he could finish dealing with the TIVO serviceman.[163] The combination, Jewish male–Christian female lead characters and the unappealing Jewish woman, serves to reinforce popular culture's long history of reversing Jewish emasculation through interfaith romance and marriage. David's claim, "I may loathe myself, but it has nothing to do with the fact that I'm Jewish," suggests that producers of popular culture know that their Jewishness is seen more as a disability than a strength,[164] and his fictionalized life suggests that self-love through intermarriage has everything to do with his being Jewish.[165] This ongoing trend influences cinema productions equally as it does television.

Actor Ben Stiller may be considered the Casanova of interfaith romance in American film. He stars in the most movies with Jewish man–Christian woman couples, including *Along Comes Polly, Keeping the Faith,* the trilogy *Meet the Parents, Meet the Fockers, and Little Fockers,* and the remake of *The Heartbreak Kid,* among others.[166] He was raised Jewish by his father Jerry Stiller and mother Ann Meara, who converted

Jerry Stiller and Anne Meara photographed on the *The Ed Sullivan Show* (November 7, 1966). *CBS/Landov.*

to Judaism after marriage. When Ben hosted *Saturday Night Live* on the evening of Yom Kippur 2011, he joked about feeling "woozy" from fasting, then added, "My father's Jewish and my mother's Irish Catholic. According to every Torah, I'm not Jewish; but according to every mirror, I am."[167] The monologue segued into a skit that played off of Stiller's Jew-

The Jewish Costanzas (Estelle Harris, Jason Alexander, and Jerry Stiller) in *Seinfeld* (1990–1998). *NBC TV/The Kobal Collection.*

ish identity, with a Willy Wonka character singing "Pure Imagination" and a wonderland created out of Jewish foods. Interviewed by fellow comedian Jon Stewart on *The Daily Show,* Ben credited his mother the most for his Jewish upbringing: "She knows more about Judaism than our entire family combined."[168] Anne Meara's experience, like some of the Christian-born women I interviewed, illustrates how Jews-by-choice can become more invested in Judaism than Jews-by-birth.

Ben Stiller followed in his father's footsteps in two significant ways: he became a comedian and he married a woman raised Catholic, comedic actress Christine Taylor, in 2000.[169] Together the couple has two children, a son and a daughter.[170] Although Ben's wife has not converted at the time of this writing, he made clear to Stewart in the interview that their daughter Ella had learned the ten plagues of Passover and would be attending a Seder that same evening. Whereas in life he emphasized his Jewish identity, including attending a school where matzah was provided and mentioning his bar mitzvah during a roast for his father, his onscreen persona is far less concerned with ethnic or religious heritage.[171] Not until the final scene of *Little Fockers,* when a Christmas tree stands in one corner of the living room counterbalanced by an equal-size menorah in another, is a Jewish element made explicit. Even then the scene suggests that syncretism is really the goal as both sets of grandparents unload their gifts on the twin children.[172]

Like son, like father—but with a twist. The success of Jerry Stiller's acting career was in part due to the seven years he and his wife performed in front of a live television audience on *The Ed Sullivan Show.* Stiller and Meara's breakthrough skit was one that emphasized the differences between a Jewish man and an Irish woman, "Hershey Horowitz" and "Mary Elizabeth Doyle." The acting agency representing them at the time thought that Sullivan would never allow it on the air because most of the country was Protestant; Sullivan gave it his blessing, and they made their first appearance on the show on April 7, 1963. Long before the era of online dating services, the skit consisted of the dialogue between two people, matched up by a computer dating service, meeting for the first time. The fictional characters live on the same block of East Forty-Second Street, yet as they compare their friends' names, they discover that they do not know any of the same people.[173] Stiller and Meara's success played on their ability to put their ethnic differences in sharp contrast with each other. In one skit, for example, they alternate calling each other names: "Matzah Head" / "Shillelagh Shiksa" / "Bensonhurst Blintz" / "Meshugenah Mother McCree" / "Cockamamie Knish." Their press photo shows Stiller holding a bagel and Meara holding an enlarged shamrock.[174] His Jewishness continued to be part of the characters Stiller played, including the role for which Jerry Stiller is best known, Frank Costanza, George's father on *Seinfeld.* The elder Costanza is always mad, at what no one is quite sure. The same goes for his ethnicity. People asked him, "How can people who eat kasha, and *knedelach,* and matzahs have the name Costanza?" One day he came up with the line: "Well, they're a Jewish family in the Witness Protection Plan." They never talked about it, what was the Costanzas' background; "but we all knew."[175] The fact that George, played by Jason Alexander, is often in pursuit of non-Jewish women on the show reinforces the stereotype of Jewish men seeking women with "shiksappeal."[176]

Ben Stiller, Dustin Hoffman, and Barbra Streisand in *Meet the Fockers* (2004), directed by Jay Roach. *Universal/Dreamworks/The Kobal Collection/Tracy Bennet.*

In *Meet the Fockers,* Ben Stiller's screen parents "out" him as a Jew by showing off their wall of memorabilia documenting his life on the "Hall of Gaylord," including a framed tallit presumably from his bar mitzvah. While in the *Little Fockers* the audience knows that Ben Stiller's character is Jewish because his "parents" are Barbra Streisand, who throws around words like "knish" and "mitzvah," and Dustin Hoffman, in the 2007 remake of *The Heartbreak Kid* the Jewish component of the male character is evident only because Stiller the actor is Jewish. In this film, both Stillers, Jerry and Ben, play single men; the father calls the son "pussydick" because he is not involved with anyone, yet also does not enjoy the bachelor life. The jab, delivered in classic Jerry Stiller style, pokes fun at Ben's masculinity. When he meets Lila, a tall beautiful blonde, Ben tells her, "You don't look like the prototypical scientist type."[177] This signals to the audience that she is his golden shiksa, perpetuating in the process the subliminal message that *real* Jewish men intermarried. Instead of any emphasis on interfaith issues, however, the plot focuses on the potential nightmare of marrying a woman who is not at all like the person he thinks she is when they first meet.

At the dawn of the twenty-first century, Jewish-Christian marriages continue to flourish in popular culture, and as the 2000 movie *Keeping the Faith* illustrates, the Christian woman is still idealized, often at the expense of the Jewish woman. Rabbi Jake Schram (Ben Stiller) and Catholic priest Brian Finn (Edward Norton) fall in love with the same non-Jewish childhood friend, Anna Riley (Jenna Elfman). Harking back to the 1972 *The Heartbreak Kid,* this film caricatures Jewish women; Lisa Edelstein plays a desperate exercise fanatic, and Rena Sofer plays a Middle East affairs expert who is excessively intelligent, thereby negating her beauty and making the Christian woman, by contrast, seem all the more appealing, even safe. Anna is smart and financially successful, but she comes across as fun loving and non-threatening. *Keeping the Faith* also bears a strong resemblance to *The Jazz Singer,* in which Jakie Rabinowitz/Jack Robin, like Jake Schram in the year 2000, is torn between his Jewish heritage, his career, and his romantic interest. According to *Keeping the Faith* film writer and co-producer Stuart Blumberg, "The message, if there is one, is that love often ignores the dictates of religious affiliation and we must make our own decisions in this modern world."[178] Ultimately, both productions conclude with the suggestion that the men can maintain their Jewish identities and keep their Christian girl, all without losing their mother's love. The mom in *Keeping the Faith* refused to attend her elder son's wedding when he intermarried yet does not turn away from her younger son, Jake, and his romantic interest. Magnificently played by Anne Bancroft, the character is based on Rena Joy Blumberg Olshanksy, the writer and co-producer's actual mother.[179] However as Rena is quick to point out about her own intermarried son, Stuart's brother, "I went to my kid's wedding. It's a movie. You have to separate reality from the movie. . . . The main thing is not to lose your child."[180] Her comment illustrates the modern priority of maintaining a relationship with one's adult intermarried child, in contrast to the traditional mourning of a child who intermarries as if he had died.

Eli Wallach, Anne Bancroft, Jenna Elfman, and Ben Stiller in *Keeping the Faith* (2000), directed by Edward Norton. *Touchstone Pictures/ The Kobal Collection/Glen Wilson.*

The interfaith loose ends are neatly tied up when *Keeping the Faith* ends because Anna considers conversion to Judaism, an apparent leit-motif of late-century cinematic representations making Jewish women seem obsolete.[181] In Stuart Blumberg's mind and words, "Anna chose to explore Judaism because she knew it was of deep importance to the man she loved and, in addition, was a spiritual tradition well worth con-sidering in her own personal quest for meaning." Blumberg's rationale for including Anna's spiritual journey, when the plot really focuses on Jake's religious quandary, was because it illustrated the complexity of the human condition and that people do things for multiple rather than sin-gular reasons.[182] In Joseph Greenblum's comparative analysis between the 1927 and 1980 productions of *The Jazz Singer,* he illustrates how Jess Rabinovitch, the cantor played by Neil Diamond in the remake, per-sonifies Jewishness that is sufficiently strong to establish the religious identity of the interfaith relationship; "Jewish identity and American modernity are compatible."[183] Diamond, known by some as the Jewish Elvis, followed a similar path as the Hollywood producers when he divorced his first wife, who was Jewish, and subsequently remarried a Christian woman.[184] Likewise, *Keeping the Faith* suggests that as long as a Jewish man remains Jewish, intermarriage is acceptable today. The film mirrors the lives of non-celebrity men who, although not rabbis like Jake Schram, maintained Jewish identities, thereby making intermarriage seem more acceptable than if they had ceased being Jews. The evolving religious identity of the born-Christian woman, Anna Riley, reflects the spiritual explorations of some non-celebrity women who married Jewish men. In these regards, art actually depicts life.

While continuing to exalt Jewish men's fascination with non-Jewish women, the 2005 film *Prime* also reinterprets the Jewish mother stereotype, broadens the professional possibilities for American Jewish men, and redefines what it means to be one. Written and directed by Ben Younger, a former yeshiva student raised "in a traditional Jewish community where professions like doctors or lawyers were seen as more important than others," *Prime* offers a creative retelling of the interfaith narrative.[185] Twenty-three year-old David (played by Bryan Greenberg, who related personally to the character's strong Jewish identity), a struggling artist, falls in love with Rafi (Uma Thurman), a thirty-seven-year-old recent divorcée.[186] Reinforcing the idea that Jewish men make good husbands, Rafi tells her therapist that David is "eager to please" and the sex is amazing: "You were so right about Jewish men, he's so attentive!" Younger's male character shows a new Jewish man who is both sensitive and strong, eschewing the Woody Allen-esque figure for a combination that more closely resembles his reality.[187] Rafi's therapist, Lisa, brilliantly played by Meryl Streep, figures out that her patient is involved with her son.[188] Eventually overcoming their mutual angst about the situation, mother/therapist and girlfriend/patient enjoy a family Shabbat dinner together. When Rafi raises a glass to celebrate the sale of David's first paintings, he adds, "You should all know that this is what I'm going to be doing for the rest of my life. No CPA, no law degree, no paging Dr. Bloomberg. . . ." Lisa thanks Rafi for opening her eyes to her son's true vocation. Rafi describes Lisa's love and involvement in her children's lives positively, as closeness; "We should all be so lucky," she tells her friends.[189] Part homage to *Annie Hall,* and in contrast to *Keeping the*

Faith, the *Prime* lovers ultimately do not marry, suggesting that sometimes love is not enough—at least when there is a fourteen-year age difference between an older female and a younger male.[190]

Early-twenty-first-century literature continues the trend with *Club Revelation,* written by Allan Appel in 2001, which focuses on three Jewish men–Christian women couples; the females joke about becoming not "just women married to Jewish men," but "Osmosed Jews." Appel's book, however, stretches creativity and gender roles farther by concluding with the news that William Harp, the young Southern evangelist character, has fallen in love with Rena, an Orthodox Jewish woman, and *he* plans to convert to Judaism.[191] More recent works further develop a reader's deeper appreciation for the value of Judaism and Jewish life. Joshua Halberstam's superb tale *A Seat at the Table: A Novel of Forbidden Choices* introduces Elisha, who journeys away from Orthodoxy, through interfaith romance, to find his authentic Jewish self. Interweaving Hasidic stories with Elisha's inner turmoil and relationship with his father, Halberstam paints a portrait of the tensions between tradition and modernity, love and faith, self and family.[192] The most recent addition to my interfaith shelf, *The Conversation: A Novel* (2011) by Joshua Golding, suggests that Jewish men *can* find Jewish women and Judaism attractive, choosing them over an initial attraction to a Christian woman.[193] Whether this illustrates a new literary trend among male novelists and characters remains to be seen. It follows a pattern begun decades earlier by female novelists whose characters, more often than not, were attracted to men of varied ethnic and religious backgrounds but settled down with "a nice Jewish boy."[194]

The single exception to the glorification of intermarriage in contemporary filmmaking to date is *Two Lovers* (2008), starring Joaquin Phoenix. In "the best American drama of the year," according to the *Hollywood Reporter,* Jewish Leonard is recovering from his depression over a broken engagement with a Jewish woman when he meets two women: Jewish Sandra Cohen (played by Vinessa Shaw), daughter of the man merging dry-cleaning businesses with Leonard's father, an Israeli immigrant, and Christian Michelle (Gwyneth Paltrow). Torn between a woman who loves him unconditionally, Sandra, and a woman whom he falls in love with, Michelle, the film keeps viewers in suspense about which woman Leonard will ultimately choose until the very end. When the fantasy of his escape to San Francisco with Michelle evaporates because she gets back together with her former lover, Leonard presents the engagement ring he had bought for Michelle to Sandra. It is an all but inadvertent Jewish-Jewish engagement, the right "choice" for his "future family," as Sandra's father says. The Jewish mother, too, is depicted in an uncharacteristically positive light. Played beautifully by Isabella Rossellini, Leonard's mother assures him as he prepares to elope with Michelle that his parents only want him to be happy and he can return home anytime. She lets him go and then stays silent as he reenters the apartment to propose to Sandra. The mother-son moments are poignant, as is Leonard's acceptance of his "fate." Although the conclusion supports Jewish continuity, it does so through Leonard's emotional anguish, suggesting that he has subordinated his true desire for the sake of making others happy.[195]

The male focus influenced social understanding. Rarely depicting Jewish women who intermarried in films and television programs suggested to American audiences that few Jewish women left the fold. Cultural representations of a gender disparity in intermarriage illustrated the extent to which it was considered more commonplace for Jewish men to intermarry than for Jewish women. The lack of representation of Jewish-Jewish marriages indicates that marrying within the tribe is not a burning issue for creators of popular culture as it is for Jewish communal leaders. Jewish-Jewish marriage does not produce immediate conflict, at least not on the surface, which is the stuff of drama and comedy. The few portrayals of Jewish-Jewish romance connote either a failed marriage, such as on the 2002 television sitcom *Will and Grace*[196] or an engagement by default (as in the film *Two Lovers*).[197] There is also the painful-to-watch film *Breaking Upwards* (2009), depicting a Jewish-Jewish couple's negotiations to slowly and by mutual consent extricate from their co-dependent relationship, eliminating the possibility of marriage.[198]

How intermarriage among Jews has been portrayed in popular culture has changed significantly since the beginning of the twentieth century. From 1910 to 1928, films portrayed Jewish women marrying away from Judaism. However, in the years to follow, film productions increasingly starred Jewish men characters; these movies gained both more attention and longevity. Between 1930 and 1960, with the exception of *Tevye* in 1939, Jewish men who intermarried eclipsed intermarried Jewish women on screen and in print. While Hollywood initially depicted almost exclusively happy endings to intermarriage, novelists more often focused on the negative consequences of Jewish-Christian unions. Although representations of interfaith romance increased in number over the course of the twentieth century, their attention to actual religious and cultural differences between Jews and Christians decreased. By the end of the twentieth century and the beginning of the twenty-first, Jewish men and the perceived "threat" of Christian women are ever-present themes on prime-time television.[199]

Mirroring concerns about actual intermarried Jewish men, popular culture continues to perpetuate the Jewish communal fear that intermarried Jewish men do not raise Jewish children. Aside from the fictional cases in which twins are born and one of the children is raised Jewish, discussed above, the cases of singleton children reinforce the idea that these offspring of Jewish men and Christian women are "lost" to the Jewish people or otherwise confused. Creators of cultural representations of interfaith marriage seem not to be aware of the Reform movement's patrilineal descent decision. The ethno-religious identities of Jewish men's children are absent in their portrayals of intermarriage. In the 2005 film *Transamerica*, for example, the son notices a small Christmas tree in his father-turned-mother's house and asks, "I thought you said we were Jewish." The lead character responds, "Half Jewish, through my father so it's technically the wrong half. You're only a quarter, the wrong quarter."[200] "The wrong quarter" does not constitute much progress from Judy Blume's *Are You There God? It's Me Margaret* (1970); published before "patrilineal Jew" even became a label, Margaret, the daughter of a Jewish father, has "no religion."[201]

Television emphasizes the same assumption of discontinuity. In the final episode of the TV series *Boston Legal* (2004–2008), the opening scene starts with "Jingle Bells" playing in the background as the camera finds its way into a church where a rabbi and priest verbally duke it out at Shirley (Candice Bergen) and Carl's (John Larroquette) wedding rehearsal. After the priest accidentally refers to the rabbi as "the Jew" and

offers his apology, the rabbi states, "May I be really honest, Father? I'm
not happy at all with this union. There's a very old joke: You know what
they call the child of a Jew and a Christian? A Christian!" Within the first
seventy-five seconds of the show, Christmas, assimilation, antisemitism,
oppression, the Holocaust, the Catholic Church, and Israel's existence
are all put on the table as actor William Shatner, himself intermarried,
calls out, "Uh-oh, Holy War!"[202] Hence, children of intermarried Jewish
men either do not count in terms of the Jewish population or religious
syncretism rules the screen. "The Best Christmukkah Ever" episode on
the Fox television show *The O.C.*, for example, has Seth Cohen combining his parents' dual holiday traditions. A Jewish male patient on
Grey's Anatomy is treated for a head injury sustained from falling off his
roof hanging "Hannumas lights" as his three mixed-faith children sing
Christmas songs in his hospital room.[203] There are undoubtedly other
such subplots.

Beginning in the early twentieth century and continuing today,
Jewish-Christian couples have been used in popular culture to illustrate
that Jews can indeed marry into America, first assuaging nativist fears
about immigrants and then diminishing the social currency of antisemitism. Depictions of interfaith romance, Jews, and gender changed over
time from overrepresentation of women to overrepresentation of men.
This gendered shift had an important and unanticipated consequence:
representations of intermarriage in popular culture have constructed
Jewish-Christian unions as both a male prerogative and an objective
for Jewish men. The profound influence on American popular culture
wrought by works such as *Abie's Irish Rose*, *Gentleman's Agreement*, and
Exodus continues with the 2006 production of *Ira and Abby*. This time
the Jewish lead is a neurotic depressant, playing on the stereotype made
famous by actor Woody Allen, who finds happiness with the Christian
woman who turns tradition on its head by proposing marriage to him
within hours of meeting. This romantic comedy won numerous awards,
suggesting that the Jewish man–Christian woman theme continues to
entertain American audiences.[204]

The second decade of the twenty-first century shows Jewish men
who are a bit less nebbish than their fathers were, but equally enthralled
with non-Jewish women. *The Five-Year Engagement*, released in spring

2012, starred co-writer Jason Segel as Tom, who bends his knee for Catholic Violet (Emily Blunt). Like his real-life creator, Tom has a "Jewish drawer" where he keeps his yarmulke and which he opens only for the High Holy Days. The drawer acts as a metaphor for the character's Jewishness—indeed that of most leading Jewish male characters—it is kept mostly out of sight and merits little attention.[205] Segel was raised Jewish by his Jewish father and Episcopalian mother. He recalls hearing at Hebrew school, "If your mother's not Jewish, you don't get it [God]"; nevertheless, he celebrated a bar mitzvah. Segel's childhood experience convinced him that exclusivity in religion is not right.[206] Unwed at the time of this publication, time will tell whether he becomes a father and raises Jewish children. "Am I man . . . or a muppet?"—a song Segel sings in *The Muppets* (2011)—could be a metaphor for men deciding how to self-identify as Jews. "Today, I am a clown," Krusty declared at his midlife bar mitzvah ceremony on *The Simpsons* television show, and later, "I'd rather be a happy *shnook* [simpleton] than a noble *shlumpf* [sucker]," as he floated down the Seine in Paris after marrying Princess Penelope, a Congregationalist.[207]

The tenacity of intermarried Jewish men in popular culture suggests that despite the prevalence of intermarriage in America, it is still seen as involving sufficient conflict for drama and comedy. Jewish writers, producers, and directors may also still be proving themselves if not as Americans, then perhaps as men, husbands, and fathers, just as non-celebrities renegotiate what these roles mean on a daily basis. Writing in 1991, film critic Michael Melved prophesized, "Eventually, movies on Jewish themes may catch up with offscreen developments: as more and more Hollywood figures make personal contact with the renewal of Jewish life, films may begin to present a more balanced and dynamic view of the Jewish present and future."[208] His theory has yet to be realized, at least with regard to intermarriage in America.[209] Perhaps popular culture will represent the real-life stories of Jewish men who intermarry and raise Jewish children when more fathers are equally empowered and responsible for parenting as are mothers. Stay tuned.

Conclusion

Self-understanding is an essential first step for men today. If a man is to be a good father to his son, or a good husband to his wife, he needs to know what he got, or wanted and didn't get, from his own father; how he was both strengthened *and* wounded by that relationship; how it has influenced his own fathering style and his own identity as a man.

—Samuel Osherson

Intermarried Jewish men *can* raise Jewish children equally effectively as can Jewish women. However, given that gender seems to trump ethnicity, it remains to be seen whether they will and, if they do, whether the organized Jewish community will accept their offspring as Jews. After comparing intermarried men and intermarried women, this chapter emphasizes how the issues of men's involvement in Jewish parenting and the Jewish community need to be looked at in their fuller contexts, including interactions with Jewish leaders and spending less hours with their families than do women. Lastly, I suggest a new model for Jewish identity that validates Jewish men's intermarried experiences, while challenging them to step up to the fatherhood plate, along with all American men. Finally ending the ongoing "battle of the sexes" would require that men and women work together to truly level both the professional playing field and the home court. As Princeton professor of politics and international affairs Anne-Marie Slaughter wisely stated in the *Atlantic*, "Let us presume, as I do with my sons, that they will understand 'supporting their families' to mean more than earning money."[1]

This book on intermarried Jewish men reinforces the findings in my book on intermarried Jewish women with regard to gender, suggesting that Jewish gender is at work whether a couple includes a Jewish woman–Christian man or a Jewish man–Christian woman. In the former combination, as I discuss at length in *Still Jewish: A History of Women and Intermarriage in America*, Jewish women were both the deciders and the doers, increasingly over the twentieth century making sure that their children would be raised as Jewish. In the case of Jewish men, they were often the deciders, but the bulk of the domestic and childcare burdens, including Jewish education, remained on the shoulders of their Christian-born wives. What makes Jewish gender all the more significant for me, however, is that these fathers are in the awkward position of trying to fulfill their roles as men that are sometimes at odds with being Jewish with regard to home religion and children's day-to-day involvement in the Jewish community. Moreover, just as Jewish women who intermarried during the mid-twentieth century and were "still Jewish" regardless of whether they chose to identify otherwise, women born Christian who married Jewish men, converted to Judaism, and raised Jewish children had "interfaith families" because their parents and siblings were still Christian.

Four striking similarities between intermarried Jewish men and intermarried Jewish women merit some discussion here. First is the most obvious point: men who married "out" were, like women, still Jewish. Second, the influence of becoming a parent on men's and women's Jewish identities was similar, heightening their awareness of being Jewish. Men who intermarried may have switched denominations from more traditional to more liberal, but this change over time entailed an enhancement, not diminishment, of their Jewish identity. Third, both men and women were influenced by a parent's intermarriage, reflecting national demographic data that Jewish adults who were the children of intermarriages were three times more likely to marry non-Jews themselves.[2] Since none of the men or women participated in the Taglit-Birthright Israel program, however, it is unknown whether having that experience would have influenced their marital choices or family lives.[3] Lastly, and perhaps more significantly for in-marriage advocates who argue that intermarriages more often end in divorce, in the cases where intermarried Jewish men and intermarried Jewish women divorced, both did so for reasons unrelated to religious differences and most often involving adultery, financial issues, or problems with substance abuse. While religious differences did not drive couples apart, further study is needed to determine the powerful role that cultural differences may play in marital disunion.[4]

Differences between intermarried Jewish men and intermarried Jewish women were also significant. The most profound difference between men and women regarded denominational shifting: intermarried Jewish women maintained the denominational affiliations in which they were raised after marriage, whereas a majority of the men switched. The experiences of intermarried Jewish mothers and intermarried Jewish fathers were distinct due to traditional family structures and ongoing gender disparity in the workforce. The Holocaust factored differently into intermarried men and women's lives. For women, the decimation of Eastern European Jewry encouraged their raising Jewish children but did not influence their feelings about Judaism per se. In contrast, the legacy of the Holocaust played a much more significant role in men's consciousness with regard to their relationships with Judaism, challenging them to define what being Jewish meant to them. In addition, men had much shorter fuses when rabbis declined to officiate at their wedding or they felt ostracized by the organized Jewish community, whereas women did not take such great offense. During the course of interviews with men, they used expletives far more freely than did women. They also raised the topic of sex and the importance of physical attraction and intimacy; women did not. Men encouraged me to speak to their wives, whereas women did not suggest that I interview their husbands, suggesting that men recognized the important responsibilities of their born-Christian wives.

There is a long way to go before American society accepts men as full-fledged parents and they have all the support, resources, and wherewithal that they need. Parenting together requires a restructuring of fatherhood that has long been influenced by a psychological process known as reproducing motherhood: basically, for centuries daughters have been taught to remain connected with their family of origin and become mothers, and sons to separate from their parents and go out in the world.[5] This enduring phenomenon undermines intermarried Jewish fathers, as it does all fathers, and continues to reinforce a culture centered on the mothering role. Study participant Greg Marin, who was determined to do everything his wife did (short of breastfeeding) for their daughter born in 2008, lamented the lack of paternity magazines. He commented sarcastically that his favorite phrase was "the involved dad." "Like what the hell is 'an involved dad'? Is there an 'involved mom'?"[6] No, but there is a "breadwinner mom," illustrating how women's large presence in the labor force is disproportionate to men's domestic participation.[7] As the second decade of the twenty-first century proceeds, there are increasingly more online resources for American fathers; however, they are slow to take hold of consumers and gain widespread visibility.[8] Until men and women in heterosexual partnerships co-parent equally, "involved dads" will remain the exception rather than the rule. Currently, even among shared parenting families striving for a fifty-fifty household division of labor, women *are* parents while men *do* parenting.[9] Progress co-exists with the need for more change, which may only be possible in subsequent generations of intermarried couples parenting together. Although the principle of equal parenting suggests that mothers and fathers are equally invested in parenting, gender role socialization continues to be influenced by the ways in which contemporary mothers and fathers were themselves parented.

Men who intermarried most recently seem the most invested in trying to balance their career pursuits with fatherhood. Forgoing business travel and other activities that would take him away from parenting, a participant who intermarried in 1991 prioritized his son's happiness, success, and comfort and helping him become a good young man: "That's what I consider my number one job."[10] According to Allan Benjamin, who intermarried in 2003, once his son was born, his life began anew; it became centered on his role as a father and doing everything for his son and eventually his daughter, too.[11] However much men may want to be involved in their children's lives, the social reality in which they currently live makes prioritizing family life a challenge. Charles Revkin's Christian wife was glad to have a Jewish family but told him that to the extent that they're Jewish, he would have to do the work to make that happen. The rationale did not reflect feminist thinking but rather ignorance and inexperience. Charles pointed out, "The only problem with that theory is that I'm at work sixty or seventy hours every week," which does not leave much time to ensure his children's Jewish cultural or religious education.[12] The upshot is that the children attended the Jewish day school in Ann Arbor from kindergarten through second grade, where they were exposed to more Judaic content than their father had. The family transitioned the children to a public school in 2010, and their home life does not include much consistent Jewish ritual or observance; hence it remains to be seen to what extent this father will be able to foster his children's developing Jewish identities without the built-in support of a day school environment. Synagogue affiliation will help him.

The question that I continue to wrestle with is this: to what extent do men actually *want* to be more involved in the day-to-day care and education of their children—that is, the grunt work—that their demanding jobs inhibit, and to what extent does their work provide a means of escape from what is less rewarding according to the model of masculinity that judges men by their paycheck, the size of their homes, and the number of their big-boy toys? Perhaps an inadvertent consequence of the male breadwinning ideology persisting over the twentieth century and into the twenty-first is the justification for men's less-than-equal commitment to childcare.[13] A brave man to my mind, Nathan Bloomer acknowledged that his long hours at the office were partly of his own device: "I was working for Arthur Anderson and admit to male workaholism as a form of childcare avoidance; 'I gotta go to work now, honey,' you know, that kind of thing."[14] Charles Revkin always envisioned that he would be a progressive husband doing half of the domestic work, from dish washing to child raising, and that his wife would work outside the home. In reality, however, his life is far more traditional than he had anticipated; he leads a medical department, and his wife does 75 to 90 percent of everything else. Asked if there was anything within his control that he could change, Charles replied, "I would need a brain transplant."[15] He feels trapped and anticipates regretting not having more time at home and with his children, but also feels unable to change behavioral patterns. He is not alone.

Sometimes it took a major life change for men to alter their habits. When he got divorced, Kalman Long dedicated himself to modeling for his children all types of domestic labor. He believed that his children

How Should I Know?

A Program for Jewish Men with
Spouses/Partners of Other Religious Backgrounds
www.howshouldiknow.org

"How Should I Know?" program for Jewish men by the Jewish
Outreach Institute. *Jewish Outreach Institute/Paul Golin.*

needed to see him do everything. "A male needs to be responsible for everything that keeps the male alive," he urged while single. Yet when he remarried, more of the domestic labor shifted to his wife. Admitting white male privilege, Kalman stated, "I am in no way egalitarian in my view as much as I would like to be. I just am not living in a society where I think I could possibly be."[16] Whether Jewish men want to cut back on their paid labor hours and increase the hours with their families depends intimately on how they envision their roles as American men and fathers. More deeply, it depends on how they want to be Jewish fathers.

In the so-called post-feminist age, what is an intermarried Jewish man to do when his wife agrees to raise their children as Jews yet expects him to do what it takes? Several of the men who married in the first decade of the twenty-first century faced this exact challenge. Gary Michaels, who married in 2006 and had a son the same year, had this conversation with his wife:

> Gary: I want my kids to be Jewish or to identify as Jewish people.
> Wife: Okay. What does that mean?
> Gary: I don't really know. Well, I want them to be Jewish.
> Wife: Fine. What are you going to do about it?

Although Gary did not expect his wife to introduce their son to Jewish religion, education, and culture, he had not yet determined how he would do it at the time of the interview, in 2009. He surmised, "I started a family late in life. I can resolve my relationship to Judaism late in life."[17] His experience illustrates the meaning of intermarriage for Jewish men: while his wife's non-identification with religion made Judaism the easy choice, it also made figuring out Jewish parenting *his* issue. For many men, particularly those without substantial Jewish education, what and how to teach their children remained perplexing. This presents a tremendous opportunity for the organized Jewish community to offer creative programming for single and intermarried Jewish men that could shape the future of American Jewry. "How Should I Know?" a pilot program launched in 2010 by the Jewish Outreach Institute designed specifically for men involved in interfaith relationships will, if it continues to be funded, provide support and information for fathers looking to explain basic Judaism to their partners and children.[18] To be truly effective there also needs to be a nationwide initiative that educates people about the relationship between intermarriage and gender roles. None of the men I interviewed had access to such resources at the time of their interview, which their experiences illustrate.

One respondent resolved this gender quandary by moving from the South, where he had met his wife, back to Ann Arbor to live near his mother so she could help him nurture his children's Jewish identities. However, a Jewish grandmother for his children was not a substitute for a Jewish wife for himself. Morton Langfeld, who married in 2008, confessed how he wished his wife would "take over," but that was not going to happen and so he complained, "Why doesn't the house smell like a Jewish home should?" He worked full-time, his wife did not earn an income, and although he insisted, "I'm not like some traditional guy who needs a wife to be cooking all day long," he also contended, "We do have roles here."[19] Whether his wife's cooking would smell sufficiently Jewish for him given that she did not know how to replicate the childhood memory of this meaning-packed scent is doubtful. Her comment to him, "You're not going to make me your mother," indicates resistance on her part to even try to learn what his mother used to cook. Morton's geographic move and his position that his wife should be the one to make their home "smell Jewish" illustrate his lack of participation in making that happen himself, as well as perhaps his unconscious inability to envision himself in that role.

There is likely a relationship between the country's preoccupation with getting fathers to play with their children and what some Judaic studies scholars report about the "'disappearance' of Jewish men from lay leadership positions in Reform congregations, with the exception of the office of temple president, and the difficulty of attracting them to the professional workforce in the Jewish community, suggesting that Jewish men became less communally involved over time."[20] Some scholars have gone so far as to blame men's decreasing involvement on women's greater involvement in liberal Judaism, an argument I find particularly problematic because it oversimplifies American men's experiences—never mind that it blames women for men's inaction.[21] Some of the men in my study are highly involved in the Jewish community. In addition to serving on temple committees and boards of Jewish organizations, they have worked creatively to build a more inclusive Jewish community. Other men, who have focused more exclusively on career building or supporting their family, declare that they hope to be more involved when they retire from full-time employment. A highly successful physician commented most sincerely, "I'd like to be more involved with the community—but I barely have time to go to the bathroom!"[22] Although obviously an exaggeration, this statement indicates how strapped he felt for discretionary time.

The ongoing issue of gender inequity in American society at large and the Jewish communal world continues to influence intermarried Jewish men's identities, lives, and families. The pay disparity is as true for Fortune 500 companies as for nonprofits. In 2004, women CEOs in charities with budgets over $50 million earned 37 percent less than male CEOs.[23] The wage gap between men and women has narrowed by only less than half a cent per year since 1963 when President Kennedy signed the Equal Pay Act. In 2008, women earned seventy-seven cents to men's dollar.[24] According to the March 2011 report prepared for the White House Council on Women and Girls, white women earned only 79 percent as much as white men in 2009.[25] In the Conservative and Reform rabbinates, there are compensation gaps between men and women rabbis, with male rabbis earning more and serving more of the large congregations on a full-time basis.[26] Controlling for years of education, years in the field, title of job, and number of supervisees, women working in the Jewish community earned on average $20,000 less than their male counterparts. Women's careers are affected by the interruption of raising children; women, more than men, stop working altogether or significantly reduce the number of hours of paid employment and as a result lag behind in the race for higher positions. "There may be something to learn from the behavior of women" about creating work-life balance, commented sociologist Steven M. Cohen. "And if that's the case . . . then it behooves the Jewish communal world, if not all of American society, to learn something from women, *and* to create those positions that can afford work-life balance so that we can indeed use the talents of all of our people in all of those jobs." If the gender gap is due to discrimination, Cohen argued, "it is incumbent upon all of us to eliminate this gender gap."[27] On these points, Cohen and I agree.[28]

The issues of men's involvement in Jewish parenting and in the Jewish community need to be looked at in their fuller contexts, which include interactions with members of Jewish leadership and the ongoing American reality of men spending more hours away from their families and earning more than women for the same work. Women's success in college and the professions apparently has not eliminated the pressure many men feel to be the major breadwinners, nor has it changed women's focus on being the primary parent. A lot has changed, in some ways. One of the study participants remarked that over the course of his lifetime, he went from attending a segregated first grade to having a black president;[29] yet the goal of securing gender equity remains unmet. Equal communal involvement will only occur once the wage gap between women and men (of all race and ethnic groups) ceases to exist and both genders fully envision themselves *as* full-fledged parents, not just as *doing* parenting. Those who care deeply about Jewish continuity must try to understand both men and women as well as level the professional playing field and the domestic one so that regardless of whether they intermarry, Jewish men will be empowered to raise Jewish children. Jennifer A. Thompson's research illustrates that women raised Christian who marry Jewish men and agree to raise their children as Jews wield considerable power as religious leaders in their families.[30] What about when the Christian women agree to having Jewish children but also insist that the Jewish husbands must lead the way as the Jewish parent in the family? Active Jewish fathering needs to be seen as equally important as providing. Gender will persist in influencing the disproportionately low transmission rate of Jewish identity to children of intermarried Jewish men compared to intermarried Jewish women so long as "men's work" outside the home continues to be socially valued more highly than "women's work" inside it—and men's identities continue to be fashioned by what they *do* rather than who they *are*.

ENDING THE BATTLE OF THE SEXES

Is there an ongoing backlash against women, or are men the ones who are stiffed? In her 1991 book about the "undeclared war against American women" and then the 1999 book about "the betrayal of the American man," journalist Susan Faludi chronicled how women have remained the second sex while men likewise have languished at the hands of corporate America. According to Faludi, "Men and women both feel cheated of lives in which they might have contributed to a social world; men and women both feel pushed into roles that are about little more than displaying prettiness or prowess in the marketplace."[31] Although published more than a decade ago, Faludi's appraisal of the status of the sexes persists in many ways, largely because of the failure of both sexes to fully figure out what it means to be simultaneously human and in conversation with each other about their humanity . . . and about domestic labor. Most significantly, with growing exceptions in parts of the country such as the San Francisco Bay Area, there continues to be a shortage of egalitarian marriages in which both spouses have rewarding careers and embrace caregiving. Facebook chief operating officer Sheryl Sandberg's 2013 book *Lean In* is primarily written for and marketed to women, but it also includes significant wisdom about and for men: "If we make it too easy for women to drop out of the career marathon, we also make it too hard for men." Men, opines Sandberg, need social encouragement to be ambitious in their homes, to lean in at the kitchen table, and women need to help empower them by allowing men's greater responsibility.[32]

News headlines and academic studies illustrate the near constant preoccupation with whether men or women carry the heaviest burden on their shoulders. "Poll Finds Women's Gains Have Taken Personal Toll," the *New York Times* headlined in 1989. Reporting that women made up 45 percent of the labor force, compared to 38 percent in 1970, the poll depicted women in couples in which both husband and wife worked as doing much more than half of the grocery shopping, cooking, cleaning, and bill paying.[33] This imbalance created what sociologist Arlie Hochschild described in her book *The Second Shift*.[34] More than twenty years later, not much had changed in this respect. In 2008, University of Michigan researchers conducting a study funded by the National Science Foundation found that while men were doing more housework than they had in 1976, husbands created an additional seven hours a week of housework for wives, whereas wives saved husbands an hour a week.[35] Aiming to put this long-term debate to rest, *Time* magazine's August 2011 cover claimed, "Chore Wars: Let It Go. Make Peace. Men and Women, It Turns Out, Work the Same Amount." While making an effort to dismantle the tenacious idea that women do more at home than do men, the author simply reinterprets the old argument to mean that women experience a high cost due to a deficit in leisure time relative to men. However, *Time* author Ruth Davis Konigsberg also makes the valid point that so long as women leave work early to relieve the babysitter or pick up children and start dinner, they allow men to continue working late.[36] Although this recent argument seems to "blame the victim" for accommodating her spouse, it does highlight the fact that women continue to sacrifice their careers for the sake of their families more than do men. Perhaps as more highly visible men cut back on work in order to spend more time with their children, as did the Obama administration deputy secretary of state James Steinberg and the deputy secretary of defense William Lynn, men of all stations will feel more comfortable joining the cause for greater career-family balance, and both genders will benefit. "We'll create a better society," writes a former director of policy planning at the State Department, when we focus on "how we can help all Americans have healthy, happy, productive lives, valuing the people they love as much as the success they seek."[37]

The stalled men's movement of the 1970s and 1980s may be reigniting in the twenty-first century as more men are looking for new ways to integrate work and family. In 2010, researchers cited statistics for what they consider to be a decline in the power base of men: (1) over the past three decades, women have achieved unprecedented success in higher education; (2) for the first time in American history, women now make up slightly more than half of the labor force; (3) young men and women share the same desire for jobs with greater responsibility; (4) there is a decrease of the "traditional family" consisting of one working parent and one stay-at-home parent; and (5) work-life conflict is felt more strongly by fathers than mothers.[38] The upside of the greater impact of the 2008–2010 recession on men, challenges of dual-career couples, and the increases in employed single-parent households is that men have had no other choice than to reevaluate their roles as fathers. Released in 2011 by the Boston College Center for Work & Family, *The New Dad: Caring, Committed and Conflicted* explored the role of worker and caregiver from the perspectives of nearly one thousand fathers. Lead author Brad Harrington and his co-researchers found that men under forty were less likely to see being a good father as solely or even primarily about being the financial provider, while men over forty were slightly more likely to do so. Three aspects ranked higher than providing financial security: providing love and emotional support; being involved and present in their child's life; and being a teacher, guide and coach. Breadwinning ranked equally with providing discipline. The one aspect of parenting that ranked lowest was doing their part in the day-to-day childcare tasks![39] Although fathers perceived teaching, guiding, and coaching as significant aspects of parenting, there was a disconnect between these aspirations and the practice of them through daily involvement in caregiving. Reasons for not seeing the relationship between the two could include a difference in definitions of caregiving between spouses and the fact that most men do not experience the hands-on parenting that women do who take significantly more time off from work after the birth of a child. Hence there continues to be, according to the Boston College study, "a noteworthy gap between what fathers desire, and what they seem able to do to adjust their work lives after their children are born, both in an immediate sense (e.g., through taking leave) and an ongoing sense (e.g., through flexible work arrangements)."[40] How and to what extent this gap decreases will depend on whether men and women work together to strike a more equitable balance between their roles as professionals and parents.

Enabling intermarried Jewish men, along with all American men, to better integrate work and family is a feminist goal, and reaching it will benefit both sexes. It is time, as Jeremy Adam Smith, author of *The Daddy Shift* wrote, "to go on the offensive."[41] Encouraging men of all denominational stripes to invest in raising Jewish children is not about men getting in touch with their feminine side. It *is* about acknowledging that while American men contribute more at home than they did in years past, they still do far less than women on the domestic front. It also requires confronting the reality that intermarried Jewish men have been shortchanged in the realm of domestic Judaism, sometimes inadvertently ousted by their wives, who pick up the slack, and neglected by a Jewish community that erroneously assumed they did not come back after becoming b'nai mitzvah because their Jewishness was unimportant to them or because women were present. "Gender equality," in the words of sociologist Michael Kimmel on how he became a feminist, "is the only way for men to have the sorts of relationships we say we want to have—with women, with men, and with our children."[42]

Redefining Jewish fatherhood will not only create happier intermarried Jewish families; it will also ensure Jewish continuity and end the battle of the sexes once and for all by eliminating a sex-gender system based on inequality, creating room for one that is truly socially advanced.[43] The new model of Jewish identity and fatherhood that emerges will include active involvement in the day-to-day responsibility of parenting Jewish offspring that happens in the home as well as in the synagogue or Jewish community center. Just as important, however, it will encourage Jewish men to incorporate fathering into their Jewish identities as contributing parts of their inner essence, just as it is for Jewish mothers. When that happens, a new psychological process will reproduce neither motherhood nor fatherhood, allowing instead for equal parenthood to empower both sexes and, subsequently, their offspring of both sexes. Let us, men and women, act now to complete the unfinished business of the feminist and fatherhood movements by creating a society where "family values" actually means something that benefits all of its citizens.

Notes

PREFACE

1. Shulamit Reinharz, Welcome Lunch, Hadassah-Brandeis Institute, Women's Resource Center, Brandeis University, 22 September 2011.

2. David Mogul, Federation of Jewish Men's Clubs *Keruv* Initiative Retreat, 19 May 2012.

INTRODUCTION

The epigraph comes from John Steinbeck, journal entry (1938), quoted by Susan Shillinglaw in her introduction to *Of Mice and Men* by Steinbeck (New York: Viking Penguin, 1994 [1938]), vii.

1. "Jewish Mothers," Curlicues, accessed 8 December 2008, http://www.curlicues .com/jokes.htm.

2. According to sociologists Sylvia Barack Fishman and Daniel Parmer, "Jewish men, [in contrasts to Jewish women], tend to be reactive in inter-dating and intermarriage, not talking about the religion of the household or of the eventual children until children are born or ready for religious school." Sylvia Barack Fishman and Daniel Parmer, *Matrilineal Ascent/Patrilineal Descent: The Gender Imbalance in American Jewish Life* (Waltham, MA: Brandeis University, 2008), 4.

3. Fishman and Parmer, *Matrilineal Ascent/Patrilineal Descent*, 77.

4. Within intermarried families, affiliated Jewish intermarried mothers (32 percent) were twice as likely as affiliated intermarried Jewish fathers (15 percent) to say religion is "very important." Among the unaffiliated intermarried population, the ratio is even sharper, with only 9 percent of Jewish fathers compared to 27 percent of Jewish mothers. Fishman and Parmer, *Matrilineal Ascent/Patrilineal Descent*, 41.

5. "Pick-a-Little, Talk-a-Little," *Sex and the City*, season 6, episode 4, starring Evan Handler as Harry Goldenblatt and Kristen Davis as Charlotte York, aired 13 July 2003.

6. Alan M. Dershowitz, *The Vanishing American Jew: In Search of Jewish Identity for the Next Century* (Boston: Little, Brown, 1997), 42.

7. Nathan Jeffrey, "An $800,000 Israel Ad Campaign to Save 'Lost' Diaspora Jews Falls Flat and Dies," *Forward*, 9 September 2009. See also Pini Herman, "Unintended Intermarriage between Jews?," *Jewish Journal*, 6 December 2011, accessed 28 February 2012, http://www.jewishjournal.com/demographic_duo/item/unintended_intermarriage _between_jews_20111206/.

8. Prior to 1940, the rate of Jews married to non-Jews was estimated to be between 2 and 3.2 percent, doubling to approximately 6 percent between 1941 and 1960. The percentage of Jews marrying non-Jews increased roughly as follows: from less than 13 percent before 1970 to 28 percent in 1970–1979, then from 38 percent in 1980–1984 to 43 percent in 1985–1995, and reaching an all-time high of 47 percent in 1996–2001. If one applies a definition of "born Jews," a category that includes non-Jews who had at least one Jewish parent and were raised in a non-Jewish religion, the intermarriage rate among those married in 1985–1990 was 52 percent, 53 percent in 1991–1995, and 54 percent in 1996–2000. The percentage of Jews who intermarried in 2000–2013 was 58 percent. Laurence Kotler-Berkowitz et al., *The National Jewish Population Survey 2000–01: Strength, Challenge and Diversity in the American Jewish Population* (New York: United Jewish Communities, 2003), 16–17; Pew Research Center's Religion & Public Life Project, *A Portrait of Jewish Americans: Findings from a Pew Research Center Survey of U.S. Jews* (Washington, DC: Pew Research Center, 2013), 9, 35. Pew's survey, released when this book was in production at the publisher, provoked a torrent of news headlines in the national and Jewish press, response columns, and electronic discussions among social scientists. It will likely continue to be analyzed for many years to come.

9. "Ivanka's Big Day," *New York Post,* 10 September 2009, accessed 5 October 2009, http://www.nypost.com/p/pagesix/ivanka_big_day_uVwzXKGheUqhuGoyErRaAN.

10. William Norwich, "Western Union: Lauren Bush and David Lauren's Wedding," *Vogue,* 11 November 2011, accessed 7 November 2013, http://www.vogue.com/culture/article/western-union-lauren-bush-and-david-laurens-wedding/#1; Roxanne Roberts and Amy Argetsinger, "Ashley Biden Weds Howard Krein in Delaware," *Washington Post,* posted 3 June 2012, http://www.washingtonpost.com/blogs/reliable-source/post/ashley-biden-weds-howard-krein-in-delaware-photo/2012/06/03/gJQA7XaKBV_blog.html.

11. C. David Heyman, *American Legacy: The Story of John and Caroline Kennedy* (New York: Atria Books, 2007), 288. See also "Biden Wedding: Father of the Bride Joe Biden Does the Hora," *Huffington Post,* posted 7 June 2012, http://www.huffingtonpost.com/2012/06/07/biden-wedding_n_1578784.html.

12. *The Bachelorette,* ABC, season 7, finale, episode 11, aired 1 August 2011.

13. Virginia Yans-McLaughlin, *Family and Community: Italian Immigrants in Buffalo, 1880–1930* (Ithaca: Cornell University Press, 1971), 22.

14. Werner Sollors, ed., *The Invention of Ethnicity* (New York: Oxford University Press, 1989), xiii–xv.

15. I refer here to Richard D. Alba's useful conception of ethnic identity. See *Ethnic Identity: The Transformation of White America* (New Haven: Yale University Press, 1990), 25. Regarding "flux and choice in American ethnicity," see Mary C. Waters, *Ethnic Options: Choosing Identities in America* (Berkeley: University of California Press, 1990), 16–17.

16. "Winning isn't everything, it's the only thing"—Vince Lombardi. "Nice guys finish last"—Leo Durocher. In Frank Pittman, *Man Enough: Fathers, Sons, and the Search for Masculinity* (New York: Berkley Publishing Group, 1993), 49.

17. Betty Friedan, *The Feminine Mystique* (New York: W. W. Norton, 1963).

18. Jewish manhood and representations of Jewish masculinity have a tumultuous history, beginning in ancient times. See Benjamin Maria Baader et al., eds., *Jewish Masculinities: German Jews, Gender, and History* (Bloomington: Indiana University

Press, 2012); Michael Brenner and Gideon Reuveni, eds., *Emancipation through Muscles: Jews and Sports in Europe* (Lincoln: University of Nebraska Press, 2006); Harry Brod and Shawn Israel Zevit, eds., *Brother Keepers: New Perspectives on Jewish Masculinity* (Harriman, TN: Men's Studies Press, 2010); Lori Lefkowitz, "Coats and Tales: Joseph Stories and Myths of Jewish Masculinity," in *A Mensch among Men: Explorations in Jewish Masculinity,* ed. Harry Brod (Freedom, CA: Crossing Press, 1988); Daniel Boyarin, *Unheroic Conduct: The Rise of Heterosexuality and the Invention of the Jewish Man* (Berkeley: University of California Press, 1997); Michael Chabon, *Manhood for Amateurs: The Pleasures and Regrets of a Husband, Father, and Son* (New York: HarperCollins, 2009); Paula E. Hyman, *Gender and Assimilation in Modern Jewish History: The Roles and Representation of Women* (Seattle: University of Washington Press, 1995); Warren Rosenberg, *Legacy of Rage: Jewish Masculinity, Violence, and Culture* (Amherst: University of Massachusetts Press, 2001); and Beth S. Wenger, "Constructing Manhood in American Jewish Culture," in *Gender and Jewish History,* ed. Marion A. Kaplan and Deborah Dash Moore (Bloomington: Indiana University Press, 2011), 350–363.

19. Karen Egolf, "President Obama: Take Time to Be a Dad; New PSAs Encourage Men to Be Responsible Fathers," *Advertising Age,* 19 June 2009, http://adage.com/goodworks/post?article_id=137465, accessed 4 October 2009.

20. President Barack Obama, "The Most Important Job," Father's Day electronic communication to author, 20 June 2010.

21. Milton M. Gordon, *Assimilation in American Life: The Role of Race, Religion, and National Origins* (New York: Oxford University Press, 1964), 228–229.

22. Marshall Sklare, "Intermarriage and the Jewish Future," *Commentary,* April 1964, 46–52.

23. See Eddie Fisher, *Eddie: My Life, My Loves* (New York: Harper and Row, 1981); and William Shatner, *Up Till Now: The Autobiography* (New York: St. Martin's Press, 2008), 265.

24. In contemporary times, labeling a Jewish-Jewish marriage as "intermarriage" is bad form. See, for example, the failed publicity campaign in Israel to categorize Israeli Jewish and American Jewish marriages as intermarriage. Pini Herman, "Unintended Intermarriage between Jews?," *Jewish Journal,* 6 December 2011, accessed 28 February 2012, http://www.jewishjournal.com/demographic_duo/item/unintended_intermarriage_between_jews_20111206/.

25. Ira M. Sheskin, *The 2005 Detroit Jewish Population Study* (Jewish Federation of Metropolitan Detroit, December 2006), Main Report, vol. 1, ch. 6, pp. 90–92.

26. Sheskin, *The 2005 Detroit Jewish Population Study,* 90.

27. Ariela Keysar, Barry A. Kosmin, Nava Lerer, and Egon Mayer, *Exogamy in First Marriages and Remarriages: An Analysis of Mate Selection in First and Second Marriages among American Jews in the 1990s, and Its Theoretical Implications* (Association for the Social Scientific Study of Jewry [ASSJ], 1991).

28. Danielle Kurtzleben, "The 10 Most Educated U.S. Cities: Boulder, Ann Arbor, Washington, D.C., Top the List," *U.S. News and World Report,* 30 August 2011.

29. Gordon, *Assimilation in American Life,* 161–162.

30. Ron French and Mike Wilkinson, "Leaving Michigan Behind: Eight-Year Population Exodus Staggers State," *Detroit News,* 2 April 2009, accessed 12 June 2013, http://www.detroitnews.com/article/20090402/METRO/904020403.

31. "U.S. Census Bureau Delivers Michigan's 2010 Census Population Totals," released 22 March 2011, accessed 12 June 2013, http://www.census.gov/newsroom/ releases/archives/2010_census/cb11-cn106.html.

32. Kofi Myler, "Detroit's Population from 1840 to 2012 Shows High Points, Decades of Decline," *Detroit Free Press,* 23 July 2013, accessed 2 November 2013, http://www.freep .com/interactive/article/20130723/NEWS01/130721003/detroit-city-population; Jim Schaefer et al., "Detroit Files for Bankruptcy, Setting Off Battles with Creditors, Pensions, Unions," *Detroit Free Press,* 19 July 2013, accessed 2 November 2013, http://www .freep.com/article/20130718/NEWS01/307180107/; Nancy Kaffer et al., "Detroit Files for Bankruptcy Protection," *USA Today,* 18 July 2013, accessed 2 November 2013, http:// www.usatoday.com/story/news/nation/2013/07/18/detroit-prepares-bankruptcy-filing -friday/2552819/.

33. Estimated median household income in 2009 was $50,291 for Ann Arbor and $45,255 for Michigan; estimated median house or condo value in 2009 was $239,200 for Ann Arbor compared to $132,200 for Michigan. City-Data.com, accessed 13 June 2013, http://www.city-data.com/city/Ann-Arbor-Michigan.html.

34. Races in Ann Arbor (2009): white 82,328 (72.1 percent); Asian 16,028 (14 percent); black 7,391 (6.5 percent); two or more races 4,768 (4.2 percent); and Hispanic 3,570 (3.1 percent). Races in Michigan (2009): white 7,703,149 (77.3 percent); black 1,372,264 (13.8 percent); Hispanic 422,831 (4.2 percent); Asian 240,892 (2.4 percent); and two or more races 170,298 (1.7 percent). "Races in Ann Arbor, Michigan, Detailed Stats," City-Data.com, accessed 13 June 2013, http://www.city-data.com/races/races -Ann-Arbor-Michigan.html.

35. "Robert J. Harris," *Wikipedia,* accessed 14 June 2013, http://en.wikipedia.org/ wiki/Robert_J._Harris; Horace Martin Woodhouse, *101 Things You Didn't Know About Ann Arbor, Michigan* (New York: Curiosity Company, 2010), 66; "Ann Arbor, Michigan," *Wikipedia,* accessed 13 June 2013, http://en.wikipedia.org/wiki/Ann_Arbor,_Michigan.

36. Robert Faber, "Anti-war protests of the 1960s and '70s changed the political face of Ann Arbor," AnnArbor.com, 15 February 2012, accessed 13 June 2013, http://www .annarbor.com/news/how-the-anti-war-protests-of-the-1960s-and-'70s-changed-the -political-face-of-ann-arbor/; "Hash Bash 2013," *High Times,* 8 April 2013, accessed 14 June 2013, http://www.hightimes.com/read/hash-bash-2013-0; "Thousands Rally for Marijuana Legalization at Annual Hash Bash in Ann Arbor," *Detroit Free Press,* 6 April 2013, accessed 14 June 2013, http://www.freep.com/article/20130406/ NEWS05/130406025/Thousands%20rally%20for%20marijuana%20legalization%20 at%20annual%20Hash%20Bash%20in%20Ann%20Arbor.

37. "Human Rights Party (United States)," *Wikipedia,* accessed 13 June 2013, http:// en.wikipedia.org/wiki/Human_Rights_Party_(United_States).

38. ArborWeb, Ann Arbor City Guide, Religion, accessed 13 June 2013, http://arbor web.com/cg/to064.html. Washtenaw County (including Ann Arbor, Ypsilanti, Saline, Milan, and Chelsea) has considerably more congregations and denominations. "Washtenaw County, Michigan Religion Statistics Profile," City-Data.com, accessed 13 June 2013, http://www.city-data.com/county/religion/Washtenaw-County-MI.html.

39. Ira M. Sheskin, *The 2010 Update to the 2005 Detroit Jewish Population Study* (Mandell L. Berman North American Jewish Data Bank, April 2011), accessed 9 August 2011, http://www.jewishdatabank.org/Archive/C-MI-Detroit-2005-Slide_Set_L_2010 _Update_Presentation.pdf.

40. The ratio was 50.58 percent females to 49.42 percent males. "Ann Arbor Michigan Population and Demographics Resources," U.S. Census 2000, accessed 6 August 2011, http://annarbor.areaconnect.com/statistics.htm.

41. Paula Gardner, "Ann Arbor Is 6th Largest Michigan City and Other Washtenaw County Facts from New U.S. Census Data," *Ann Arbor News,* 22 March 2011, accessed 6 August 2011, http://annarbor.com/business-review/ann-arbor-is-6th-largest-michigan -city-and-other-washtenaw-county-facts-from-new-us-census-data/?cmpid=NL_DH _topheadlines.

42. *The American Jewish Year Book* 2006 has 7,000 Jews in Ann Arbor; it's grown since then. Phone conversation with David Shtulman, executive director of the Jewish Federation of Washtenaw County, 18 December 2008.

43. Sheskin, *The 2005 Detroit Jewish Population Study,* table 4–10, 25. See also Irwin J. Cohen, *Echoes of Detroit's Jewish Communities: A History* (Lainsburg, MI: Boreal Press, 2003).

44. Thanks to study participant Gary Michaels for introducing me to the term "hidden *yidden.*"

45. Jane and Michael Stern, "Bread Alone: In Search of the Best Rye Bread in America," *Saveur,* 16 March 2011, accessed 7 June 2013, http://www.saveur.com/article/Travels/ best-rye-breads-in-america.

46. Phone conversation with David Shtulman, executive director of the Jewish Federation of Washtenaw County, 26 June 2013.

47. The Hebrew Day School of Ann Arbor is formally affiliated with the Schechter Day School Network, part of the United Synagogue of Conservative Judaism, but "serves the entire range of religious and cultural Jewish expressions in Ann Arbor and the surrounding area." "Our Mission," Hebrew Day School of Ann Arbor, accessed 3 June 2013, http:// hdsaa.org/mission.php.

48. Roy Thomas, interview by author, 4 March 2009, Ann Arbor, MI.

49. Morton Langfeld, interview by author, 13 March 2009, Ann Arbor, MI.

50. According to Sheskin, "The Detroit Jewish community contains 18,903 married couples. 76% (14,329 married couples) of married couples involve in-marriages between two persons born or raised Jewish, 8% (1,493 married couples) involve conversionary in-marriages, and 16% (3,081 married couples) involve intermarriages. . . . The couples intermarriage rate differs according to age: decreasing from 22% for married couples in households under age 35 to 18% for married couples in households age 35–64 and 10% for married couples in households age 65 and over." His explanation about rates of intermarriage is exemplary: Intermarriage rates may be reported based on married couples or individuals. As an illustration, imagine that two weddings occur. In wedding one, Moshe (a Jew) marries Rachel (also a Jew). In wedding two, Abraham (a Jew) marries Christine (a non-Jew). Thus, there are two married couples, one of whom is intermarried. In this illustration, the couples intermarriage rate is 50 percent. Another method of calculating an intermarriage rate, however, is to note that there are three Jews (Moshe, Rachel, and Abraham) and one of the three (Abraham) is married to a non-Jew (Christine). In this illustration, the individual intermarriage rate is 33 percent. Sheskin, *The 2005 Detroit Jewish Population Study,* Main Report, vol. 1, ch. 6, p. 91.

51. Sheskin, *The 2005 Detroit Jewish Population Study,* Main Report, vol. 1, 90–92. See Table 6–29 on pp. 94–96. The comparative perspective in this report is based on data from 1986–2005. In Sheskin's 2010 New Haven Jewish population report, which is

based on 1993–2010, Detroit maintained its position in fourth place. Ira M. Sheskin, *The 2010 Greater New Haven Jewish Population Study* (Jewish Federation of Greater New Haven, June 2011), "Intermarriage Comparison with Other Communities," ch. 6, table 30, 96–98.

52. Stuart Kamden, interview by author, 9 January 2009, Ann Arbor, MI.

53. Morton Langfeld, interview by author, 13 March 2009, Ann Arbor, MI.

54. Matthew Boxer, "Community Size and Identity," *Sh'ma*, June 2007, 7. See also Matthew Boxer, "Jewish Identity on All Frontiers: The Effect of Jewish Community Size on Jewish Identity" (PhD dissertation, University of Wisconsin-Madison, 10 October 2013).

55. Larry Rush, interview by author, digital recording, 15 December 2008, Ann Arbor, MI.

56. Ben Levine, interview by author, digital recording, 8 January 2009, Ann Arbor, MI.

57. Lauren Apteker, interview by author, digital recording, 18 January 2010, Ann Arbor, MI.

58. Gary Brodin, interview by author, digital recording, 19 November 2008, Ann Arbor, MI.

59. Samuel Isserman, interview by author, digital recording, 8 December 2008, Ann Arbor, MI.

60. Allan Benjamin, interview by author, digital recording, 21 November 2008, Ann Arbor, MI.

61. Mark Entennman, interview by author, digital recording, 9 December 2008, Ann Arbor, MI.

62. Michael Bellow, interview by author, digital recording, 10 December 2008, Ann Arbor, MI.

63. Bellow, interview.

64. Walter Chatham, interview by author, digital recording, 23 January 2009, Ann Arbor, MI.

65. Felix Garrison, interview by author, digital recording, 11 December 2008, Ann Arbor, MI.

66. Sue Fishkoff, "New Jew Cool," *Reform Judaism* 33, no. 1 (Fall 2004).

67. Paul Chazen, interview by author, digital recording, 8 January 2009, Ann Arbor, MI.

68. Morris Aker, interview by author, digital recording, 15 December 2008, Ann Arbor, MI.

69. Laura M. Holson and Nick Bilton, "Facebook's Royal Wedding," *New York Times*, 25 May 2012.

70. Of Asians, 27.7 percent intermarried, compared to 25.7 percent of Hispanics, 17.1 percent of blacks, and 9.4 of whites. Wendy Wang, *The Rise of Intermarriage: Rates, Characteristics Vary by Race and Gender* (Washington, DC: Pew Research Center, 2012); Hope Yen, "Interracial Marriage in the U.S. Climbs to New High, Study Finds," *Huffington Post*, 16 February 2012, http://www.huffingtonpost.com/2012/02/16/interracial-marriage-in-us_n_1281229.html.

71. Dana Evan Kaplan, "How Did We Lose Him?," *Forward*, 8 June 2012, 9.

72. "Zuckerberg's Dinners with Girlfriend Help Spur Life-Saving Facebook Tool," *ABC News*, 1 May 2012; Keren McGinity, "Mazel Tov Mark Zuckerberg," unpublished

letter to the editor. See also Kevin Lincoln, "Priscilla Chan Is Not 'Mrs. Zuckerberg,'" *Buzzfeed* (n.d).

73. Doug Gross, "Facebook's Zuckerberg Is Nation's No. 2 Charitable Donor," *CNN*, 12 February 2013, accessed 23 October 2013, http://www.cnn.com/2013/02/12/tech/social-media/zuckerberg-top-philanthropist.

74. Joshua Henkin, "Guest Blogger: Joshua Henkin on Stereotypes of Jewish Men and Jewish Women," *Jewess: The Tribe's Better Half*, 9 October 2007, accessed 23 October 2013, http://jewess.canonist.com/?p=623.

75. Clare O'Connor, "Mark Zuckerberg's Wife Priscilla Chan: A New Brand of Billionaire Bride," *Forbes*, 20 May 2012, accessed 23 October 2013, http://www.forbes.com/sites/clareoconnor/2012/05/20/mark-zuckerbergs-wife-priscilla-chan-a-new-brand-of-billionaire-bride/.

76. My understanding is that, according to the school, others were also excluded.

77. Noah Feldman, "Orthodox Paradox," *New York Times Magazine*, 22 July 2007.

78. Norman Lamm, "A Response to Noah Feldman," *Forward*, 2 August 2007, web exclusive, http://www.forward.com/articles/11308/, accessed 13 April 2011; "Letters," *New York Times Magazine*, 5 August 2007; "Noah Feldman *New York Times* Controversy" (Orthodox Union letters to and responses from the *New York Times*, OU reply to *New York Times* Editor's Message; initial OU response printed in *New York Times Magazine*), 3 August 2007, Institute for Public Affairs, accessed 22 May 2009. http://advocacy.ou.org/2007/noah_feldman_as_the_jewish_jayson_blair/#.TnkKo3P-SX0.

79. Feldman, "Orthodox Paradox."

80. My gratitude to Jonathan D. Sarna and his Near Eastern and Judaic Studies students in the course "Judaism Confronting America" for raising this important point about JDate after my guest lecture 6 October 2011 at Brandeis University. My meteorology reference is a small way of paying homage to the legacy of sociologist Egon Mayer, *z"l*, who once opined that fighting intermarriage in an open, democratic pluralistic society was like opposing the weather: "You can't change it." See Keren R. McGinity, *Still Jewish: A History of Women and Intermarriage in America* (New York: NYU Press, 2009), 206–207.

81. Kathy Seal, "Raising Children on Kugel and Kimchi, and as Jews: New Study Suggests That Asian-Jewish Families May Be Likely to Raise Jewish Children," *Forward*, 27 May 2011, front page, 7.

82. Helen Kim and Noah Leavitt, "It's Not Just about the Food: Jewish American and Asian American Marriages" (paper presented at Association for Jewish Studies Conference, December 2009). Thanks to Noah and Helen for sharing their work with me and for their intellectual camaraderie. See also Helen Kim and Noah Leavitt, "The Newest Jews? Understanding Jewish American and Asian American Marriages," *Contemporary Jewry* (Springer) 32, no. 2 (July 2012): 135–166; and "Second-Generation Asian Americans and Judaism," in *Sustaining Faith Traditions: Race, Ethnicity, and Religion among the Latino and Asian American Second Generations*, ed. Carolyn Chen and Russell Jeung (New York: NYU Press, 2012), 69–90.

83. Kathy Seal, "To Have and to Hold: A New Study Explores the Prevalence of Asian-Jewish Coupling," *KoreAm*, 3 June 2011, accessed 27 July 2011. http://iamkoream.com/june-issue-examining-asian-jewish-marriages/.

84. Amy Chua, "Why Chinese Mothers Are Superior: Can a Regimen of No Playdates, No TV, No Computer Games and Hours of Music Practice Create Happy Kids? And What Happens When They Fight Back?," *Wall Street Journal*, 8 January 2011.

85. Blogger Chris Abraham, transcript of interview of Amy Chua by John McLaughlin on "One to One," weekend May 22–23, 2004, accessed 26 July 2011, http://chrisabraham.com/2007/07/29/i-am-amazed-by-amy-chua/.

86. Julie Wiener, "Roaring Back at the Tiger Mom: Jewish Mothers Get in Some Parenting Licks in Favor of Guilt, Play, Community," *Jewish Week*, 18 January 2011, accessed 24 January 2011, http://www.thejewishweek.com/news/new_york/roaring_back_tiger_mom; Julie Gruenbaum Fax, "Amy Chua's Tiger Mom Has Jewish Moms Ready for Battle," *Jewish Journal*, 19 January 2011, accessed 24 January 2011, http://www.jewishjournal.com/bloggish/item/amy_chuas_tiger_mom_has_jewish_moms_ready_for_battle_20110119/; and Beth Kissileff, "An Open Letter to Amy Chua," *Raising Kvell*, 21 January 2011, accessed 24 January 2011, http://www.kveller.com/blog/parenting/an-open-letter-to-amy-chua/.

87. Robin Wilson, "Study of Asian-Jewish Couples Finds Few Tiger Moms," interview with Helen Kim and Noah Leavitt, *Chronicle of Higher Education* 57, no. 25 (25 February 2011): A4.

88. "Soy Vay: Our History," accessed 27 July 2011, http://www.soyvay.com/index.php?main_page=page&id=5&chapter=0.

89. "Soy Vay: In the Press," *San Diego Jewish Press*, 17 February 1995, accessed 27 July 2011, http://www.soyvay.com/index.php?main_page=page&id=17&chapter=0.

90. Thanks to Ethan, Miho and Naomi Segal for granting me permission to describe their lovely card tradition.

91. Jamie Narva converted to Judaism before the couple wed. The 1,001 cranes symbolize long life, fidelity, peace, celebration, joy, and good luck. I am grateful to Shari Mae Narva for showing me this beautiful example of Japanese Judaica and to Josh and Jamie for their permission to mention it.

92. Paul Golin, "Jewish Intermarriage Myth Busted?," *Huffington Post*, 16 July 2011, accessed 24 January 2011, http://www.huffingtonpost.com/paul-golin/if-differences-can-streng_b_807727.html.

93. Paul Golin, "My Jewpanese Wedding," *InterfaithFamily.com*, accessed 27 September 2011, http://www.interfaithfamily.com/life_cycle/weddings/My_Jewpanese_Wedding.shtml; Paul Golin, "Proud 'Jewpanese' Americans," *InterfaithFamily.com*, accessed 27 September 2011, http://www.interfaithfamily.com/relationships/marriage_and_relationships/Proud_Jewpanese_Americans.shtml.

94. Golin, "My Jewpanese Wedding."

95. Golin, "Proud 'Jewpanese' Americans."

96. Eli Valley, "Bucky Shvitz: Sociologist for Hire," *Forward*, 4 June 2010, 13.

97. Paul Spickard, *Mixed Blood: Intermarriage and Ethnic Identity in Twentieth-Century America* (Madison: University of Wisconsin Press, 1989), 158.

98. Nat Lehrman's mother softened as soon as she actually met his fiancée, who learned to make matzah ball soup and used chopsticks to flip latkes, and the couple remained married for more than fifty years. Josh Lambert, "My Son, the Pornographer," *Tablet*, 24 February 2010, accessed 25 October 2013, http://www.tabletmag.com/jewish-arts-and-culture/books/26418/my-son-the-pornographer.

99. "No More Jewish Husbands," *Asian Week*, 15 November 2008, accessed 18 March 2010, http://www.asianweek.com/2008/11/15/no-more-jewish-husbands/.

100. Wilson, "Study of Asian-Jewish Couples Finds Few Tiger Moms."

101. Seal, "To Have and to Hold."

102. Gish Gen, *Mona in the Promised Land: A Novel* (New York: Vintage Books, 1996).

103. Amy Tan, *The Joy Luck Club* (New York: Penguin Group, 1989), 33–34. For an interesting oral history about Jews in China dating back more than a thousand years, see Xu Xin with Beverly Friend, *Legends of the Chinese Jews of Kaifeng* (Hoboken, NJ: Ktav, 1995).

104. See, for example, "Why Davids Desire Debs: Forbidden Fruit," in *The Jewish American Prince Handbook,* by Sandy Toback and Debbie Haback (Chicago: Turnbull and Willoughby, 1986), 106.

105. Rahm Emanuel, quoted in *The Nastiest Things Ever Said about Democrats,* ed. Martin Higgins (Guilford, CT: Lyons Press, 2006), 49. Also cited by Ben Smith and John F. Harris, "Emanuel Pick Sends Powerful Signal," *Politico,* 6 November 2008, http://www.politico.com/news/stories/1108/15388_Page2.html.

106. I am grateful to several people who convinced me that using "Christian" was preferable to "gentile," including Deborah Dash Moore, Maura Epstein, Anne Bellows, and Rachael Koehler. See also Sarah Bunim Benor, "Do American Jews Speak a 'Jewish Language'? A Model of Jewish Linguistic Distinctiveness," *Jewish Quarterly Review* 99, no. 2 (Spring 2009): 230–269.

107. McGinity, *Still Jewish*. See also Jonathan D. Sarna, "Intermarriage in America: The Jewish Experience in Historical Context," in *Ambivalent Jew: Charles Liebman in Memoriam,* ed. Stuart Cohen and Bernard Susser (New York: Jewish Theological Seminary of America, 2007). For a global perspective, see Shulamit Reinharz and Sergio DellaPergola, eds., *Jewish Intermarriage around the World* (New Brunswick, NJ: Transaction Publishers, 2009).

1. PROFESSIONAL MEN

Epigraph: Rabbi Shmuley Boteach, *The Broken American Male: And How to Fix Him* (New York: St. Martin's Press, 2008), 43.

1. Morris Aker, interview by author, digital recording, 15 December 2008, Ann Arbor, MI.

2. Locating these interviewees was accomplished in several different ways. Advertisements were placed in publications that attracted attention from both the religiously affiliated and the unaffiliated. In lieu of some print publications whose classified rates are prohibitive, electronic bulletin boards and mailing lists were utilized to target more local populations. I submitted copy to select synagogues and churches with the request that it be included in their newsletters and displayed on their bulletin boards. I also posted flyers. And I conducted snowball sampling whereby I asked respondents to refer me to other men they know who are intermarried to further diversify the sample.

3. Jennifer A. Thompson found the same pattern in her fieldwork about intermarried couples: "Jewish men . . . insisted that their children had to be raised in Judaism." Jennifer A. Thompson, "'He Wouldn't Know Anything': Rethinking Women's Religious Leadership," *Journal of the American Academy of Religion,* 25 April 2013, 9. See also Jennifer A. Thompson, *Jewish on Their Own Terms: How Intermarried Couples Are Changing American Judaism* (New Brunswick, NJ: Rutgers University Press, 2014).

4. This paragraph paraphrases my book *Still Jewish: A History of Women in America* (New York: NYU Press, 2009), 64.

5. The reported figures were 6.7 percent in 1941–1950 and between 6.4 and 5.9 percent in 1951–1960. Fred Massarik et al., *National Jewish Population Study: Intermarriage,*

Facts for Planning (New York: Council of Jewish Federations and Welfare Funds, 1971), 10. These figures indicate the percentages of Jewish persons who intermarried by time period.

6. "Holmes Says Love Overcomes Mixed Marriage Difficulties," *New York Times*, 26 January 1931, 13.

7. Dorothy Barclay, "Mixed-Religion Marriage Called Difficult to Sustain," *New York Times*, 2 April 1957, 60.

8. Renee C. Romano, *Race Mixing: Black-White Marriage in Postwar America* (Cambridge, MA: Harvard University Press, 2003), 3, 123–124. See also William S. Cohen with Janet Langhart Cohen, *Love in Black and White: A Memoir of Race, Religion, and Romance* (Lanham, MD: Rowman & Littlefield, 2007).

9. This paragraph and the one that follows it paraphrase my book *Still Jewish*, 156–157.

10. Calvin Goldscheider, "Are American Jews Vanishing Again?," *Contexts* 2 (Winter 2003): 18–24; editorial, "The 52% Fraud," *Forward*, 12 September 2003; Jason Nielsen, "Long-Awaited Population Study Offers Mixed Verdict," *Jewish Advocate*, 12–18 September 2003; Calvin Goldscheider, "Why the Population Survey Counts," *Forward*, 11 October 2002, 11.

11. Barry A. Kosmin et al., *Highlights of the CJF 1990 National Jewish Population Survey* (New York: Council of Jewish Federations, 1991), 14; Fred Massarik et al., *National Jewish Population Study: Intermarriage, Facts for Planning* (New York: Council of Jewish Federations and Welfare Funds, 1971), 10.

12. Laurence Kotler-Berkowitz et al., *The National Jewish Population Survey 2000–01: Strength, Challenge and Diversity in the American Jewish Population* (New York: United Jewish Communities, 2003), 16–17.

13. Sherry Israel, *Boston's Jewish Community: The 1985 Demographic Study* (Boston: Combined Jewish Philanthropies of Greater Boston, 1987), 58; and Sherry Israel, *Comprehensive Report on the 1995 Demographic Study* (Boston: Combined Jewish Philanthropies of Greater Boston, 1997), 114; Morris Axelrod, Floyd J. Fowler, Jr., and Arnold Gurin, *A Community Survey for Long Range Planning: A Study of the Jewish Population of Greater Boston* (Boston: Combined Jewish Philanthropies, 1967), 168–169, table 15.2; Floyd J. Fowler, Jr., *1975 Community Survey: A Study of the Jewish Population of Greater Boston* (Boston: Combined Jewish Philanthropies, 1975), 67, table 5.16.

14. The majority from the two largest ancestry groups, English and Germans, did not marry outside their ethnic groups in part due to larger numbers of potential partners and their concentration. Richard Alba, "Intermarriage and Ethnicity among European Americans," in *Jewish Intermarriage and Its Social Context*, ed. Paul Ritterband (New York: Jewish Outreach Institute and Center for Jewish Studies, Graduate School of the City University of New York, 1991), 5–8. Material in the paper I cite was originally taken from the author's book *Ethnic Identity: The Transformation of White America* (New Haven, CT: Yale University Press, 1990).

15. The normalization of inter-ethnic marriage occurred despite the fact that the census did not provide information about people's religion because the findings were part of a larger trend that included interfaith marriage patterns. Richard D. Alba and Reid M. Gordon, "Patterns of Ethnic Marriage in the United States," *Social Forces* 65, no. 1 (September 1986): 213. See also Richard D. Alba, quoted by Glenn Collins in "A New Look at Intermarriage in the US," *New York Times*, 11 February 1985, C13.

16. Alba, "Intermarriage and Ethnicity among European Americans," 8.

17. Rabbi Jeffrey K. Salkin, *Searching for My Brothers: Jewish Men in a Gentile World* (New York: Berkley Publishing Group, 1999), 112–113.

18. Aviva Cantor, *Jewish Women/Jewish Men* (San Francisco: HarperCollins, 1995), 130. The theory that Jewish men were good husbands may have, inadvertently, helped disguise some Jewish men's involvement in wife beating and desertion. Although none of the men I interviewed admitted physically abusing their wives, some did admit emotional neglect and infidelity. By and large, however, the respondents were—according to their own self-evaluations—model husbands. The full American population of Jewish men, however, we know to have been less than perfect. See Mimi Scarf, "Marriages Made in Heaven? Battered Jewish Wives," in *On Being a Jewish Feminist: A Reader,* ed. Susanna Heschel (New York: Schocken Books, 1983), 51–64; Abraham Twersky, *The Shame Born of Silence: Spouse Abuse in the Jewish Community* (Pittsburgh: Mirkov Publications, 1996); and Naomi Graetz, *Silence Is Deadly: Judaism Confronts Wifebeating* (Northvale, NJ: Jason Aronson, 1998).

19. See Joyce Antler, *You Never Call! You Never Write! A History of the Jewish of the Jewish Mother* (Oxford: Oxford University Press, 2007).

20. Sandy Toback and Debbie Haback, *The Jewish American Prince Handbook: From Bris to Bar Mitzvah and Beyond* (Chicago: Turnbull and Willoughby Publishers, 1986), 105.

21. Toback and Haback, *The Jewish American Prince Handbook,* cover.

22. Ben Levine, interview by author, digital recording, 8 January 2009, Ann Arbor, MI.

23. Philip Roth, *Portnoy's Complaint* (New York: Random House, 1969), 153.

24. Leslie A. Fiedler, "The Jew as Mythic American," *Ramparts,* Autumn 1963, 35.

25. Approximately 5 percent of the 750,000 members of JDate, the Jewish online matchmaking site, are not Jewish. "Why Do Jews Intermarry, and Who Wants to Marry a Jew, Anyway?," *JTA,* 22 May 2013, accessed 28 May 2013, http://www.jta.org/2013/05/22/life-religion/why-do-jews-intermarry-and-who-wants-to-marry-a-jew-anyway. I contacted JDate twice to discern the gender breakdown of the 5 percent, to no avail.

26. Peter N. Stearns, *Be A Man! Males in Modern Society,* 2nd ed. (New York: Homes & Meier, 1990), 161.

27. Cited in Robert L. Griswold, *Fatherhood in America: A History* (New York: Basic Books, 1993), 187.

28. Robert E. Gould, "Measuring Masculinity by the Size of a Paycheck," cited in *Men and Masculinity,* ed. Joseph H. Pleck and Jack Sawyer (Englewood Cliffs, NJ: Prentice-Hall, 1974), 98.

29. Chaim I. Waxman, "The Jewish Father: Past and Present," in *A Mensch among Men: Explorations in Jewish Masculinity,* ed. Harry Brod (Freedom, CA: Crossing Press, 1988), 65, 72n21; Fred L. Strodbeck, "Family Integration, Values, and Achievement," in *Education, Economy, and Society: A Reader in the Sociology of Education,* ed. A. H. Halsey, Jean Floud, and C. Arnold Anderson (New York: Free Press, 1961).

30. Rachel Kranson, "What Kind of Job Is *That* for a Nice Jewish Boy?' Grappling with Jewish Masculinity in an Era of Affluence, 1945–1967," excerpt from "Grappling with the Good Life: Jewish Anxieties over Affluence in Postwar America" (PhD dissertation, New York University, 2012).

31. Norman Podhoretz, *Making It* (New York: Random House, 1967), 25. I am indebted to Gina Morantz-Sanchez for bringing this book to my attention.

32. Larry King, quoted in Abigail Pogrebin, *Stars of David: Prominent Jews Talk about Being Jewish* (New York: Broadway Books, 2005), 320, 322.

33. Kirk Edwards, interview by author, digital recording, 5 December 2008.

34. Stearns, *Be A Man!*, 161.

35. Stephanie Coontz, *The Way We Never Were: American Families and the Nostalgia Trap* (New York: Basic Books, 1992), 25.

36. Elaine Tyler May, *Homeward Bound: American Families in the Cold War Era* (New York: Basic Books, 1999), 187.

37. Mirra Komarovsky, "Cultural Contradictions and Sex Roles: The Masculine Case," *American Journal of Sociology*, 78, no. 4 (January 1973): 883.

38. Judith Porter and Alex A. Albert, "Attitudes toward Women's Role: Does a 'Jewish Subculture' Exist in America?," *Gratz College Annual of Jewish Studies* 5 (1976): 132–133.

39. Marilyn Yalom, *A History of the Wife* (New York: Harper Collins, 2001), 366, 371; Nancy F. Cott, *Public Vows: A History of Marriage and the Nation* (Cambridge, MA: Harvard University Press, 2000), 204.

40. Michael Gold, "The Real Jewish Father," in *A Mensch among Men: Explorations in Jewish Masculinity*, ed. Harry Brod (Freedom, CA: Crossing Press, 1988), 85.

41. May, *Homeward Bound*, 200–203.

42. Rhona Rapoport and Robert N. Rapoport, "The Dual Career Family: A Variant Pattern and Social Change," *Human Relations* 22 (1969): 3–30, cited in Yalom, *A History of the Wife*, 380.

43. Paul C. Glick of the U.S. Census Bureau, cited in Jon Norheimer, "The Family in Transition: A Challenge from Within," *New York Times*, 27 November 1977, 74.

44. Stearns, *Be a Man!*, 161–167.

45. Fred Stevens, interview by author, digital recording, 12 December 2008, Ann Arbor, MI. His sentiments toward Jewish women illustrated his being intimidated by their intellect and ambition: "My view of Jewish women was that they were *really* smart, smarter than me."

46. Seth Roller, interview by author, digital recording, 15 December 2008, Ann Arbor, MI.

47. Edward S. Shapiro, *A Time for Healing: American Jewry since World War II* (Baltimore: Johns Hopkins University Press, 1992), 125.

48. Shapiro, *A Time for Healing*, 143.

49. Deborah Dash Moore, *At Home in America* (New York: Columbia University Press, 1981), 85, 254n33; *Forward*, 4 July 1926, as translated and quoted by *Jewish Daily Bulletin*, 7 July 1926.

50. May, *Homeward Bound*, xviii.

51. James H. S. Bossard, "Residential Propinquity as a Factor in Marriage Selection," *American Journal of Sociology*, 38 no. 2 (September 1932): 219–224; Ruby Jo Reeves Kennedy, "Premarital Residential Propinquity and Ethnic Endogamy," *American Journal of Sociology* 48, no. 5 (March 1943): 580–584; John L. Thomas, "The Factor of Religion in the Selection of Marriage Mates," *American Sociological Review* 16, no. 4 (August 1951): 491.

52. Marshall Sklare, *Jewish Identity on the Suburban Frontier: A Study of Group Survival in the Open Society* (Chicago: University of Chicago Press, 1979), 270–271. Sklare's observation is pertinent to Jewish men meeting Christian women, although it should be noted that interfaith marriage was not predominantly the case in Lakeville, Minnesota.

53. Ellen K. Rothman, *Hands and Hearts: A History of Courtship in America* (New York: Basic Books, 1984), cited in Howard Chudacoff, *The Age of the Bachelor: Creating an American Subculture* (Princeton: Princeton University Press, 1999), 71.

54. Frank Morton, interview by author, digital recording, 16 January 2009, Ann Arbor, MI.

55. Bert Feldman, interview by author, digital recording, 16 December 2008, Ann Arbor, MI.

56. Roger Levine, *In Search of the Golden Shiksa* (self-published, 22 October 2010). E-mail communication to author, 23 September 2009. I am grateful to Roger Levine for sharing his book manuscript and candor.

57. "50 Years After the Kinsey Report," CBS News, 11 February 2009, Associated Press.

58. Christopher Blazina, *The Secret Lives of Men: What Men Want You to Know about Love, Sex, and Relationships* (Deerfield Beach, FL: Healthfield Communications, 2008), 207.

59. Nathan Bloomer, interview by author, digital recording, 22 January 2009, Ann Arbor, MI.

60. Frank Morton, interview by author, digital recording, 16 January 2009, Ann Arbor, MI.

61. In one passage, Wylie goes to the extreme of comparing American mothers to Hitler! Philip Wylie, *Generation of Vipers* (Champaign, IL: Dalkey Archive Press, 2007), 194–217.

62. Felix Phillips, interview by author, digital recording, 10 December 2008, Ann Arbor, MI.

63. Ben Levine, interview by author, digital recording, 8 January 2009, Ann Arbor, MI.

64. Blazina, *The Secret Lives of Men*, 207.

65. Stephanie Coontz, *The Way We Never Were: American Families and the Nostalgia Trap* (New York: Basic Books, 1992), 222.

66. Brian Geller, interview by author, digital recording, 16 February 2009, Ann Arbor, MI.

67. Stearns, *Be A Man!*, 172.

68. Felix Phillips, interview by author, digital recording, 10 December 2008, Ann Arbor, MI.

69. Nathan Bloomer, interview by author, digital recording, 22 January 2009, Ann Arbor, MI.

70. Bloomer, interview. "Righteous Gentiles" is the phrase used for non-Jews who risked their lives to save Jews during the Holocaust.

71. Helen Epstein, *Children of the Holocaust: Conversations with Sons and Daughters of Survivors* (New York: Penguin, 1979), 209–210.

72. Susan Simpson Geroe, *The Silence of the Parents: A Novel* (McKinleyville, CA: Fithian Press, 2006), frontispiece.

73. Gary Gerstle, *American Crucible: Race and Nation in the Twentieth Century* (Princeton, NJ: Princeton University Press, 2001), 8, 126–127.

74. Arthur Hertzberg, *The Jews in America: Four Centuries of An Uneasy Encounter* (New York: Columbia University Press, 1997), 290–291.

75. Michael E. Staub, *Torn at the Roots: The Crisis of Jewish Liberalism in Postwar America* (New York: Columbia University Press, 2002), 8–9. Staub cites Edward S.

Shapiro, *A Time for Healing: American Jewry since World War II* (Baltimore: Johns Hopkins University Press, 1992), 3; Peter Novick, *The Holocaust in American Life* (Boston: Houghton Mifflin, 1999) 1; and Irving Howe, *World of Our Fathers* (New York: Harcourt, Brace, Jovanovich, 1976), 627.

76. Hasia Diner, *We Remember with Reverence and Loves: American Jews and the Myth of Silence after the Holocaust, 1945–1962* (New York: NYU Press 2009), 5–6, 9.

77. Hasia R. Diner, *The Jews of the United States, 1654–2000* (Berkeley: University of California Press, 2004), 264.

78. James Rubin, quoted by Pogrebin, *Stars of David,* 58.

79. Charles Revkin, interview by author, digital recording, 11 January 2009, Ann Arbor, MI.

80. Epstein, *Children of the Holocaust,* 210.

81. Epstein, *Children of the Holocaust,* 210.

82. Aaron Hass, *In the Shadow of the Holocaust: The Second Generation* (Ithaca, NY: Cornell University Press, 1990), 115.

83. Gary Brodin, interview by author, digital recording, 19 November 2008, Ann Arbor, MI.

84. Interviews by author with Bob Melton, December 11, 2008; Kobie Martin, March 9, 2009; and George Maze, December 4, 2008; digital recordings.

85. Kalman Long, interview by author, digital recording, 4 December 2008, Ann Arbor, MI.

86. Long, interview.

87. Mark Entennman, interview by author, digital recording, 9 December 2008, Ann Arbor, MI.

88. "For most of the last half of the twentieth century, this was a position that Reform had either shared with or conceded to Conservative Judaism. Orthodoxy, which for much of the past 50 years had experienced numerical declines, seems to have stabilized as a denominational preference and appears demographically poised for future growth." Jonathon Ament, *United Jewish Communities Report Series on the National Jewish Population Survey 2000–2001: American Jewish Religious Denominations,* report 10, (February 2005), 8; and table 3, "Childhood and Current Denominational Preferences," 10.

89. Pew Research Center's Religion & Public Life Project, *A Portrait of Jewish Americans: Findings from a Pew Research Center Survey of U.S. Jews* (Washington, DC: Pew Research Center, 2013), 10.

90. Sixty-seven percent of Reform households made more than $75,000 a year compared to 57 percent of Conservative Jewish households. Pew Forum on Religion and Public Life, *U.S. Religious Landscape Survey* (Washington, DC: Pew Research Center, 2008), "Summary of Key Findings" and "Income Level by Religious Tradition," 5; appendix 1, "Detailed Data Tables," 78. See also David Leonhardt, "Is Your Religion Your Financial Destiny?," *New York Times Magazine,* 15 May 2011, 18.

91. George Maze, interview by author, digital recording, 4 December 2008, Ann Arbor, MI.

92. Kobie Martin, interview by author, digital recording, 9 March 2009, Ann Arbor, MI.

93. See Keren R. McGinity, "Outreach versus In-reach," in *Still Jewish,* 203–209.

94. Gal Beckerman, "New Study Finds That It's Not a Lack of Welcome That's Keeping the Intermarrieds Away," *Forward,* published 7 July 2010, issue of 16 July 2010.

95. Rabbi Levy, quoted in Julie Wiener, "Should Rabbis Say 'I Do' to Intermarriage?," *InterfaithFamily.com*, reprinted from the *New York Jewish Week*, 20 July 2007.

96. Julie Wiener, "Are More Rabbis Saying 'I Do' to Interfaith Weddings?," *New York Jewish Week*, 29 September 2010.

97. The couple must commit to establishing a Jewish home and raising Jewish children. Rabbi Keith Stern, "Intermarriage: A Reappraisal," Rosh Hashanah 5767 (2006), Temple Beth Avodah, Newton, MA.

98. "The Central Conference of American Rabbis Task Force on the Challenges of Intermarriage for the Reform Rabbi, March 2010." I am grateful to Rabbi Ralph Mecklenburger for sharing this document with me, and to Jim Deutchman for forwarding the opinion of Rabbi Reeve Robert Brenner from the 2010 CCAR Convention of Reform Rabbis. See also "Reform Rabbis, Largest Group of Jewish Clergy, Address Intermarriage at 121st Convention of the CCAR," press release, 8 March 2010, San Francisco, CA.

99. E-mail communication from Rabbi Robert D. Levy to author, 17 May 2013.

100. Rabbi Robert D. Levy, quoted in Karen Schwartz, "People to People: Ann Arbor Interfaith Families Say Their Community Is Especially Welcoming," *InterfaithFamily.com*, reprinted with permission of the *Detroit Jewish News*, accessed 20 October 2008.

101. Another described his first impression of the rabbi: "I really liked him, he makes jokes, he's well dressed, he's my age." Alvin Mitchells, interview by author, digital recording, 4 December 2008, Ann Arbor, MI.

102. Penny Schwartz, "More Reform Rabbis Agreeing to Officiate at Intermarriages," *Jewish Telegraphic Agency*, 3 July 2012. For a detailed summary of the earlier history of rabbinic debates about officiation, see McGinity, *Still Jewish*, 40–41, 127–130.

103. "Becoming a Member," Temple Beth Emeth, accessed 18 May 2013, www.temple bethemeth.org/about/join.

104. The 2000–2001 National Jewish Population Study (NJPS) reported that 33 percent of the children in households with one non-Jewish spouse were being raised Jewish, a slight increase from 1990, when the estimate reported was 28 percent. (The 2000–2001 data are based on the randomly selected children of all currently intermarried Jews that are being raised as Jewish, 38 percent of children; the 33 percent in the NJPS was based on a multiple response analysis of all children in the household.) Kotler-Berkowitz et al., *National Jewish Population Survey 2000–01*, 3–4, 18; Kosmin et al., *Highlights of the CJF 1990 National Jewish Population Survey*, 16.

105. I am grateful to Gregory A. Smith for responding to my queries about gender. Unfortunately, insufficient sample size thwarted gender analysis of intermarried Jews raising their children as Jewish according to these definitions or as not Jewish. E-mail communication from Gregory A. Smith, director of U.S. Religion Surveys at Pew Research Center, 15 November 2013; Pew Research Center's Religion & Public Life Project, *A Portrait of Jewish Americans*, 67–68. Taking an inclusive approach to identity, the Jewish Outreach Institute interpreted these numbers to mean that 61 percent of Jewish interfaith families are raising their children with a Jewish identity. "Half Full or Half Empty?," JOI Blog, 14 October 2013, accessed 3 November 2013, http://joi.org/blog/?p=3584.

106. Thanks to Len Saxe for his take-away messages from Pew's study and enlightened interpretations. E-mail communication to author, 17 November 2013; e-mail to the Association for Social Scientific Study of Jewry list, 13 November 2013.

107. Theodore Sasson, "New Analysis of Pew Data: Children of Intermarriage Increasingly Identify as Jewish," *Tablet,* 11 November 2013, accessed 12 November 2013, http://www.tabletmag.com/jewish-news-and-politics/151506/young-jews-opt-in.

108. A 2005 Boston survey estimated that the proportion of children being raised Jewish by religion was 60 percent, considerably higher than in New York or Pittsburgh. Len Saxe et al., *The 2005 Boston Jewish Community Survey: Preliminary Findings* (Waltham, MA: Steinhardt Social Research Institute, November 2006), 12. See also Ira M. Sheskin, *The 2001 Jewish Community Study of Bergen County and North Hudson* (Teaneck, NJ: UJA Federation of Bergen County and North Hudson, 2002), vi, 36; and McGinity, *Still Jewish,* 185–186.

109. An analysis of the 2000–2001 National Jewish Population Survey found that of the roughly third of the children of all currently intermarried Jews being raised Jewish, it was 47 percent of children among intermarried women and 28 percent among intermarried men. The 2005 Boston Jewish Community Survey authors described: "Intermarried households where the Jewish parent is female are significantly more likely to raise their children as Jews. Jewish mothers married to non-Jews are near-universal in reporting that they raised their children as Jews. In contrast, Jewish fathers in interfaith relationships are much less likely to report that they are raising their children as Jews." In a qualitative sample of ninety young adult children of the intermarried, 77 percent of the respondents with Jewish mothers indicated that their Jewish parent encouraged them to "identify with the Jewish religion," compared to 45 percent of respondents with Jewish fathers. E-mail communication from Laurence Kotler-Berkowitz, NJPS research director at United Jewish Communities, via Sherry Israel, 5 January 2006; Saxe et al., *2005 Boston Jewish Community Survey,* 11–12; Pearl Beck, *A Flame Still Burns: The Dimensions and Determinants of Jewish Identity among Young Adult Children of the Intermarried* (New York: Jewish Outreach Institute, June 2005), 28–29. See also Linda J. Sax, *America's Jewish Freshman: Current Characteristics and Recent Trends among Students Entering College* (Los Angeles: Higher Education Research Institute, UCLA, June 2002), 52.

110. Sylvia Barack Fishman, *Double or Nothing? Jewish Families and Mixed Marriage* (Waltham, MA: Brandeis University Press, 2004).

111. Griswold, *Fatherhood in America,* 184.

112. Morris Aker, interview by author, digital recording, 15 December 2008, Ann Arbor, MI.

113. Keith Soller, interview by author, digital recording, 9 December 2008, Ann Arbor, MI.

114. Stevens, interview.

115. Aaron Brown, quoted in Pogrebin, *Stars of David,* 177.

116. Brian Geller, interview by author, digital recording, 16 February 2009, Ann Arbor, MI.

117. Fisher married Debbie Reynolds, Elizabeth Taylor, and Connie Stevens (all born Christian). Eddie Fisher, *Eddie: My Life, My Loves* (New York: Harper and Row, 1981), 156, 159.

118. Cokie Roberts and Steven V. Roberts, *From This Day Forward* (New York: William Morrow, 2000), 16.

119. Egon Mayer, *Love and Tradition: Marriage between Jews and Christians* (New York: Schocken Books, 1985), 267, citing Central Conference of American Rabbis, "Resolution of the Status of Children of Mixed Marriages," adopted March 15, 1983, mimeograph.

120. Jonathan D. Sarna, *American Judaism* (New Haven, CT: Yale University Press, 2004), 322–323. Sarna notes that Reconstructionism comprised less than 2 percent of the American Jewish population, which might explain why the 1968 decision received little attention.

121. Rabbi J. Simcha Cohen, *Intermarriage and Conversion: A Halakhic Solution* (Hoboken, NJ: Ktav, 1987), 3, 83.

122. Nadia Siritsky, "The Human Face of Intermarriage: A Rabbi's Pastoral Reflections," *InterfaithFamily.com*, May 11, 2009, accessed 29 September 2009. In the original, the word was "[their]."

123. Cohen, *Love in Black and White*, 24–25.

124. David A. M. Wilensky, "A Patrilineal Jew's Lament: What Would *You* Call Me?," *Forward*, 20 April 2012, 9.

125. Naomi Zeveloff, "30 Years On, Still Dissent on Patrilineal Descent," and "Patrilineal Jews Still Find Resistance: Denominations Stick to Traditional Definition of Who Is Jewish," *Forward*, 6 April 2012, cover story.

126. Kayla Higgins, "Jewish Enough," *Forward*, 13 April 2012, 16.

127. A total of 204 adults in their twenties and thirties were surveyed. Zohar Rotem et al., *Listening to the Adult Children of Intermarriage: What Jews with One Parent Need and Want from the Jewish Community* (New York: Jewish Outreach Institute, October 2013), 11–12.

128. Laurel Snyder, ed. *Half/Life: Jew-ish Tales from Interfaith Homes* (Brooklyn: Soft Skull Press, 2006), 6.

129. Informant A.B., entry in "The Silent Revolution: Autobiography, Soviet-Jewish Émigrés and Jewish Migration in the 21st Century," by Rebecca Kobrin, Columbia University. My gratitude to Rebecca, whose paper "Giving Voice to the Silent Revolution: Autobiographies of Russian-Jewish Émigrés" brought this entry to my attention. Biennial Scholars Conference on American Jewish History, June 11–13, 2012, Center for Jewish History, New York City.

130. Shira Belle McGinity gets full credit for encouraging me to read *Harry Potter!*

131. *Star Trek*, Paramount Pictures (2009), directed by J. J. Abrams, color, 127 min. My sincere thanks to Alex Romano for presenting a clip illustrating Spock's quandary at the Federation of Jewish Men's Clubs Retreat I attended in May of 2012.

132. Samuel Isserman, talk at *Kol Nidre* service, Fall 2008, shared with author. His son made aliyah to Israel and e-mailed his father the same day I interviewed him the documents from the Orthodox authority that performed his conversion to Judaism.

133. Zeveloff, "30 Years On, Still Dissent on Patrilineal Descent," and "Patrilineal Jews Still Find Resistance."

134. Naomi Schaefer Riley, *'Til Faith Do Us Part: How Interfaith Marriage Is Transforming America* (New York: Oxford University Press, 2013), 93.

135. Steve Solomon, "My Mother's Italian, My Father's Jewish & I'm In Therapy," recorded live at the Brentwood Theater, Los Angeles, CA, 2007, compact disc.

136. Yisrael Campbell, "Circumcise Me: A New Comedy on the Cutting Edge," Ryna Greenbaum JCC Center for the Arts, 17 March 2012, Newton, MA.

137. Jon Fisch, "Moo Shu Jew," 24 December 2012, China Pearl, Boston, MA.

138. Leonard Saxe et al., *Jewish Futures Project: The Impact of Taglit-Birthright Israel: 2010* Update (Waltham, MA: Brandeis University, Cohen Center for Modern Jewish Studies, 2011), 19–20. See also Leonard Saxe et al., *Generation Birthright Israel: The Im-*

pact of an Israel Experience on Jewish Identity and Choices (Waltham, MA: Brandeis University, Cohen Center for Modern Jewish Studies, 2009).

139. Bethamie Horowitz, *Connections and Journeys: Assessing Critical Opportunities for Enhancing Jewish Identity*, rev. ed. (New York: UJA Federation of Jewish Philanthropies, 2003).

140. Mirroring intermarried Jewish men's experiences, see story about son of intermarried father being rejected as Jewish by rabbi described by Cohen, *Love in Black and White*, 21–24.

141. While Jewish women expressed frustration or hurt, Jewish men more often severed ties. See McGinity, *Still Jewish*, 130. See also Egon Mayer, *Intermarriage and Rabbinic Officiation* (New York: American Jewish Committee, 1989); Bruce A. Phillips, "Interfaith Couples: Rabbinic Wedding Officiation and Subsequent Jewish Engagement," 40th Conference of the Association for Jewish Studies, 21 December 2008, Washington, DC; Rabbi Lawrence Raphael, "Embracing Interfaith Couples Only Strengthens Congregations," *JWeekly, Covering the San Francisco Jewish Bay Area*, 20 January 2006; Sue Fishkoff, "To Officiate or Not? Mixed Marriage on Agenda at Reform Rabbis Convention," *InterfaithFamily.com*, 22 June 2006.

142. Edward Cohen, *The Peddler's Grandson: Growing Up Jewish in Mississippi* (New York: Dell, 2002), 105. Thanks to Kirsten Fermaglich for recommending this title.

143. Morris Aker, interview by author, digital recording, 15 December 2008, Ann Arbor, MI.

144. Stuart Kamden, interview by author, digital recording, 9 December 2008, Ann Arbor, MI.

145. Kamden, interview.

146. Entennman, interview.

147. George Maze, interview by author, digital recording, 4 December 2008, Ann Arbor, MI.

148. Diane Ehrensaft, *Parenting Together: Men and Women Sharing the Care of the Their Children* (Urbana: University of Illinois Press, 1987); Sharon Meers and Joanna Strober, *Getting to 50/50: How Working Couples Can Have It All by Sharing It All* (New York: Bantam Books, 2009); Kim Parker and Wendy Wang, "Modern Parenthood: Roles of Moms and Dads Converge as They Balance Work and Family," *Social and Demographic Trends* (Washington, DC: Pew Research Center, 14 March 2013).

149. Shira Offer and Barbara Schneider, "Revisiting the Gender Gap in Time-Use Patterns: Multitasking and Well-Being among Mothers and Fathers in Dual-Earner Families," *American Sociological Review*, vol. 76, no. 6 (2011): 809–833; *Women in America: Indicators of Social and Economic Well-Being* (Washington, DC: U.S. Department of Commerce, Economics and Statistics Administration, 2011); Liana C. Sayer, "Gender, Time and Inequality: Trends in Women's and Men's Paid Work, Unpaid Work and Free Time," *Social Forces*, vol. 84, no. 1 (2005): 285–303.

150. Stevens, interview.

151. Although both fathers and mothers spend more time with their children than they did in the 1960s, the gender gap persists; mothers spend 13.5 hours compared to 7.3 hours for fathers. Parker and Wang, "Modern Parenthood," 6.

152. Griswold, *Fatherhood in America*, 248.

153. Beth S. Wenger, "Constructing Manhood in American Jewish Culture," in *Gender and Jewish History*, ed. Marion A. Kaplan and Deborah Dash Moore (Bloomington: Indiana University Press, 2011), 350.

2. SEX AND MONEY

Epigraph: Steve Jobs (1955–2011), as quoted in the *Wall Street Journal,* 25 May 1993.

1. This paragraph and the one that follows it paraphrase my book *Still Jewish: A History of Women and Intermarriage in America* (New York: NYU Press, 2009), 155, 157.

2. Although Gallup polls in 2000 and in 1980 showed that a consistent proportion of the population, 57 percent, thought religion was "very important," I believe that identification and membership are better measurements of religious engagement. Gallup Poll, conducted 24–27 August 2000, telephone interviews with a national adult sample of 1,019; Gallup Poll (AIPO), conducted 15–18 August 1980, personal interviews with a national adult sample of 1,600. I am grateful to Sarah Dutton, deputy director of surveys at CBS News, for the Gallup information. Barry A. Kosmin, Egon Mayer, and Ariela Keysar, *American Religious Identification Survey* (New York: Graduate Center of the City University of New York, 2001), 10–11, 13–15, Exhibit 1: "Self Described Religious Identification of U.S. Adult Population 1990–2001" and Exhibit 2: "Reported Household Membership in Church, Temple, Synagogue, or Mosque for Selected Religious Groups." ARIS cites aggregated survey data about a sample of 1,481 American adults from the General Social Survey 1972–1994, National Opinion Research Center, University of Chicago. ARIS is available online at http://www.gc.cuny.edu/studies/aris_index.htm.

3. Pew Forum on Religion & Public Life, *"Nones" on the Rise: One-in-Five Adults Have No Religious Affiliation* (Washington, DC: Pew Research Center, 2012). See also Katherine Ozment, "Losing Our Religion," *Boston Magazine,* January 2013, 70–79; and Barry A. Kosmin and Ariela Keysar, *American Religious Identification Survey, ARIS 2008 Summary Report* (Hartford, CT: Trinity College, March 2009), 3–4.

4. Between 2000 and 2010 the number of Jews who identified by non-religious criteria increased from 857,888 to 974,374. Leonard Saxe, *U.S. Jewry 2010: Estimates of the Size and Characteristics of the Population* (Waltham, MA: Maurice and Marilyn Cohen Center for Modern Jewish Studies and Steinhardt Social Research Institute, 20 December 2010). While older U.S. adults identified as Jewish by religion significantly more than younger adults, one in five Jews (22 percent) described "themselves as having no religion" by 2013. Pew Research Center's Religion & Life Project, *A Portrait of Jewish Americans: Findings from a Pew Research Center Survey of U.S. Jews* (Washington, DC: Pew Research Center, 2013), 7.

5. Although the ratio of intermarriage as it correlated to gender fluctuated with age, with men under the age of thirty-five and above the age of fifty-five more likely to have intermarried than women in the same age bracket, equal proportions of women and men intermarried in the thirty-five through fifty-four age bracket. Laurence Kotler-Berkowitz et al., *The National Jewish Population Survey 2000–01: Strength, Challenge and Diversity in the American Jewish Population* (New York: United Jewish Communities, 2003), 17. See also Sergio DellaPergola, "Go to School, Work, Marry, Have Children: Jewish Women and Men in the U.S., France, and Israel" (paper presented at International Conference on Gender, Identity, and the Jewish family, Brandeis University, Waltham, MA, 2007).

6. Larry Rush, interview by author, digital recording, 15 December 2008, Ann Arbor, MI.

7. Charles Revkin, interview by author, digital recording, 11 January 2009, Ann Arbor, MI.

8. I use the *New Yorker* cover by Art Spiegelman to illustrate physical attraction between a Jewish man and a woman of color, and relationships of mutual consent. The con-

textual history behind the cover is more complex, and reaction to it was mixed despite the artist's good intentions. It was originally published after a period of considerable tension between Hasidic Jews, Guyanese immigrants, and African Americans in the Crown Heights section of Brooklyn, New York, that resulted in riots and death. Read Edward S. Shapiro, *Crown Heights: Blacks, Jews, and the 1991 Brooklyn Riot* (Waltham, MA: Brandeis University Press, 2006), 210–211.

9. Hugh Hefner, a Protestant, served as the public face of *Playboy*, but a team of Jewish editors "reinvigorated the publication, embracing and fomenting the sexual revolution." Josh Lambert, "My Son, the Pornographer," *Tablet*, 24 February 2010, accessed 25 October 2013, *http://www.tabletmag.com/jewish-arts-and-culture/books/26418/my-son -the-pornographer*; Beth L. Bailey, *From Front Porch to Back Seat: Courtship in Twentieth-Century America* (Baltimore: Johns Hopkins University Press, 1988), 142; Ellen K. Rothman, *Hands and Hearts: A History of Courtship in America* (Cambridge: Harvard University Press, 1987), 307–308.

10. Gary Brodin, interview by author, digital recording, 19 November 2008, Ann Arbor, MI.

11. Allan Benjamin, interview by author, digital recording, 21 November 2008, Ann Arbor, MI.

12. Greg Marin, interview by author, digital recording, 6 January 2009, Ann Arbor, MI.

13. Morton Langfeld, interview by author, digital recording, 13 March 2009, Ann Arbor, MI.

14. Rush, interview.

15. Brodin, interview.

16. Revkin, interview.

17. Rush, interview.

18. Brodin, interview.

19. Chaim I. Waxman, "The Jewish Father: Past and Present," in *A Mensch among Men: Explorations in Jewish Masculinity,* ed. Harry Brod (Freedom, CA: Crossing Press, 1988), 65.

20. Amy Sales, associate director, Center for Modern Jewish Studies, Brandeis University, e-mail communication to author, 14 December 2004.

21. Pew Forum on Religion & Public Life, *U.S. Religious Landscape Survey: Religious Beliefs and Practices; Diverse and Politically Relevant* (Washington, DC: Pew Research Center, 2008), 23–24. See also Pew Forum on Religion & Public Life, *Religion among the Millennials: Less Religiously Active Than Older Americans, But Fairly Traditional in Other Ways* (Washington, DC: Pew Research Center, 2010).

22. Revkin, interview.

23. Benjamin, interview.

24. Ludwig Lewisohn, *The Island Within* (New York: Harper & Brothers, 1928), 272, 346.

25. Rush, interview; Revkin, interview.

26. David Frum, "Latkes and Caviar, Doughnuts with Champagne!," *Moment* 33, no. 6 (November/December 2008): 12.

27. Jon Stewart, "Faith Off—Easter vs. Passover," *The Daily Show,* 9 April 2012.

28. Langfeld, interview.

29. Bruce Davidson, interview by author, digital recording, 5 December 2008, Ann Arbor, MI.

30. The first man quoted intermarried in 1968. Bert Feldman, interview by author, 16 December 2008. The second man quoted intermarried in 1995. Davidson, interview.

31. Rush, interview.

32. Walter Chatham, interview by author, digital recording, 23 January 2009, Ann Arbor, MI.

33. According to this study participant, the son of a Jewish mother and Christian father, a rabbi questioned his Jewish identity when he was growing up in Benton Harbor, MI, and required him to convert to Judaism. All other participants had two Jewish parents.

34. Brodin, interview.

35. Michelanne Forster quoting her father in Jon Kalish, "The Road from Casablanca: A Playwright Explores the Real-Life Drama in her Hollywood Family's Past," *Forward,* 3 August 2012, 18.

36. Roland C. Warren, "What Can Happen When Too Many Dads Choose Comfort Rather Than Courage," *The Father Factor* (blog of National Fatherhood Initiative, Washington, DC), 14 March 2011, accessed 31 March 2011, http://thefatherfactor.blogspot.com/2011/03/what-can-happen-when-too-many-dads.html.

37. Benjamin, interview.

38. Rush, interview; and Felix Garrison, interview by author, digital recording, 11 December, 2008, Ann Arbor, MI.

39. Davidson, interview.

40. Bo Burlingham, "The Coolest Small Company in America," *Inc.,* 1 January 2003, accessed 19 October 2013, *http://www.inc.com/magazine/20030101/25036.html*; Micheline Maynard, "The Corner Deli That Dared to Break Out of the Neighborhood," *New York Times,* 3 May 2007; "Traveler's Guide to Matzo Ball Soup," Zingerman's, 2 May 2013, accessed 7 June 2013, http://www.zingermansbakehouse.com/?utm_source=community&utm_medium=zinglink&utm_campaign=zcobbar; "Community Giving," accessed 7 June 2013, http://www.zingermanscommunity.com/about-us/community-giving/.

41. Glenn Aker, interview by author, digital recording, 13 January 2009, Ann Arbor, MI.

42. Benjamin, interview.

43. Greg Marin, interview by author, digital recording, 6 January 2009, Ann Arbor, MI.

44. Dan Zevin, *Dan Gets a Minivan: Life at the Intersection of Dude and Dad* (New York: Scribner, 2012), 54.

45. Mark Oppenheimer, *Thirteen and a Day: The Bar and Bat Mitzvah across America* (New York: Farrar, Straus and Giroux, 2005), 17.

46. Simon Bronner, "Father and Sons: Rethinking the Bar Mitzvah as an American Rite of Passage," *Children's Folklore Review* 31 (2008–2009): 28, 27.

47. Oppenheimer, *Thirteen and a Day,* 4.

48. Samuel Osherson, *Finding Our Fathers: How a Man's Life Is Shaped by His Relationship with His Father* (New York: Contemporary Hill, McGraw Books, 2001), 18–24.

49. Samuel G. Freedman, *Jew vs. Jew: The Struggle for the Soul of American Jewry* (New York: Simon & Schuster, 2000), 114.

50. Barry A. Kosmin and Ariela Keysar, *"Four Up": The High School Years 1995–1999; The Jewish Identity Development of the B'nai Mitzvah Class of 5755* (New York: Jewish Theological Seminary, Ratner Center for the Study of Conservative Judaism, 2000), 49.

51. Len Saxe, "Jewish Youth: At Best, the Cup is 'Half Full,'" in *"Four Up": The High School Years 1995–1999,* 56.

52. Sarah Singer, "Where Have All the Young Men Gone?," *Washington Jewish Week,* 25 October 2007, B21–B22.

53. The study was conducted by the Center for the Study of Boys' and Girls' Lives for Moving Traditions. Rahel Musleah, "Where the Boys Are," *Hadassah Magazine,* June/July 2012.

54. Barry A. Kosmin, "Coming of Age in the Conservative Synagogue: The Bar/Bat Mitzvah Class of 5755," in *Jews in the Center: Conservative Synagogues and Their Members,* ed. Jack Wertheimer (New Brunswick, NJ: Rutgers University Press, 2002), 232–268; cited by Simon Bronner, "Father and Sons: Rethinking the Bar Mitzvah as an American Rite of Passage," *Children's Folklore Review* 31 (2008–2009), 9.

55. Rabbi Dan Moskowitz and Rabbi Perry Netter, *The Men's Seder: A Haggadah-Based Exploration of Contemporary Men's Issues* (New York: Men of Reform Judaism, 2007).

56. Federation of Jewish Men's Clubs, accessed 24 March 2011, http://www.fjmc.org/.

57. Moving Traditions, "Campaign for Jewish Boys," accessed 14 May 2009 and 24 March 2011, http://www.movingtraditions.org/index.php?option=com_content&task=view&id=45&Itemid=64. See also William Pollak, quoted in Gary Rosenblatt, "Where the Boys Aren't," *New York Jewish Week,* 9 September 2008.

58. "Men, Mikveh and Malt," 25 April 2013, accessed 26 May 2013, http://www.mayyimhayyim.org/Events-Classes/Men-s-Benefit-Event; "The Mikveh Lady Has Left the Building," blog by Jordan Braunig, accessed 26 May 2013, http://mayyimhayyimblog.com/2013/05/20/great-questions-ive-been-asked-while-working-as-an-intern-at-mayyim-hayyim/.

59. Temple Beth Avodah Brotherhood, Newton, MA, 30 May 2013.

60. Sylvia Barack Fishman and Daniel Parmer, *Matrilineal Ascent/Patrilineal Descent: The Gender Imbalance in American Jewish Life* (Waltham, MA: Hadassah-Brandeis Institute, Maurice and Marilyn Cohen for Modern Jewish Studies, 2008), 4.

61. Sue Fishkoff, "Reform Trying to Lure Men Back," *JTA,* 18 December 2007.

62. See also Hara E. Person et al., eds., *The Gender Gap: A Congregational Guide for Beginning the Conversation about Men's Involvement in Synagogue Life* (New York: URJ Press, 2009); Doug Barden, *Wrestling with Esau and Jacob: Fighting the Flight of Men, A Modern Day Crisis for the Reform Movement* (New York: Men of Reform Judaism, 2005); and the "Jewish Men's Storytelling Project" (2006), cited in *The Still Small Voice: Reflections on Being a Jewish Man,* ed. Michael G. Holzman (New York: URJ Press, 2008), ix–xi.

63. Rabbi Charles Simon, "The Status of Jewish Men in the Conservative/Masorti Movement," *Involving Men in Jewish Life,* Federation of Jewish Men's Clubs, accessed 28 March, 2011, www.fjmc.org/index.php?option=com_content&view=article&id=308. See also Rabbi Charles E. Simon, *The Diminishing Role of Jewish Men in Jewish Life: Addressing the Challenge,* 2011 Hearing Men's Voices Monographs (New York: Federation of Jewish Men's Clubs, 2011); Rabbi Charles Simon, "The Next Wave of Jewish Feminism: Engaging Jewish Men in Communal Life," *Huffington Post,* Religion, posted 27 October 2011, accessed 19 October 2013, http://www.huffingtonpost.com/rabbi-charles-simon/the-next-wave-of-jewish-feminism_b_1031092.html.

64. FJMC Keruv Initiative Advanced Training Conference, Pearlstone Retreat Center, Reisterstown, MD, 18–20 May 2012.

65. Doug Barden, *How to Plan and Conduct a Successful MRJ Men's Seder* (New York: Men of Reform Judaism, 2007).

66. Benjamin, interview.

67. For a detailed survey of the American rabbinate on the officiation issue (conducted by the Levitt Foundation) using a questionnaire method and a representative sample of 650 pulpit Orthodox, Conservative, Reform, and Reconstructionist rabbis, go to http://www.joi.org/library/research/rabbis.shtml.

68. Aker, interview.

69. Rabbi Howard Jaffe, quoted in Penny Schwartz, "More Reform Rabbis Agreeing to Officiate at Intermarriages," *JTA*, 3 July 2012.

70. Edmund Case, phone conversation with author, 28 May 2013.

71. Rabbi and Jewish Clergy Officiation Request, accessed 29 May 2013, http://www .interfaithfamily.com/jml/index.php?option=com_civicrm&view=Profiles&Itemid =62&rd=2.

72. Jeremy Gillick, "The Coming of the Intermarried Rabbi," *newvoices,* 23 April 2009, accessed 25 June 2013, http://newvoices.org/2009/04/23/0007-3/; Brandon Bernstein and Daniel Kirzane, "Rabbinic Life Partners: Do They Have to Be Jewish?," *Sh'ma: A Journal of Jewish Ideas,* posted 3 April 2013, accessed 25 June 2013, http://shma .com/2013/04/rabbinic-life-partners-do-they-have-to-be-jewish/; Dana Evan Kaplan, "Is Reform Judaism Losing Its Religion?," *Forward,* 26 April 2013; Ellen Lippman, "A Reform Rabbis Plea for Openness," *Forward,* 24 May 2013, 9; Joel Alperson, "If Rabbis Are Allowed to Intermarry," *Forward,* 31 May 2013.

73. Rush, interview.

74. Aker, interview.

75. Freedman does an excellent job of explaining the three causes underlying the conflict between Jews in modern America: Israel, lack of a common single foe, and unprecedented acceptance. Freedman, *Jew vs. Jew,* 23, 26.

76. Paul Berger, "Lopatin Gets a Prickly Welcome from Orthodox," *Forward,* 1 November 2013, 1, 6. In March 2009, Sara Hurwitz was ordained with the title "maharat" by Avi Weiss, who subsequently changed her title to "rabba" in January 2010. E-mail communication from Rabba Sara Hurwitz, 6 November 2013. Abigail Pogrebin, "The Rabbi and the Rabba," *New York Magazine,* 11 July 2010, accessed 6 November 2013, *http://nymag.com/news/features/67145/.* See, also, *http://www.makers.com/sara -hurwitz.*

77. Aker, interview.

78. Freedman, *Jew vs. Jew,* 26.

79. Rabbi Moshe Waldoks, "What's the Difference between a Temple, Synagogue and a Shul?," *Ask a Rabbi,* 10 July 2012, JewishBoston.com, http://www.jewishboston .com/Ask-A-Rabbi/blogs/3729-whats-the-difference-between-a-temple-synagogue -and-a-shul.

80. Kalman Long, interview by author, digital recording, 4 December 2008, Ann Arbor, MI.

81. Although I wrote this paragraph before reading Rabbi Charles Simon's essay "The Status of Jewish Men in the Conservative/Masorti Movement" (Federation of Jewish Men's Clubs website), I would like to share credit with him for the analogy between men's need to demonstrate confidence and Jewish literacy.

82. Chatham, interview.

83. Two notable exceptions are books by Rabbi Tirzah Firestone, *With Roots in Heaven: One Woman's Passionate Journey into the Heart of Her Faith* (New York: Dutton, 1998), and by Harold Berman and Gayle Redlingshafer Berman, *Doublelife: One Family Two Faiths and a Journey of Hope* (New York: Longhill Press, 2013). Firestone describes her voyage from an Orthodox upbringing, through intermarriage, to leadership in the Jewish Renewal movement. The Bermans' book is written as a series of letters to each other as members of an interfaith couple who together navigate adoption, conversion, and aliyah, eventually becoming an Orthodox Jewish family.

84. Bruce Davidson, interview by author, digital recording, 5 December 2008, Ann Arbor, MI.

85. Rabbi Simon indicated that the Wrap program is geared toward women as well as men of all ages, and that the Build-a-Pair program is focused on fifth through seventh graders. E-mail communication to author, 28 February 2011.

86. "Introduction to Judaism," Union for Reform Judaism, accessed 28 February 2011, http://urj.org/learning/classes/intro/.

87. Kevin Stephens, interview by author, digital recording, 13 February 2009, Ann Arbor, MI.

88. Brodin, interview.

89. Langfeld, interview.

90. Long, interview. Note that this respondent was quoted in the preceding chapter because he was born in 1957; his second marriage was interfaith and occurred in 1998.

91. Barbara Dafoe Whitehead and David Popenoe, "Why Men Won't Commit: Exploring Young Men's Attitudes About Sex, Dating and Marriage," *The State of Our Unions: The Social Health of Marriage in America* (New Brunswick, NJ: National Marriage Project at Rutgers University, 2002), 2.

92. Mireya Navaro, "The Bachelor Life Now Includes a Family," *New York Times*, 7 September 2008, accessed 7 April 2011, http://www.nytimes.com/2008/09/07/fashion/07single.html?pagewanted=2.

93. "Single Men Turning to Surrogates," CNN, 23 December 2008. See also Peggy Drexler, *Raising Boys without Men: How Maverick Moms Are Creating the Next Generation of Exceptional Men* (Emmaus, PA: Rodale, 2005); and Rosanna Hertz, *Single by Chance, Mothers by Choice: How Women Are Choosing Parenthood without Marriage and Creating the New American Family* (Oxford: Oxford University Press, 2006).

94. Rabbi Levi Brackman and Rivkah Lubitch, "Being a Religious Single Mother," *ynet news.com, Jewish World*, accessed 7 April 2011, http://www.ynetnews.com/articles/0,7340,L-3942580,00.html.

95. Langfeld, interview. Also, Judith Walzer Leavitt, *Make Room for Daddy: The Journey from Waiting Room to Birthing Room* (Chapel Hill: University of North Carolina Press, 2009).

96. "Facts for Features," U.S. Census Bureau News, U.S. Department of Commerce, Washington, DC 20233, 10 June 2005, accessed 7 April 2011, http://www.census.gov/newsroom/releases/archives/facts_for_features_special_editions/cb05-ff08.html.

97. "Facts for Features," U.S. Census Bureau News, U.S. Department of Commerce, Washington, DC 20233, 20 April 2010, accessed 7 April 2011, http://www.census.gov/newsroom/releases/archives/facts_for_features_special_editions/cb10-ff11.html.

98. "Facts for Features," U.S. Census Bureau News, U.S. Department of Commerce, Washington, DC 20233, 9 March 2009, accessed 7 April 2011, http://www.census.gov/

newsroom/releases/pdf/cb10-ff09.pdf; "Facts for Features," U.S. Census Bureau News, U.S. Department of Commerce, Washington, DC 20233, 5 January 2009, accessed 7 April 2011, http://www.census.gov/newsroom/releases/pdf/cb09-ff03.pdf.

99. "Silly Season," *The Good Wife*, CBS, aired February 1, 2011.

100. Langfeld, interview.

101. Chatham, interview.

102. Chatham, interview.

103. Gary Michaels, interview by author, digital recording, 5 March 2009, Ann Arbor, MI.

104. Jeremy Adam Smith, *The Daddy Shift: How Stay-at-Home Dads, Breadwinning Moms, and Shared Parenting Are Transforming the American Family* (Boston: Beacon Press, 2009).

105. Catherine Rampell, "As Layoffs Surge, Women May Pass Men in Job Force," *New York Times*, 5 February 2009, accessed 15 April 2011, http://www.nytimes.com/2009/02/06/business/06women.html?pagewanted=all&_r=0.

106. *The State of Our Unions 2000: The Social Health of Marriage in America* (New Brunswick, NJ: National Marriage Project, Rutgers University, 2000), 25–26, figure 6.

107. Jerold S. Heiss, "Interfaith Marriage and Marital Outcome," *Marriage and Family Living* 23, no. 3 (August 1961): 229, 233.

108. Harold T. Christensen and K. Barber, "Interfaith Versus Intrafaith Marriage in Indiana," *Journal of Marriage and the Family* 29, no. 3 (August 1967): 461–469; Howard M. Bahr, "Religious Intermarriage and Divorce in Utah and the Mountain States," *Journal for the Scientific Study of Religion* 20 no. 3 (1981): 251–261; Tim B. Heaton, Stan I. Albrecht, and Thomas K. Martin, "The Timing of Divorce," *Journal of Marriage and the Family* 47, no. 3 (August 1985): 631–639; Cited in Barry A. Kosmin, Nava Lerer, and Egon Mayer, *Intermarriage, Divorce and Remarriage among American Jews 1982–1987* (New York: North American Jewish Data Bank, CUNY Graduate Center, 1989), 4.

109. Kosmin et al., *Intermarriage, Divorce, and Remarriage among American Jews, 1982–87*, executive summary 1–2. Something that deserves further analysis is that women who intermarried had a divorce rate higher than men: 38 percent compared to 25 percent.

110. Sylvia Barack Fishman and Sergio DellaPergola, e-mails to Association for Social Scientific Study of Jewry member list, 3 April 2012.

111. My thanks to Jennifer Thompson, whose exceptional scholarship on the discourse of intermarriage and her reference to a "continuity of conflicts" inspired me to conceive of the debate about intermarriage and divorce as a discourse of discord. Thompson cites Bernard Lazerwitz et al., *Jewish Choices: American Jewish Denominationalism* (Albany: State University of New York Press, 1998).

112. Marshall Sklare, "Intermarriage and Jewish Survival," *Commentary* 49, no. 3 (March 1970): 53.

113. E-mail to author and Association for Social Scientific Study of Jewry member list, 4 April 2012. I am deeply grateful to Harriet Hartman for responding with precise clarity when I asked her about intermarriage and divorce, for modeling the highest level of scholarship, and for her leadership. See Harriet Hartman and Moshe Hartman, *Gender and American Jews: Patterns of Work, Education, and Family in Contemporary Life* (Waltham, MA: Brandeis University Press, 2009), 232–233, table 10.2. The Hartmans' analysis was based on the 2000–01 National Jewish Population Study.

114. Josh Mintz, "The Real Reason Why Interfaith Marriages Fail," Jewish World Blogger, *Haaretz.com,* 15 March 2012, accessed 19 October 2013, http://www.haaretz.com/jewish-world/the-jewish-thinker/the-real-reason-why-interfaith-marriages-fail-1.418812.

115. Esther Perel, cited in "Divorce Rates Among Inter-Faith Marriages," accessed 25 June 2013, http://www.religioustolerance.org/ifm_divo.htm. See also Esther Perel, "Ethnocultural Factors in Marital Communication Among Intermarried Couples" (presented at the Paul Cowan Memorial Conference on Intermarriage, Conversion and Outreach at the City University of New York, 14 October 1989), *Journal of Jewish Communal Service,* January 1990: 244–253.

116. Janice McDavit-Aron, "Ingredients for a Happy Marriage: Religious Homogamy and Its Interaction with Strength of Faith" (PhD dissertation, California School of Professional Psychology, 2009), 104, 112.

117. Naomi Schaefer Riley, *'Til Faith Do Us Part: How Interfaith Marriage Is Transforming America* (New York: Oxford University Press, 2013), 122, 128, 211 n.1.

118. Rebecca Goldberg, "Intrafaith Marriage: Making It Work" (unpublished MA thesis, Hebrew Union College–Jewish Institute of Religion, Los Angeles, CA, April 2011).

119. Aker, interview.

120. Warren Alt, interview by author, digital recording, 7 April 2010, Ann Arbor, MI.

121. Kotler-Berkowitz et al. *The National Jewish Population Survey 2000–01,* 18.

122. Leonard Saxe, Fern Chertok, and Benjamin Phillips, *It's Not Just Who Stands Under the Chuppah: Intermarriage and Engagement* (Waltham, MA: Steinhardt Social Research Institute, 2008), 1–2. See also Ariela Keysar and Barry A. Kosmin *"Eight Up": The College Years; The Jewish Engagement of Young Adults Raised in Conservative Synagogues, 1995–2003* (New York: Jewish Theological Seminary, Ratner Center for the Study of Conservative Judaism, 2004), 41.

123. Leonard Saxe et al., *Generation Birthright Israel: The Impact of an Israel Experience on Jewish Identity and Choices* (Waltham, MA: Maurice and Marilyn Cohen Center for Modern Jewish Studies, 2009), 27–31. See also Shaul Kelner, *Tours That Bind: Diaspora, Pilgrimage, and Israeli Birthright Tourism* (New York: NYU Press, 2010).

124. Leonard Saxe et al., *Jewish Futures Project: The Impact of Taglit-Birthright: 2010 Update* (Waltham, MA: Maurice and Marilyn Cohen Center for Modern Jewish Studies, 2011), 13, 19. See also www.brandeis.edu/cmjs/publications.html for further updates.

125. Sylvia Barack Fishman contended, "Jewish mixed-married households are twice as likely to end in divorce as Jewish inmarried households," and that of American families, "interfaith households are three times more likely to end in divorce as families in which both parents share the same faith." She continued, "For years, parents of mixed-married couples have accused Jewish communal leaders who articulate a principled preference for endogamy of contributing to the marital friction of mixed-married households through their intransigence and insensitivity. The ARIS data, however suggest that religious differences themselves contribute to great spousal tensions. Marital problems within mixed marriage probably arise from internal—rather than external—sources." *Double or Nothing: Jewish Family and Mixed Marriage* (Waltham, MA: Brandeis University Press, 2004), 44–45. However, the statistical estimates are not confirmed by the original sources Fishman cited, the 1990 National Jewish Population Survey and the 2001 American Religious Identification Survey. More exhaustive research unearthed a *USA Today* article from December 5, 2002, that made a mixed-married divorce versus same-faith divorce comparison. Ariela Keysar, a demographer

and the co-author of both reports, could not confirm the statistics for the NJPS 1990 and stated that ARIS did not publish divorce rates for mixed-faith versus same-faith couples. Information about marital status and religious composition of couples was given to Cathy Grossman, the *USA Today* reporter who requested that the researchers cross-tabulate their findings for the purposes of her article. Keysar further clarified that the data required more in-depth analysis, namely by age, gender, and more specific religious groups, something that *USA Today* did not address and that she might do in the future. Ariela Keysar to author, e-mail communication, 12 April 2004; Cathy Grossman to author, e-mail communication, 4 May 2004.

126. Barry A. Kosmin, Nava Lerer, and Egon Mayer, *Intermarriage, Divorce, and Remarriage among American Jews, 1982–87*, Family Research Series 1 (New York: North American Jewish Data Bank, 1989), 9.

127. Seth Roller, interview by author, digital recording, 15 December 2008, Ann Arbor, MI.

128. Alt, interview.

129. Linda Robayo, "Child Custody and Religion," NoLo.com, accessed 15 April 2011, http://www.nolo.com/legal-encyclopedia/child-custody-religion-29887.html.

130. Judith Erger, "Interfaith Divorce in an Imperfect World," InterfaithFamily.com, accessed 31 July 2007, http://www.interfaithfamily.com/relationships/marriage_and _relationships/Interfaith_Divorce_in_an_Imperfect_World.shtml.

131. Neela Banerjee, "Religion Joins Custody Cases, to Judges' Unease," *New York Times*, 13 February 2008, accessed 13 April 2011, http://www.nytimes.com/2008/02/13/ us/13custody.html.

132. Dahlia Lithwick, "Whose God Wins? For Divorcing Parents, It's Not Clear," *Newsweek* online, 26 February 2010; Cara Hogan, "Father Says 'Catholic,' Mother Says 'Jewish'," *Jewish Advocate*, 19 February 2010; Julie Wiener, "For Interfaith Couple, a Baptism by Fire," *Jewish Week*, 9 March 2010; and Lauren Pearle, Felicia Patinkin, Teri Whitcraft, and Sunny Antrim, "Exclusive: Chicago Father Faces Jail for Bringing Daughter to Church," *ABC News*, 26 February 2010.

133. Lauren Pearle, Felicia Patinkin, Teri Whitcraft, and Sunny Antrim, "Exclusive: Chicago Father Faces Jail for Bringing Daughter to Church," *ABC News*, 26 February 2010.

134. Manya A. Brachear, "Child Custody and Religion: A Judge in Divorce Case Won't Let a Father Take His Daughter to Easter Services," *Los Angeles Times*, 24 March 2010, accessed 14 April 2011, http://articles.latimes.com/print/2010/mar/24/nation/la-na -easter25–2010mar25; "Judge Denies Easter Mass for Jewish Girl," *JTA*, 25 March 2010, accessed 13 May 2010, http://jta.org/news/article/2010/03/25/1011366/judge-denies -easter-mass-for-jewish-girl.

135. Jay Andrew Allen, "Joseph Reyes and Rebecca Shapiro Are Damning Their Child to Hell," The Zero Boss, accessed 10 March 2010. Site no longer available.

136. Lauren Pearle, "Judge Rules Joseph Reyes Can Take Daughter to Church," *ABC News*, 15 April 2010.

137. "Joseph Reyes Can Take Jewish Daughter to Catholic Church, Judge Rules in Dad's Favor," *Huffington Post*, accessed 25 May 2013, http://www.huffingtonpost.com/2010/04/ 13/joseph-reyes-can-take-jew_n_536311.html.

138. Rush, interview.

139. Enid Weiss, "Appeals Court Backs Jewish Dad's Bid in Custody Battle," *New Jersey Jewish News*, 2005, reprinted on InterfaithFamily.com, accessed 31 July 2007, http://

www.interfaithfamily.com/relationships/marriage_and_relationships/Appeals_Court
_Backs_Jewish_Dads_Bid_in_Custody_Battle.shtml.

140. Marshall S. Zolla and Deborah Elizabeth Zola, "Religious Divide," *California Lawyer*, 1 June 2002, updated January 2004, accessed 28 July 2012, http://www.callawyer.com/cle/cle_story.cfm?eid=447002&evid=1&qVersionID=158&qTypeID=7&qcatid=22. Thanks to Lisa Fishbayn Joffe, director of the Project on Gender, Culture, Religion and the Law at the Hadassah-Brandeis Institute, who educated me about family law matters and shared this article.

141. Ellen Schur Brown, "After Divorce: Will the Children Still Be Raised Jewish?," *Cleveland Jewish News*, reprinted 25 January 2007 on InterfaithFamily.Com, accessed 31 July 2007, http://www.interfaithfamily.com/relationships/marriage_and_relationships/After_Divorce_Will_the_Children_Still_be_Raised_Jewish.shtml.

142. Chatham, interview.

143. Salvatore Arena, "Perelman Wins Custody Round Ex-Wife Hit in Passover 'Sacrilege,'" *New York Daily News*, 27 February 1999, accessed 25 May 2013, http://www.nydailynews.com/archives/news/perelman-wins-custody-ex-wife-hit-passover-sacrilege-article-1.824731.

144. Ronald Perelman, cited in Abigail Pogrebin, *Stars of David: Prominent Jews Talk about Being Jewish* (New York: Broadway Books, 2005), 90–91.

3. SHIKSAPPEAL

Epigraph: Ann Bancroft, http://dameonline.blogspot.com/2008/05/anne-bancroft-and-mel-brooks.html.

1. Nate Bloom, "Interfaith Celebrities: Mel Brooks Honored at Kennedy Center," *InterfaithFamily.com*, 22 December 2009, accessed 20 October 2013, http://www.interfaithfamily.com/arts_and_entertainment/popular_culture/Interfaith_Celebrities_Mel_Brooks_Honored_at_Kennedy_Center.shtml.

2. The joke has been told using either a Jewish man or a Jewish woman who intermarries. See Bernard Rosenberg and Gilbert Shapiro, "Marginality and Jewish Humor," *Midstream* 4, no. 2 (1958): 72–73; and Steve Solomon, *My Mother's Italian, My Father's Jewish & I'm In Therapy*, recorded live at the Brentwood Theater, Los Angeles, CA, 2007, compact disc.

3. Mel Brooks, quoted by James Robert Parish in *It's Good to Be King: The Seriously Funny Life of Mel Brooks* (Hoboken, NJ: John Wiley & Sons, 2007), 161.

4. Sheri and Bob Stritof, "Anne Bancroft and Mel Brooks Marriage Profile," *About.com*, accessed 20 October 2013, http://marriage.about.com/od/entertainmen1/p/bancroftbrooks.htm.

5. Max Brooks married a Jewish woman and is raising a Jewish son. Nate Bloom, "Interfaith Celebrities: Mel Brooks Honored at Kennedy Center," *InterfaithFamily.com*, 22 December 2009, accessed 20 October 2013, http://www.interfaithfamily.com/arts_and_entertainment/popular_culture/Interfaith_Celebrities_Mel_Brooks_Honored_at_Kennedy_Center.shtml.

6. "Son, Promise Me You Won't Marry a Shiksa," Gentile Jokes, accessed 25 January 2010, http://www.gentilejokes.com/son-promise-me-you-wont-marry-a-shiksa/gentile-jokes.

7. Christine Benvenuto, *Shiksa: The Gentile Woman in the Jewish World* (New York: St. Martin's Press, 2004), 270.

8. I mention Marilyn Monroe only briefly, as she is a topic of considerable attention in other work. See Lila Corwin Berman, *Speaking of Jews: Rabbis, Intellectuals, and the Creation of an American Public Identity* (Berkeley: University of California Press, 2009), 143–151.

9. Philip Roth, *Portnoy's Complaint* (New York: Random House, 1969), cited in Frederic Cople Jaher, "The Quest for the Ultimate Shiksa," *American Quarterly* 35, no. 5 (Winter 1983), 522. For more on Roth, see Lauren S. Cardon, *The "White Other" in American Intermarriage Stories 1945–2008* (New York: Palgrave Macmillan 2012).

10. B. H. Litwack, *The Last Shiksa* (New York: Putnam, 1978), book flap.

11. "The Serenity Now," *Seinfeld* (1989–1998), season 9, episode 159, originally aired on 9 October 1997, NBC, accessed 25 January 2010, http://www.seinfeldscripts.com/TheSerenityNow.htm.

12. "The Serenity Now," *Seinfeld*.

13. Laurie Graff, *The Shiksa Syndrome: A Novel* (New York: Broadway Books, 2008); Kristina Grish, *Boy Vey! The Shiksa's Guide to Dating Jewish Men* (New York: Simon Spotlight Entertainment, 2005); and Tracy McArdle, *Confessions of a Nervous Shiksa* (New York: Downtown Press, 2005).

14. Oren Gutfeld, conversation with author, 29 January 2010.

15. Anita Norich, "Isaac Bashevis Singer and the Yiddish Difference, or: Why Yentl Sings," 22 January 2010, Frankel Center for Judaic Studies, Ann Arbor, MI.

16. "The Yiddish Handbook: 40 Words You Should Know," *Daily Writing Tips* (blog), accessed 21 January 2010, http://www.dailywritingtips.com/the-yiddish-handbook-40-words-you-should-know/. A *shaygets* means a non-Jewish boy and has the connotation of someone who is unruly, even violent.

17. Tamar Caspi, "Shiksas Are for Practice," *San Diego Jewish Journal*, 1 January 2009.

18. Milton L. Barron, "The Incidence of Jewish Intermarriage in Europe and America," *American Sociological Review* 11, no. 1 (February 1946): 8. Regarding sexual relations initiated by males and females' activities as more circumscribed, see also Robert K. Merton, "Intermarriage and the Social Structure: Fact and Theory," *Psychiatry: Journal of the Biology and the Pathology of Interpersonal Relations* 4, no. 3 (August 1941): 373–374.

19. For a thoughtfully written interpretation of the original text, see Pearl Elman, "Deuteronomy 21:10–14: The Beautiful Captive Woman," *Women in Judaism: A Multidisciplinary Journal* 1, no.1 (1997), accessed 5 January 2005, http://www.utoronto.ca/wjudaism/journal/vol1n1/v1n1elma.htm.

20. Shaye Cohen, *The Beginnings of Jewishness* (Berkeley: University of California Press, 1999), 253–255.

21. Marsha Chelm, interview by author, digital recording, 13 January 2010, Ann Arbor, MI.

22. Eli Valley, "Vader: Half-Jew," *Forward*, 2 April 2010. Valley credits Paul Golin with the idea for this last line.

23. Fred Massarik et al., *National Jewish Population Study: Intermarriage, Facts for Planning* (New York: Council of Jewish Federations and Welfare Funds, 1971), 10.

24. Roxanne Pomerantz, interview by author, digital recording, 13 January 2010, Ann Arbor, MI.

25. Julie Wiener, "In the Mix: Gentile Women and the S Word," *The Jewish Week*, 18 March 2009.

26. Nonna Gorilovskaya, "The Shiksa Revival," *Moment*, June 2006, 24.

27. See ChaeRan Y. Freeze, *Jewish Marriage and Divorce in Imperial Russia* (Waltham, MA: Brandeis University Press, 2002); Deborah Hertz, *Jewish High Society in Old Regime Berlin* (Syracuse, NY: Syracuse University Press, 2005); and Marion A. Kaplan, *The Making of the Jewish Middle Class: Women, Family, and Identity in Imperial Germany* (New York: Oxford University Press, 1991).

28. Diane Wolf, professor of sociology at University of California, Davis, quoted by Nonna Gorilovska, "The Shiksa Revival," *Moment*, June 2006, 24.

29. Dan Friedman, "Taking the Gloss Off of 'Shiksa Toes'," *Forward*, 23 April 2004.

30. Tori Avey, *The Shiksa in the Kitchen* (blog), accessed 16 November 2010, http://www.theshiksa.com/.

31. Tori Avey, "A Modern Conversion Story," *Tribe*, 28 April 2010.

32. Christy Potter Kass, *The Shiksa's Guide to Yiddish* (self-published, August 2007).

33. Allan Benjamin, interview by author, digital recording, 21 November 2008, Ann Arbor, MI; Sarah Bunim Benor, "Do American Jews Speak a 'Jewish Language'? A Model of Jewish Linguistic Distinctiveness," *Jewish Quarterly Review* 99, no. 2 (Spring 2009): 230–269.

34. Alex Piker, interview by author, digital recording, 21 January 2010, Ann Arbor, MI.

35. Barry A. Kosmin et al., *Highlights of the CJF 1990 National Jewish Population Survey* (New York: Council of Jewish Federations, 1991), "Chart 9, Age by Sex: Jews by Choice and Converts to Judaism (JBC)," 8.

36. Steven Bayme, in *Choosing Jewish: Conversations about Conversion,* by Sylvia Barack Fishman (New York: American Jewish Committee, 2006), v. Fishman states, "Of those non-Jews who have married Jews over the past three decades, fewer than one out of five converted to Judaism" (p. 3). She cites Bernard Lazerwitz, J. Alan Winter, Arnold Dashefsky, and Ephraim Tabory, *Jewish Choices: American Jewish Denomination-alism* (Albany: SUNY Press, 1990), 189. See also Keren McGinity, *Still Jewish: A History of Women and Intermarriage in America* (New York: NYU Press, 2009), 144.

37. Pomerantz, interview.

38. Fran Berman, interview by author, digital recording, 15 January 2010, Ann Arbor, MI.

39. Will Herberg, *Catholic-Protestant-Jew: An Essay in American Religious Sociology* (New York: Anchor Books, 1960), 112, 116; Michael Novak, *The Rise of the Unmeltable Ethnics: The New Political Force of the Seventies* (New York: Macmillan, 1971), 53.

40. Barbara Bartlett, *The Shiksa: A Novel* (New York: William Morrow, 1987), 225.

41. Chelm, interview.

42. Chelm, interview.

43. See, for example, Naomi Graetz, *Silence Is Deadly: Judaism Confronts Wifebeating* (Northvale, NJ: Jason Aronson, 1998), and Carol Goodman Kaufman, *Sins Of Omission: The Jewish Community's Reaction To Domestic Violence* (Boulder, CO: Westview Press, 2003). See also Marcia Cohn Speigel, *Bibliography of Sexual and Domestic Violence in the Jewish Community* (Minnesota Center Against Violence and Abuse, 2004), accessed 12 November 2010, http://www.mincava.umn.edu/documents/bibs/jewish/jewish.html. Vivian Gornick mentions a Jewish husband beating his Christian wife in her memoir *Fierce Attachments* (New York: Farrar Straus Giroux, 1987), 37.

44. Piker, interview.

45. Kristina Grish, *Boy Vey! The Shiksa's Guide to Dating Jewish Men* (New York: Simon & Schuster, 2005), 3–4.

46. "Why Do Jews Intermarry, and Who Wants to Marry a Jew, Anyway?," *JTA*, 22 May 2013, accessed 28 May 2013, http://www.jta.org/2013/05/22/life-religion/why-do -jews-intermarry-and-who-wants-to-marry-a-jew-anyway.

47. Drew Barrymore and Will Kopelman, *People*, 2 June 2012, cover photograph by David Khinda.

48. Adiv Sterman, "Barrymore to Erase Tats for Jewish Burial," *Times of Israel*, 17 February 2013, accessed 8 May 2013, http://www.timesofisrael.com/barrymore-to-erase -tats-for-jewish-burial/; Drew Barrymore, quoted in Allison Glock, "The Rebel Next Door," *Marie Claire*, February 2014, 174.

49. Renee Barnes, interview by author, digital recording, 14 January 2010, Ann Arbor.

50. Pomerantz, interview.

51. John Hartung, "Shiksa: Biblical Roots of Racism," unpublished article, accessed 29 September 2009, http://strugglesforexistence.com/?p=article_p&id=16.

52. See, for example, the story of Sidney and Louise in "Should We Intermarry?" in Roland B. Gittelsohn, *Modern Jewish Problems*, rev. ed. (New York: Union of Hebrew Congregations, 1955), 83.

53. Pomerantz, interview.

54. Barnes, interview.

55. Pomerantz, interview.

56. Piker, interview.

57. Charlotte Stevens, interview by author, digital recording, 7 January 2010, Ann Arbor, MI.

58. Chelm, interview.

59. See, for example, *Booklet for Women Who Wish to Determine Their Own Name* (Barrington, IL: Center for a Woman's Own Name, 1974); Susan J. Krupper, *Surnames for Women: A Decision-Making Guide* (Jefferson, NC: McFarland & Company, 1990); Jennifer Baker Fleming and Carolyn Kott Washburn, *For Better, For Worse: A Feminist Handbook on Marriage and Other Options* (New York: Charles Scribner's Sons, 1977); Rhona Rapoport and Robert Rapoport, "The Dual Career Family," *Human Relations* 22 (1969): 3–30; cited in Marilyn Yalom, *A History of the Wife* (New York: Harper Collins, 2001), 380.

60. Sally Srok Friedes, *The New Jew: An Unexpected Conversion* (Winchester, UK: O Books, 2009), 133.

61. Sharon Bak, Shabbat service, Temple Beth Avodah, Newton, MA, 18 June 2010. I am grateful to Sharon for e-mailing me the text of her talk and to her husband, Dan, for sharing his perspective.

62. Thanks to Jonathan D. Sarna for this keen insight.

63. Pomerantz, interview.

64. Pomerantz, interview.

65. Sharon Miller, interview by author, digital recording, Ann Arbor, 6 January 2010.

66. Benvenuto, *Shiksa*, 4.

67. Barnes, interview.

68. Barnes, interview.

69. Helen Carlton, interview by author, digital recording, Ann Arbor, MI, 4 January 2010.

70. Carlton, interview.

71. Pomerantz, interview.

72. Note, Martha Chelm also went to Israel: "It was beautiful. It was awesome. We loved Jerusalem. It's just terrific." Chelm, interview.

73. Piker, interview.

74. Jetskalina converted to Judaism under the tutelage of Rabbi Roland B. Gittelsohn of Temple Israel in Boston on February 8, 1964 and wed Robert M. Phillips the next day. She was born in Holland, lived in the Boston area for several years, and died in Kansas in December 2009. E-mail communication to author from Marietta Cambareri, Jetskalina H. Phillips Curator of Judaica, Museum of Fine Arts, Boston; "8 Questions for MFA Boston Judaica Curator Marietta Cambareri," *Chron Iconia*, 22 July 2010, accessed 17 June 2013, http://blog.chron.com/iconia/2010/07/8-questions-for-mfa-boston-judaica-curator-marietta-cambareri/; "Museum of Fine Arts, Boston, Announces Naming of Three Curatorships for Musical Instruments, South Asian and Islamic Art, and Judaica," MFA Press Release, 17 July 2010. My thanks to Marietta Cambareri for sharing copies of Jetskalina's conversion certificate and marriage-related document.

75. Friedes, *The New Jew*, 149–151.

76. Carlton, interview.

77. Chelm, interview.

78. Stevens, interview.

79. Kelly Darnell, interview by author, digital recording, 5 January 2010, Ann Arbor, MI.

80. Friedes, *The New Jew*, 77.

81. Ann Braude, "Women's History *Is* American Religious History," in *Retelling U.S. Religious History*, ed. Thomas A. Tweed (Berkeley: University of California Press, 1997), 88.

82. Barbara Welter, "The Cult of True Womanhood, 1820–1860," *American Quarterly* 18 (1966): 152–153.

83. Piker, interview.

84. Pedersen, interview. Lauren Apteker, interview by author, digital recording, 18 January 2010, Ann Arbor, MI. Note: When Lauren attended a bar mitzvah with her husband at Beth Israel, the Conservative synagogue, she overheard an elderly guest ask, "Why did he bring this shiksa in here?" referring to her. She was very hurt, and it made it very hard to return.

85. Chelm, interview.

86. Chelm, interview.

87. Pedersen, interview. Barnes, interview.

88. Chelm, interview.

89. Susan A. Glenn, "'Funny, You Don't Look Jewish': Visual Stereotypes and the Making of Modern Jewish Identity," in *Boundaries of Jewish Identity*, ed. Susan A. Glenn and Naomi B. Sokoloff (Seattle: University of Washington Press, 2010), 79.

90. Chelm, interview.

91. Apteker, interview.

92. Pomerantz, interview. Stevens, interview.

93. Piker, interview.

94. Apteker, interview.

95. Jennifer A. Thompson, "'He Wouldn't Know Anything': Rethinking Women's Religious Leadership," *Journal of the American Academy of Religion*, 25 April 2013, 14. See

also Jennifer A. Thompson, *Jewish on Their Own Terms: How Intermarried Couples Are Changing American Judaism* (New Brunswick, NJ: Rutgers University Press, 2014).

96. Chelm, interview.

97. Holly Pedersen, interview by author, digital recording, 11 January 2010, Ann Arbor, MI.

98. Statistical research indicates that 96 percent of Jews who have a Jewish spouse "say they are raising their children as Jewish" by religion. Pew Research Center's Religion & Public Life Project, *A Portrait of Jewish Americans: Findings from a Pew Research Center Survey of U.S. Jews* (Washington, DC: Pew Research Center, 2013), 8–9. One wonders, however, whether this survey response is a default position for some Jewish-Jewish couples who may actually be doing less to raise Jewish children than some interfaith couples.

99. Apteker, interview.

100. Stevens, interview.

101. See Nathan Stoltzfus, *Resistance of the Heart: Intermarriage and the Rosenstrasse Protest in Nazi Germany* (New Brunswick, NJ: Rutgers University Press, 2001).

102. Chelm, interview.

103. Chelm, interview.

104. Piker, interview.

105. The spelling of this word is a subject of debate. The contest used the version in *Webster's Third New International Dictionary*. According to linguists at the YIVO Institute for Jewish Research, considered the authority on Yiddish, the preferred spelling is *kneydl*. "How Do You Spell Knaidel?," *JTA*, 31 May 2013, accessed 3 June 2013, http://www.jta.org/2013/05/31/arts-entertainment/indian-american-boy-wins-national-spelling-bee-with-yiddish-word; Joseph Berger, "Some Say the Spelling of a Winning Word Just Wasn't Kosher," *New York Times*, 31 May 2013, accessed 3 June 2013, http://www.nytimes.com/2013/06/01/nyregion/some-say-spelling-of-a-winning-word-wasnt-kosher.html?emc=eta1. Thanks to Mae Rockland Tupa for bringing my attention to all things Yiddish.

106. Pomerantz, interview.

107. Barnes, interview.

108. Piker, interview.

109. Darnell, interview.

110. Apteker, interview.

111. Pomerantz, interview.

112. Berman, interview.

113. Darnell, interview.

114. Piker, interview.

115. Julie Wiener, "Conservatives Walking Intermarriage Tightrope," *Jewish Week*, 10 October 2012; Charles Simon, ed., *Intermarriage: Concepts and Strategies for Families and Synagogue Leaders*, A Project of the Federation of Jewish Men's Clubs (Denver, CO: Outskirts Press, 2012); Rabbi Kassel Abelson, "The Non-Jewish Spouse and Children of a Mixed Marriage in the Synagogue," Committee on Jewish Law and Standards of the Rabbinical Assembly, 1988; "Responsa 165: May a Non-Jew Light the Shabbat Eve Candles?," Central Conference of American Rabbis, January 1984. See also Rabbi Jacques Cukierkorn, "Should Gentiles Be Barred from the Mitzvah? Deliberating the Participation of Non-Jews at Life-Cycle Events," *InterfaithFamily.com*, accessed 31 May

2013, http://www.interfaithfamily.com/life_cycle/bar_mitzvah_and_bat_mitzvah/ Should_Gentiles_Be_Barred_from_the_Mitzvah_Deliberating_the_Participation _of_Non-Jews_at_Life-Cycle_Events.shtml.

116. For example, adult attitudes toward celebrating Shabbat in conversionary households was found to be significantly higher than both in-married and intermarried -without-conversion households in Fern Chertok, Benjamin Phillips, and Len Saxe, *It's Not Just Who Stands Under the Chuppah: Intermarriage and Engagement* (Waltham, MA: Steinhardt Social Research Institute, Cohen Center for Modern Jewish Studies, May 2008), figure 8, p. 14.

117. Male Jews-by-choice can become equally fervent as female Jews-by-choice. Taffy Brodesser-Akner, "My Husband, a Convert, Is More Observant Than I Am," *Tablet*, 27 May 2010, accessed 8 August 2012, http://www.tabletmag.com/jewish-life-and-religion/34444/intermarried. Yossy Goldman, "Jews by Choice," weekly sermonette, Chabad.org, http://www.chabad.org/parshah/article_cdo/aid/385671/jewish/Jews -By-Choice.htm.

118. Thompson, *Jewish on Their Own Terms*.

119. Nancy J. Chodorow, *The Reproduction of Mothering: Psychoanalysis and the Sociology of Gender*, 2nd ed. (Berkeley, CA: University of California Press, 1999), 7.

120. Johanna Ginsberg, "Jewish Kids, Non-Jewish Moms: For Interfaith Families, a Complicated Journey to Joining Community," *New Jersey Jewish News*, 25 January 2012.

121. Pedersen, interview.

122. Rabbi Janet Marder, "Blessing for Non-Jewish Spouses—Yom Kippur Morning," 25 September 2004, Congregation Beth Am, Los Altos Hills, CA. Accessed 5 November 2013, http://urj.org/cong/outreach/interfaith/honoring/?syspage=article&item_id=3707.

123. "Rabbi Janet Marder Becomes President of Central Conference of American Rabbis (CCAR)," March 26, 2003, "This Week in History," Jewish Women's Archive, accessed 12 November 2010, http://jwa.org/thisweek/mar/26/2003/janet-marder.

124. Rabbi Norman Cohen, "Blessing for Non-Jewish Spouses Rosh Hashanah 5771," Bet Shalom Congregation, Minnetonka, MN; Edgar Bronfman and Beth Zasloff, *Hope, Not Fear: A Path to Jewish Renaissance* (New York: St. Martin's Press, 2008), 41–43.

125. Edwin H. Friedman, "The Myth of the Shiksa," in *Ethnicity and Family Therapy* (New York: Guilford Press, 1982), 503.

126. Friedman, "The Myth of the Shiksa," 503.

127. Benvenuto, *Shiksa*, xxi.

128. Chelm, interview. Barnes, interview.

129. Piker, interview.

130. Jim Keen, *Inside Intermarriage: A Christian Partner's Perspective on Raising a Jewish Family* (New York: URJ Press, 2006).

131. Participant, Federation of Jewish Men's Clubs Keruv Initiative Advanced Training Conference, Pearlstone Retreat Center, Reisterstown, MD, 18–20 May 2012.

4. HEARTBREAK KID

Epigraph: Steven Spielberg, quoted by Abigail Pogrebin in *Stars of David: Prominent Jews Talk About Being Jewish* (New York: Broadway Books, 2005), 25.

1. Barry A. Kosmin, Nava Lerer, and Egon Mayer, *Intermarriage, Divorce and Remarriage among American Jews 1982–1987* (New York: North American Jewish Data Bank, CUNY Graduate Center, 1989), 9.

2. *The Heartbreak Kid,* directed by Elaine May, produced by Edgar J. Scherick, screenplay by Neil Simon, based on a story by Bruce Jay Friedman (Twentieth Century Fox, 1972), videocassette, 104 min.

3. Charles Grodin, quoted in Pogrebin, *Stars of David,* 333–334.

4. Vincent Canby, review of *The Heartbreak Kid* (Twentieth Century Fox movie), *New York Times,* 18 December 1972, 56, in *The New York Times Film Reviews* (New York: New York Times & Arno Press, 1973), 347–348.

5. Grodin, quoted in Pogrebin, *Stars of David,* 333–334. Charles Grodin, *It Would Be So Nice If You Weren't Here: My Journey through Show Business* (New York: Morrow, 1989).

6. Jane Morgan Weintraub is Jerry's second wife; his first marriage was to his Jewish high school sweetheart. He has a son from that marriage, Michael, who became a bar mitzvah. Jerry Weintraub with Rich Cohen, *When I Stop Talking You'll Know I'm Dead: Useful Stories from a Persuasive Man* (New York: Grand Central Publishing, 2010), 55, 253–258; "Stars of David: Jerry Weintraub," Jewlarious: Jewish Humor, Arts and Entertainment, aish.com, accessed 25 June 2013, http://www.aish.com/j/sod/99534354.html; "2009 UNICEF Ball Honors Producer Jerry Weintraub," accessed 25 June 2013, http://www.wlox.com/story/11660269/2009-unicef-ball-honors-producer-jerry-weintraub. Thanks to Danielle and Marc Gottesman for putting Weintraub on my radar.

7. Shaye D. Cohen, *The Beginnings of Jewishness: Boundaries: Varieties, Uncertainties* (Berkeley: University of California Press, 1999), 253–255.

8. Cohen, *The Beginnings of Jewishness,* 269.

9. Steven Spielberg's accomplishments, both credited and un-credited, are truly astounding. For full information, see http://www.filmmakers.com/artists/spielberg/, http://en.wikipedia.org/wiki/Steven_Spielberg, and the numerous biographies about him.

10. Eddie Fisher, *Eddie: My Life, My Loves* (New York: Harper & Row, 1981); William Shatner, *Up Till Now: The Autobiography* (New York: St. Martin's Press, 2008); Frank Sanello, *Spielberg: The Man, the Movies, the Mythology* (Dallas, TX: Taylor Publishing).

11. Fisher, *Eddie: My Life, My Loves,* 28.

12. Fisher, *Eddie: My Life, My Loves,* 156.

13. Steven Spielberg, quoted by Pogrebin in *Stars of David,* 25–27.

14. Dina Kraft, "Shatner Sends Disabled Iraelis Where Few Have Gone Before—On Horseback," *j.weekly.com,* 9 June 2006, accessed 23 April 2012, http://www.jweekly.com/article/full/29487/shatner-sends-disabled-israelis-where-few-have-gone-before-on-horseback/.

15. Laurence Kotler-Berkowitz et al., *The National Jewish Population Survey 2000–01: Strength, Challenge and Diversity in the American Jewish Population* (New York: United Jewish Communities, 2003), 17.

16. David Desser, "The Cinematic Melting Pot: Ethnicity, Jews, and Psychoanalysis," in *Unspeakable Images: Ethnicity and American Cinema,* ed. Lester D. Friedman (Urbana: University of Illinois Press, 1991), 393.

17. Sylvia Barack Fishman, "Cultural Contexts for Mixed Marriage among American Jews," Brandeis University Modern Jewish Studies Colloquium Paper, 25 September 2003, 3, 13.

18. Neal Gabler, Frank Rich, and Joyce Antler, "Problematics," in *Television's Changing Image of American Jews* (New York: American Jewish Committee and Norman Lear Center: 2000), 69.

19. Sonya Michel, "Jews, Gender, American Cinema," in *Feminist Perspectives on Jewish Studies,* ed. Lynn Davidman and Shelly Tenenbaum (New Haven, CT: Yale University Press, 1994), 248.

20. See David Zurawik, *The Jews of Prime Time* (Waltham, MA: Brandeis University Press, 2003).

21. One textual note: English translations of Hebrew and Yiddish words vary from one book or film to another, and sometimes within the very same work. For example, the name of the daughter in Sholem Aleichem's *Fiddler on the Roof* is sometimes spelled "Chava" and other times "Chavah." I have chosen to overlook inconsistencies in spelling, preferring to retain spellings as they originally appeared in history.

22. Keren R. McGinity, *Still Jewish: A History of Women and Intermarriage in America* (New York: NYU Press, 2009). In this book I discuss the marriages of Mary Antin, Rose Pastor, and Anna Strunsky, among many other women, who all married Protestant men.

23. Amy Kronish, "The Conflict between Jewish Tradition and the Modern World as Seen through Films on Intermarriage" (paper prepared for the Tenth World Congress of Jewish Studies, Hebrew University, Jerusalem, August 1989). I am grateful to Amy Kronish for sharing her unpublished work with me.

24. Prior to 1940, the rate of Jews married to non-Jews was estimated to be between 2.0 and 3.2 percent. These figures indicate the percentages of Jewish persons who intermarried by time period. Fred Massarik et al., *National Jewish Population Study: Intermarriage, Facts for Planning* (New York: Council of Jewish Federations and Welfare Funds, 1971), 10.

25. Riv-Ellen Prell, *Fighting to Become Americans: Jews, Gender, and the Anxiety of Assimilation* (Boston: Beacon Press, 1999), 71.

26. See Zurawik, "Intermarriage III (Some Jewish Women Get Gentile Guys)," in *The Jews of Prime Time,* 172–200.

27. Leslie A. Fiedler, "Genesis: The American-Jewish Novel through the Twenties," *Midstream,* Summer 1958, 26.

28. Mary V. Dearborn, *Pocahontas's Daughters: Gender and Ethnicity in American Culture* (New York: Oxford University Press, 1986), 103, cited in Desser, "The Cinematic Melting Pot," 394.

29. Desser, "The Cinematic Melting Pot," 396.

30. Thanks to Jonathan D. Sarna for prompting me to think about the *Merchant of Venice.* Lines for Jessica in *Merchant of Venice,* act 3, scene 5, line 1858, accessed 23 March 2012, www.opensourceshakespeare.org.

31. *None So Blind* (Arrow Film Corp., 1923), videocassette, black and white, silent, 106 min. Available from the National Center for Jewish Film at Brandeis University.

32. Tom Gunning, *Outsiders as Insiders: Jews and the History of American Silent Film* (Waltham, MA: National Center for Jewish Film, 1986), 13, cited in Sharon Pucker Rivo, "Projected Images: Portraits of Jewish Women in Early American Film," in *Talking Back: Images of Jewish Women in American Popular Culture,* ed. Joyce Antler (Waltham, MA: Brandeis University Press, 1998), 40.

33. *New York Times,* 23 February 1926, 26:5.

34. *New York Times,* 23 February 1926, 26:5.

35. Fred, *Variety,* 24 February 1926, 42.

36. *New York Times,* 23 February 1926, 26:5; Richard Pontius, National Center for Jewish Film, e-mail communication to author, 7 November 2003.

37. Richard Pontius, National Center for Jewish Film, e-mail communication to author, 7 November 2003. The 1927 film *Surrender,* directed by Edward Sloman and based on the screenplay *Lea Lyon* by Alexander Brody, was one of the few American silent feature films to depict European Jewish shtetl life. *Surrender* showed that the Jewish man could not prevent his beloved from falling in love with a Christian man. Betrothed to a Jewish suitor for the past five years, Lea Lyon (Mary Philbin) has a chance meeting with Constantin (Ivan Mosjukine), a Russian prince wearing peasant garb, and falls in love with him. Her father, Rabbi Mendel Lyon (Nigel De Bruler), tries to hide his daughter next to the Torah in the cabinet. However, the Russian prince turns the house inside out and discovers Lea. She rebuffs his advances on discovering he's a Cossack. Her Jewish suitor tries to intervene, but he is a weakling, nervously twiddling his *tzitzit* (prayer shawl tassels) before the strikingly more masculine Christian Russian, who will decide whether the Jew lives or dies. In a subsequent scene, when the avenging Jewish suitor has reclaimed his masculinity, barges in on the lovers, and alerts the community, the Jewish woman protects her Christian man from the Jewish man.

38. Anne Nichols, *Abie's Irish Rose: A Novel* (New York: Grosset & Dunlap, 1927).

39. Nichols, *Abie's Irish Rose,* 324–325.

40. Gene Brown, *Showtime: A Chronology of Broadway and the Theatre from Its Beginning to the Present* (New York: Macmillan, 1997), 56, 59, 86; *Variety,* 26 May 1922, 15; *New York Times,* 24 May 1922, 22:4; *Variety,* 9 December 1925, front page; *Variety,* 2 December 1925, front page; Jay Robert Nash and Stanley Ralph Ross, eds., *The Motion Picture Guide: H-K, 1927–1983* (Chicago: Cinebooks, 1986), 3–4; *Variety,* 25 April 1928, 28 and 26; *Variety,* December 1928, 27; *New York Times,* 20 April 1928, 26:7; *New York Times,* 23 December 1946, 19:4; *Jewish Daily Forward,* "Our English Page," 29 July 1923.

41. I am indebted to Adrian Koesters for this particular insight.

42. Prell, *Fighting to Become Americans,* 77.

43. Mari Kathleen Fielder, "Fatal Attraction: Irish-Jewish Romance in Early Film and Drama," *Eire: A Journal of Irish Studies* 20, 1985, 8–9.

44. Lester D. Friedman, *Hollywood's Image of the Jew* (New York: Frederick Unger Publishing, 1982), 53.

45. *Little House on the Prairie* (1974–1983), "Come, Let Us Reason Together," episode aired January 12, 1981. Thanks to Stephanie Chervin for bringing this particular episode to my attention. See also "TV's Nellie Oleson Biography," *Definitive Laura Ingalls Wilder and Little House on the Prairie,* accessed 19 May 2011, http://www.laurasprairiehouse.com/tvseries/tvnellie.html.

46. Arline Haas, *The Jazz Singer: A Story of Pathos and Laughter* (New York: Grosset & Dunlap, 1927), 160–161.

47. Neal Gabler, *An Empire of Their Own: How the Jews Invented Hollywood* (New York: Crown Publishers, 1988), 140–141.

48. Jessel was eventually dismissed, perhaps because he demanded an increase in pay, perhaps because of infighting among the Warner brothers, or perhaps because Jessel objected to changes to the script for the film. Gabler believes that it was because Jessel was "unmistakably and proudly Jewish." It may have been some combination of these variables. Gabler, *An Empire of Their Own,* 140–141.

49. Brown, *Showtime,* 74; "*The Jazz Singer* Has Heart Interest," *New York Times,* 15 September 1925, 29:2; *Variety,* 9 December 1925, 28; *Variety,* 16 December 1925, 27; Robert Sklar, *Movie-Made America: A Cultural History of American Movies* (New York:

Random House, 1975), 152; David Quinlan, ed., *The Film Lover's Companion: A to Z Guide to 2,000 Stars and the Movies They Made* (Secaucus, NJ: Carol Publishing Group, 1997), 252; Michael Rogin, *Blackface, White Noise: Jewish Immigrants in the Hollywood Melting Pot* (Berkeley: University of California Press, 1996), 81; *Variety,* 12 October 1927, 16. For another review, see *New York Times,* 7 October 1927, 24:4; Nash and Ross, *Motion Picture Guide,* 1449–1451.

50. Jews did not make, in historian Matthew Frye Jacobson's words, "the final transformation toward Caucasian whiteness" until after World War II. Matthew Frye Jacobson, *Whiteness of a Different Color: European Immigrants and the Alchemy of Race* (Cambridge, MA: Harvard University Press, 1998), 176–177. Amid the controversy about whiteness scholarship, Jacobson's work has been criticized by scholars who contend that the category of whiteness is ill defined, that race as a social construct is an idea accepted long ago by most academics, and that lack of focus on how African and Afro-Caribbean immigrants became black confirms blackness as "identification, authoritative, and external," whereas whiteness is merely identity. See, for example, Eric Arnesen, "Whiteness and the Historians' Imagination," *International Labor and Working-Class History* 60 (Fall 2001), 5–6; and Barbara J. Fields, "Whiteness, Racism, and Identity," *International Labor and Working-Class History* 60 (Fall 2001), 51. See also Elazar Barkan, *The Retreat of Scientific Racism: Changing Concepts of Race in Britain and the United States Between the World Wars* (Cambridge: Cambridge University Press, 1992); and Karen Brodkin, *How Jews Became White Folks & What That Says about Race in America* (New Brunswick, NJ: Rutgers University Press, 1998).

51. Eric L. Goldstein, *The Price of Whiteness: Jews, Race, and American Identity* (Princeton, NJ: Princeton University Press, 2000), 51.

52. Lary May, *The Big Tomorrow: Hollywood and the Politics of the American Way* (Chicago: University of Chicago Press, 2000), 62–64; Rogin, *White Noise,* 6, 79, 84–85, 103–104.

53. George Jessel starred in Jewish films prior to signing the contract for *The Jazz Singer* film, including *Your Best Friend, Private Izzy Murphy, Sailor Izzy Murphy,* and *Ginsberg the Great.* Gabler, *An Empire of Their Own,* 140–141.

54. Rogin, *White Noise,* 86, 112.

55. See also Irwin Edman, "Reuben Cohen Considers Marriage and Intermarriage," *Menorah Journal* 15, no. 4 (October 1928): 308–316. This fictional account seems so heavily influenced by Ludwig Lewisohn that it is as if Lewisohn wrote it using Edman as a pen name.

56. See also Emma Wolf's *Other Things Being Equal* (1892). Josh Lambert, *American Jewish Fiction* (Philadelphia: Jewish Publication Society, 2009).

57. Joyce Antler, introduction to *America and I: Short Stories by American Jewish Writers* (Boston: Beacon Press, 1990), 7.

58. Fannie Hurst, "Seven Candles," *Cosmopolitan* 75 (September 1923): 38.

59. Fannie Hurst, *Appassionata* (New York: Alfred A. Knopf, 1926), cited in Jenna Weissman Joselit, *The Wonders of America: Reinventing Jewish Culture, 1880–1950* (New York: Hill and Wang, 1994), 48.

60. The Jewish woman in the novel, Arthur's sister Hazel, is prevented from marrying an Irish Catholic due to her parents' strong opposition to both intermarriage and female conversion. Apparently, unlike the son, the daughter may still not decide whom she will wed. She is prevented from leaving the Jewish community, while the Jewish man makes

his own decision to marry outside it, though he eventually returns. Ludwig Lewisohn, *The Island Within* (New York: Harper & Brothers, 1928), 151.

61. Although he observes that Jewish women suffer from debilitating Jewish self-hatred, he also contends that they are satisfied with their position, accept the dominance of the male, rule unquestioned in their sphere, and are their husbands' most valued councilors. There was also "an indefinable element" of status: "As women grew older among Jews they were instinctively treated with a touch of unquestioning reverence as though they were repositories of some special grace or wisdom." *The Island Within* portrays Jewish women as neither crushed by pre-modern servitude nor lost like the "emancipated" Christian woman of the late 1920s; she is presented as a salve for Jewish male intermarriage. Of course, this elevation of Jewish women and rejection of Christian women must also be seen for the subordination to men that it is. Lewisohn, *The Island Within*, 255, 259–260; Fiedler, "Genesis: The American-Jewish Novel through the Twenties," 32–33.

62. Lambert, *American Jewish Fiction*, 71.

63. Josh Lambert, "Regatta Land," *Tablet*, 12 September 2007, accessed 20 October 2013, http://www.tabletmag.com/jewish-arts-and-culture/books/945/regatta-land.

64. See Helge Normann Nilsen, "The Road to Judaism: Spiritual Development in Ludwig Lewisohn's Autobiography," *MELUS* 14, no. 1 (Spring 1987): 59–71.

65. Ralph Melnick, *The Life and Work of Ludwig Lewisohn: "A Touch of Wildness"* (Detroit: Wayne State University, 1998), vol. 1, 46–48.

66. "Biographical Sketch," Ludwig Lewisohn Collection, Manuscript Collection No. 166, Jacob Rader Marcus Center of the American Jewish Archives, Cincinnati Campus, Hebrew Union College–Jewish Institute of Religion.

67. "Praises *Island Within*: Dr. Wise Says Lewisohn's Novel Is Answer to *The Melting Pot*," *New York Times*, 28 August 1928, 26.

68. Ludwig Lewisohn to Rabbi Philip Bernstein, Temple B'rith Kodesh, Rochester, New York, 6 January 1940; conversion certificate of Edna Manley signed by Rabbi Bernstein, 23 January 1940, Ludwig Lewisohn Collection, Jacob Rader Marcus Center of the American Jewish Archives, Cincinnati Campus, Hebrew Union College–Jewish Institute of Religion.

69. Ludwig Lewisohn to Edna Manley, 17 October 1938, Ludwig Lewisohn Collection, Jacob Rader Marcus Center of the American Jewish Archives, Cincinnati Campus, Hebrew Union College–Jewish Institute of Religion.

70. Ludwig Lewisohn to Rabbi Philip Bernstein, Temple B'rith Kodesh, Rochester, New York, 6 January 1940, Jacob Rader Marcus Center of the American Jewish Archives, Cincinnati Campus, Hebrew Union College–Jewish Institute of Religion.

71. Rabbi Stephen S. Wise to Rabbi Philip Bernstein, 20 November 1939, Ludwig Lewisohn Collection, Jacob Rader Marcus Center of the American Jewish Archives, Cincinnati Campus, Hebrew Union College–Jewish Institute of Religion.

72. Rogin, *White Noise*, 6, 79, 84–85, 103–104. Jolson was married four times. See Herbert G. Goldman, *Jolson: The Legend Comes to Life* (Cambridge: Oxford University Press, 1990).

73. Bob Thomas, *Crown Prince of Hollywood: The Antic Life and Times of Jack L. Warner* (New York: McGraw-Hill, 1990), 48–49.

74. Thomas, *Crown Prince of Hollywood*, 73.

75. Thomas, *Crown Prince of Hollywood*, 9–10.

76. Gabler, *An Empire of Their Own*, 147.

77. Thomas, *Crown Prince of Hollywood*; Sonya Michel, "Jews, Gender, American Cinema," 268n59. Gabler, *An Empire of Their Own*, 148–149.

78. Thomas, *Crown Prince of Hollywood*, 102.

79. Thomas, *Crown Prince of Hollywood*, 306; Gabler, *An Empire of Their Own*, 246–247.

80. Bernard F. Dick, *The Merchant Prince of Poverty Row: Harry Cohn of Columbia Pictures* (Lexington, KY: University Press, 1993), 18.

81. Harry's first wife's name was Rose Barker. Dick, *The Merchant Prince of Poverty Row*, 44.

82. Dick, *The Merchant Prince of Poverty Row*, 59.

83. Dick, *The Merchant Prince of Poverty Row*, 185.

84. Dick, *The Merchant Prince of Poverty Row*, 189.

85. Dick, *The Merchant Prince of Poverty Row*, 18, 60, 187.

86. Gwethalyn Graham, *Earth and High Heaven* (Philadelphia: J.B. Lippincott, 1944), 167.

87. Lewisohn, *The Island Within*, 221.

88. Graham, *Earth and High Heaven*, 193.

89. Frederic Cople Jaher, "The Quest for the Ultimate Shiksa," *American Quarterly* 35, no. 5 (Winter 1983): 520; Ben Hecht, *A Jew in Love* (New York: Triangle Books, 1939), 42, cited in Jaher, "The Quest for the Ultimate Shiksa," 520.

90. Charlotte Baum, Paula Hyman, and Sonya Michel, *The Jewish Woman in America* (New York: 1975), 226.

91. Examples of literature depicting Jewish male–Christian female intermarriage, all by male authors, include Sholem Asch, *East River* (New York: G.P. Putnam's Sons, 1946); Norman Katkov, *Eagle at My Eyes* (Garden City, NY: Doubleday, 1948); Myron Brinig, *Footsteps on the Stair* (New York: Rinehart: 1950); Myron S. Kaufmann, *Remember Me to God* (Philadelphia: J.B. Lippincott, 1957); and Jerome Weidman, *In the Enemy Camp* (New York: Random House, 1958). See also Bernard Cohen, *Sociocultural Changes in American Jewish Life as Reflected in Selected Jewish Literature* (Rutherford, NJ: Fairleigh Dickinson University Press, 1972), 128–135.

92. Robert Merton, "Intermarriage and Social Structure," *Psychiatry* 4, no. 3 (August 1941): 361–74.

93. *Mrs. Skeffington*, directed by Vincent Sherman, produced by Julius J. Epstein and Philip G. Epstein, (Warner Brothers Pictures, 1944), videocassette, black and white, 147 min.

94. Janine Basinger, *A Woman's View: How Hollywood Spoke to Women, 1930–1960* (Hanover, NH: Wesleyan University Press, 1993), 381–382.

95. Orville Prescott, "Books of the Times," *New York Times*, 13 June 1958, 21.

96. Asch, *East River*, 14.

97. Charles Poore, "Books of the Times," *New York Times*, 3 January 1948, 11.

98. Seymour Krim, "Problem Parlayed," *New York Times*, 18 January 1948, BR10.

99. Prell, *Fighting to Become Americans*, 156. Cites Philip Phylie, *Generation of Vipers*, 2nd ed. (New York: Holt, Rhinehart and Winston, 1960).

100. Brinig, *Footsteps on the Stair*, 107.

101. Weidman, *In the Enemy Camp*, 496–497.

102. Prell, *Fighting to Become Americans*, 145.

103. Philip Roth, *Portnoy's Complaint* (New York: Random House, 1967), 235. I discuss this work in chapter 3.

104. Literary scholar Lauren S. Cardon contends that both Philip Roth and Woody Allen "employ the shiksa character as a foil for the male protagonist to work out his own neuroses—his feelings of emasculation relating to an overpowering mother figure, his association of this mother figure with any Jewish partner, and his need for sexual and social validation from a member of the dominant culture." Cardon, *The "White Other" in American Intermarriage Stories 1945–2008* (New York: Palgrave Macmillan 2012), 76.

105. Asch, *East River*, 283.

106. *Hollywood Reporter* cited on DVD packaging. *Gentleman's Agreement*, directed by Elia Kazan, produced by Darryl F. Zanuck (Twentieth Century Fox Pictures, 1947), newsreel, videocassette, 118 min.

107. Laura Hobson, *Gentleman's Agreement* (New York: Simon and Schuster, 1947), 84.

108. For a fascinating discussion of how *Gentleman's Agreement* challenged the perception of difference between Jew and Christian while reinforcing the color line, see Jacobson, *Whiteness of a Different Color,* 128.

109. Arthur Hertzberg, *The Jews in America: Four Centuries of an Uneasy Encounter; A History* (New York: Columbia University Press, 1997), 291.

110. Thomas Schatz, *Boom and Bust: American Cinema in the 1940s* (Berkeley: University of California Press, 1999), 381.

111. Alan Gevinson, ed., *American Film Institute Catalog, Within Our Gates: Ethnicity in American Feature Films* (Berkeley: University of California Press, 1997), 379.

112. Jay Robert Nash and Stanley Ralph Ross, eds., *The Motion Picture Guide* (Chicago: Cinebooks, 1986), 991.

113. Bosley Crowther, review of *Gentleman's Agreement* (Twentieth Century Fox movie), *New York Times,* 12 November 1947, 36:2.

114. Friedman, *Hollywood's Image of the Jew,* 142.

115. Friedman, *Hollywood's Image of the Jew,* 156–157. The novel, upon which the film is based, was written by Irwin Shaw (born Shamforoff), who was Jewish. "Irwin Shaw," *Wikipedia,* accessed 6 November 2013, http://en.wikipedia.org/wiki/Irwin_Shaw.

116. Friedman, *Hollywood's Image of the Jew,* 158.

117. Friedman, *Hollywood's Image of the Jew,* 155–156.

118. *The Benny Goodman Story,* based on the life of Benny Goodman, written and directed by Valentine Davies (Universal International Pictures, 1956), color, 116 min. I am grateful to Mark Dunaevsky for bringing this film and the caviar/bagel quote to my attention.

119. *Exodus,* based on the 1958 novel by Leon Uris, produced and directed by Otto Preminger (Alpha and Carlyle Productions and distributed by United Artists, 1960), color, 3 hours, 28 min.

120. *Exodus,* based on the 1958 novel by Leon Uris, produced and directed by Otto Preminger (Alpha and Carlyle Productions and distributed by United Artists, 1960), color, 3 hours, 28 min.

121. "Sabra: Proud and Prickly with a Soft Heart," *Moment,* January/February 2012.

122. Deborah Dash Moore, "Exodus: Real to Reel to Real," in *Entertaining America: Jews, Movies, and Broadcasting,* ed. J. Hoberman and Jeffrey Shandler (New York: Jewish Museum, in association with Princeton University Press, 2003), 207–219.

123. Rachel Kranson, "'What Kind of Job Is *That* for a Nice Jewish Boy?': Grappling with Jewish Masculinity in an Era of Affluence, 1945–1967," excerpt from "Grappling

with the Good Life: Jewish Anxieties over Affluence in Postwar America" (unpublished dissertation, New York University, 2012).

124. *Fiddler on the Roof*, both the 1964 stage production and the 1971 film, is exceptional in two ways: first because threats to traditional Judaism (antisemitism, assimilation, intermarriage) is *the* central theme, and second because the wayward child is the daughter Chava.

125. The quotation is taken from the text of a talk Lori Lefkovitz kindly shared with me. See Lori Lefkovitz, "'Demand a Speaking Part!': The Character of the Jewish Father," in *Answering a Question with a Question: Contemporary Psychoanalysis and Jewish Thought*, ed. Lewis Aron and Libby Henik (Brighton, MA: Academic Studies Press, 2010), 289–312.

126. *Minnie and Moskowitz*, written and directed by John Cassavetes (Universal, 1971), videocassette, 114 min.

127. Vincent Canby, "Film by Cassavetes Takes Friendly Jabs," review of *Minnie and Moskowitz* (Universal movie), *New York Times*, 23 December 1971, 16.

128. Joseph Greenblum, "Does Hollywood Still Glorify Jewish Intermarriage? The Case of *The Jazz Singer*," *American Jewish History* 83, no. 4 (December 1995), 448–449.

129. Friedman, *Hollywood's Image of the Jew*, 256.

130. Grodin, *It Would Be So Nice If You Weren't Here*, 205.

131. Sklar, *Movie-Made America*, 322.

132. Vincent Canby, "Somber Comedy," review of *Annie Hall* (United Artists movie), *New York Times*, 21 April 1977, C22, in *The New York Times Film Reviews* (New York: New York Times & Arno Press, 1979), 40–41.

133. *Annie Hall*, directed by Woody Allen, produced by Charles H. Joffe (United Artists, 1977), videocassette, 93 min.

134. Judith Pearly, "Woody Allen: Play the Life or Living in a Screenplay?," *Jewishculture.info*, 26 December 2011, accessed 19 June 2012, http://www.jewishculture.info/culture/woody-allen-playing-the-life-or-living-in-a-screenplay.

135. J. J. Goldberg, "Woody Allen Talks Israel with (Surprise!) Love," *Forward*, 11 July 2012.

136. "The Woody Allen Israel Project," *Jewish Journal*, 17 July 2012, accessed 3 June 2013, http://jewcer.com/project/the-woody-allen-israel-project/#Updates; Nirit Anderman, "To Jerusalem with Love? Peres Tries to Lure Woody Allen to Film in Israel," *Haaretz*, 17 July 2012, accessed 5 June 2013, http://www.haaretz.com/jewish-world/jewish-world-news/to-jerusalem-with-love-peres-tries-to-lure-woody-allen-to-film-in-israel-1.451557; Rachel Hirshfield, "Wood Allen Urged to Film Next Movie in Israel," *Arutz Sheva* (Israeli National News 7), 10 July 2012, accessed 5 June 2013, http://www.israelnationalnews.com/News/News.aspx/157701#.Ua-N6-u-6Hk.

137. "Bridget Loves Bernie," http://www.kfcplainfield.com/tv/bridget.html.

138. Michael E. Staub, *Torn at the Roots: The Crisis of Jewish Liberalism* (New York: Columbia University Press, 2002), 255–256.

139. Albin Krebs, "*Bridget Loves Bernie* Attacked by Jewish Groups," *New York Times*, 7 February 1973, 79.

140. Krebs, "*Bridget Loves Bernie* Attacked by Jewish Groups," 79.

141. Betty Zoss, "Defending Freedom: *Bridget Loves Bernie*," *Sh'ma: A Journal of Jewish Responsibility* 3, no. 51 (30 March 1973): 86.

142. Richard L. Wagner, "Defending Ecumenism: *Bridget Loves Bernie*," *Sh'ma: A Journal of Jewish Responsibility* 3, no. 51 (30 March 1973): 87. Based on the content of the *Sh'ma* articles by Wagner and Zoss, I believe that the titles may have been inadvertently switched.

143. Jack Kugelmass, "First as Farce, Then as Tragedy: The Unlamented Demise of *Bridget Loves Bernie*," *Key Texts in American Jewish Culture*, ed. Jack Kugelmass (New Brunswick, NJ: 2003), 150–151.

144. Zurawik, *The Jews of Prime Time*, 78.

145. Meredith Baxter, *Untied: A Memoir of Family, Fame and Floundering* (New York: Crown Publishing, 2011).

146. Although religion is not discussed on *Mad about You*, the sitcom creator and actor Paul Reiser is an emphatically Jewish contrast to his female counterpart, Helen Hunt. Lynne Meredith Cohn, "To Be or Not to Be . . . Jewish: Some TV Shows Are More Shy Than Others about Presenting Characters in a Religious Light," *Jewish News of Greater Pheonix* (n.d.); Curt Schleier, "Paul Reiser's Career Imitates Art," *Forward*, 29 April 2011.

147. Zurawik, *The Jews of Prime Time*, 38, 99, 155.

148. Zurawik, *The Jews of Prime Time*, 185.

149. Joyce Antler, "Mixed Marriage in Cultural Contexts" (paper presented at "Double or Nothing: Jewish Families and Mixed Marriage" conference, Brandeis University, Waltham, MA, 26 April 2004).

150. Eli Valley, "When Jewish David Met Irish Eileen: Intermarriage, 1970s Style," *InterfaithFamily.com*, 30 April 2007, http://www.interfaithfamily.com/relationships/ marriage_and_relationships/JewishDavidIrishEileen.shtml, reprinted with permission of *Jewcy*.

151. Thanks to Jared Gollob for reminding me about *When Harry Met Sally*. Sheila Solomon, "What Is Jewish about the Film *When Harry Met Sally?*," *Jewish Community Examiner*, 21 July 2009, accessed 23 April 2012, http://www.examiner.com/article/ what-is-jewish-about-the-film-when-harry-met-sally.

152. Nathan Abrams, "'I'll Have Whatever She's Having': Jews, Food, and Film," in *Reel Food: Essays on Food and Film*, ed. Anne Bower (New York: Routledge, 2004), 91–93.

153. Billy Crystal is married to Janice Crystal (born Goldfinger). See Billy Crystal's hilarious and heartfelt memoir, *Still Foolin' 'Em: Where I've Been, Where I'm Going, and Where the Hell Are My Keys?* (New York: Henry Holt, 2013).

154. *A Stranger among Us*, directed by Sidney Lumet, produced by Steve Golin, Sigurjon Sighvatsson, and Howard Rosenman (Hollywood Pictures, 1992), videocassette, color, 111 min.

155. Greenblum, "Does Hollywood Still Glorify Jewish Intermarriage?," 451.

156. Fishman, "Cultural Contexts for Mixed Marriage among American Jews," 32.

157. Kera Bolonik, "Oy Gay!," *Nation*, 30 October 2003. See also Gary Susman, "Grace Expectations," *Entertainment Weekly*, 3 November 2003.

158. "Mash-Up," *Glee*, season 1, episode 8, aired 21 October 2009, Fox. Thanks to Shira Belle McGinity for insisting that I give *Glee* a chance and for watching it with me.

159. The ingenuity of the show revolves around Piper's sexuality and developing sense of self. Analysis by author. Quote cited in Margaret Eby, "Is Larry Smith the New Black?

His TV Life in (More Than) Six Words," *Forward*, 30 August 2013, 1, 10. *Orange Is the New Black*, Lionsgate Television, season 1, 2013. Based on the memoir by Piper Kerman by the same title, the show is distributed by Netflix. Kerman is married to Larry Smith, founding editor of *Smith Magazine* and of *Six-Word Memoirs on Jewish Life* (New York: Smith Magazine, 2013).

160. "Larry David," *Wikipedia*, accessed 13 June 2011, http://en.wikipedia.org/wiki/Larry_David.

161. According to *Heeb* magazine, Larry David's wife was originally supposed to be Jewish on *Curb Your Enthusiasm*, but on the first day of shooting the HBO comedy, Larry told his co-star Cheryl Hines that he did not think anybody would believe that she was Jewish, "and so Cheryl David the TV shiksa wife was born." Jessie, "The Accidental Shiksa," *Heeb*, 13 December 2007. I find this idea a bit hard to believe. Had Larry David truly wanted a fictional Jewish wife, why cast someone who did not "look Jewish"?

162. Someone quoted by Keren Engelberg, "Television in Our Image," *Hadassah Magazine*, May 2005, 34.

163. "Larry David's Divorce Mirrored on *Curb*," newsvine.com, accessed 13 June 13, 2011, http://www.newsvine.com/_news/2007/10/22/1042261-larry-davids-divorce-mirrored-on-curb.

164. Larry David, Memorable Quotes for *Curb Your Enthusiasm*, accessed 13 June 2011, Internet Movie Database, http://www.imdb.com/title/tt0264235/quotes.

165. See also *Whatever Works*, starring Larry David, written and directed by Woody Allen, in which David plays Boris Yellnikoff, a self-proclaimed genius who ends up providing shelter to and then marrying a much younger runaway from Mississippi named Melodie Saint Ann Celestine (Sony Pictures Classics Release, 2009, color, 92 min.).

166. Other films that pair Ben Stiller with non-Jewish women actresses (Patricia Arquette, Cameron Diaz, and Drew Barrymore, respectively) include *Flirting with Disaster* (1996, color, 92 min.), *There's Something about Mary* (1998, color, 119 min.), and *Duplex* (2003, color, 89 min.).

167. Ben Stiller, host, *Saturday Night Live*, NBC, 8 October 2011. Jonathan D. Sarna deserves credit for bringing Stiller's appearance on *SNL* to my attention.

168. Ben Stiller, interview by Jon Stewart, *The Daily Show*, 29 March 2010, accessed 11 May 2011, http://www.thedailyshow.com/watch/mon-march-29-2010/ben-stiller.

169. "Ben Stiller and Christine Taylor: How He Proposed, Why She Said . . . YESSS!," *Mademoiselle*, October 2001, 122–125.

170. Biography of Christine Taylor, accessed 24 May 24, 2011, http://movies.yahoo.com/movie/contributor/1800231183/bio.

171. Efforts to actually reach Ben Stiller through his agent were unsuccessful. ID Public Relations, who represents him, refused to answer questions about how Ben self-identifies, whether his wedding had any Jewish symbolism, and how he and his wife are raising their children with respect to religious and ethnic heritage. E-mail communication from Leah Smith, ID Public Relations, to author, 30 March 2012.

172. Ben Stiller, *The Little Fockers* (Universal Pictures, 2010), color, 98 min.

173. Jerry Stiller, *Married to Laughter: A Love Story Featuring Anne Meara* (New York: Simon & Schuster, 2000), 198–201.

174. Stiller and Meara, *The Official Ed Sullivan Site*, accessed 27 March 2012, http://www.edsullivan.com/stiller-mearas-1st-performance-on-ed-sullivan. A half century later, Stiller and Meara were still performing as a funny couple, speaking their minds

online about everything from "MariHuana" to Justin Bieber in a web series directed by their son. "Stiller & Meara," season 1, 26 webisodes, 2010–2011, http://www.imdb .com/title/tt1745952/epcast; "Meet Ben Stiller's Parents on New Yahoo! Web Show," *TV Guide*, 24 June 2010, accessed 7 November 2013, http://www.tvguide.com/News/ Stiller-Parents-Yahoo-1019875.aspx.

175. "Jerry Stiller Discusses 'Frank Constanza,'" accessed 27 March 2012, Archive of American Television, http://www.emmytvlegends.org/interviews/people/jerry -stiller.

176. Daniel Garrihy, "Jerry Seinfeld, Larry David and the Modern Jew," *Media, Film, Music, Religion* (blog), 3 November 2008, accessed 19 June 2012, http://religionand mediacourse.blogspot.com/2008/11/jerry-seinfeld-larry-david-and-modern.html. Garrihy cites Marsha Woodbury, "Jewish Images That Injure" in *Images That Injure: Pictorial Stereotypes in the Media*, 2nd ed. (London: Praeger, 2003), 121–130.

177. Ben Stiller, *The Heartbreak Kid* (Dreamworks, 2007), color, 114 min.

178. Stuart Blumberg, e-mail communication to author, 2 June 2012.

179. Rena Joy Blumberg Olshansky, conversation with author, Brandeis Faculty Club, Waltham, MA, 14 December 2011.

180. Rena Joy Blumberg Olshansky, phone conversation with author, 19 March 2012.

181. *Keeping the Faith*, directed by Edward Norton, co-produced by Edward Norton and Stuart Blumberg (Touchstone Pictures, 2000), videocassette, color, 131 min.

182. Stuart Blumberg, e-mail communication to author, 2 June 2012.

183. Greenblum, "Does Hollywood Still Glorify Jewish Intermarriage?," 467–468.

184. Diamond was married to his high school sweetheart, Jayne Posner, then a pro-duction assistant, Marcia Murphey, and lastly his manager, Katie McNeil, who is thirty years his junior. William Langley, "Neil Diamond: the Loves of a Lifelong Mr. Lonely," *Telegraph*, 10 September 2011, accessed 2 April 2012, http://www.telegraph.co.uk/ culture/music/rockandpopfeatures/8754848/Neil-Diamond-the-loves-of-a-lifelong -Mr-Lonely.html. See also "Neil Diamond," *Wikipedia*, http://en.wikipedia.org/wiki/ Neil_Diamond; "Neil Diamond and Katie McNeil Are Married in Quiet L.A. cere-mony," *Los Angeles Times*, 23 April 2012, accessed 6 June 2013, http://articles.latimes .com/2012/apr/23/entertainment/la-et-mg-neil-diamond-married-katie-mcneil.

185. "Ben's Open Road," Roadtrip Nation, Biography, accessed 17 June 2013, http:// roadtripnation.com/leader/ben-younger; Ariel Levy, "Bard of the Boiler Room," *New York Magazine*, accessed 17 June 2013, 17 January 2000, http://nymag.com/nymetro/ movies/features/1850/.

186. Emanuel Levy, "The 'Prime' of Ben Younger," *Jerusalem Post*, 27 October 2005, accessed 17 June 2013, http://www.jpost.com/Arts-and-Culture/Entertainment/ The-Prime-of-Ben-Younger.

187. Ariel Levy, "Bard of the Boiler Room," *New York Magazine*, 17 January 2000, ac-cessed 17 June 2013, http://nymag.com/nymetro/movies/features/1850/; "Ben Younger, Director, *Prime*," *Gothamist*, accessed 17 June 2013, http://gothamist.com/2005/10/28/ ben_younger_director_prime.php.

188. The plot idea came to Younger when he was dating a woman in therapy and mo-mentarily imagined that she could be seeing his mother, an actual "shrink," without re-alizing it because they have different names. "Ben Younger, Director, *Prime*," *Gothamist*, accessed 17 June 2013, http://gothamist.com/2005/10/28/ben_younger_director _prime.php.

189. *Prime,* written and directed by Ben Younger (Universal Pictures, 2005), color, 105 min.

190. Ariel Levy, "Bard of the Boiler Room," *New York Magazine,* 17 January 2000, accessed 17 June 2013, http://nymag.com/nymetro/movies/features/1850/.

191. Allan Appel, *Club Revelation* (Minneapolis: Coffee House Press, 2001), 55, 334.

192. Joshua Halberstam, *A Seat at the Table: A Novel of Forbidden Choices* (Naperville, IL: Sourcebooks, 2009).

193. Joshua Golding, *The Conversation: A Novel* (Jerusalem: Urim Fiction, 2011). For two other takes on intermarriage, see Joshua Henkin, *Swimming across the Hudson* (New York: G.P. Putnam's Sons, 1997) and *Matrimony* (New York: Vintage Books, 2007).

194. Josh Lambert, *American Jewish Fiction* (Philadelphia: Jewish Publication Society, 2009), 6.

195. *Two Lovers* (Magnolia Films, 2008), color, 110 min.

196. Fishman, "Cultural Contexts for Mixed Marriage among American Jews," 32.

197. The Jewish engagement by default is the result of the male protagonist proposing to the Jewish woman only after the non-Jewish woman rejects him. *Two Lovers* (Magnolia Films, 2008), color, 110 min.

198. *Breaking Upwards* (Daryl Wein Films, 2009), color, 88 min. I am grateful to Howard Zilber for bringing this production to my attention.

199. See, for example, the 1997 *Seinfeld* and 2003 *Sex and the City* episodes I mention in the introduction and chapter 3.

200. *Transamerica* (IFC Films and the Weinstein Company, released 14 February 2005), videocassette, color, 103 min. Thanks to Jared Gollob, who recited this line from the movie and inspired me to watch it.

201. Judy Blume, *Are You There God? It's Me, Margaret* (New York: Yearling, 1970). The daughter of a Christian mother and a Jewish father, Margaret's quest for a single religious affiliation is equally fervent as her wish to develop physically.

202. "Last Call," *Boston Legal* (2004–2008), series 5, episode 13, aired 8 December 2008, ABC.

203. "The Best Christmukkah Ever," *The O.C.* (2003–2007), season 1, episode 13, aired 3 December 2003, Fox Television, http://en.wikipedia.org/wiki/The_Best _Chrismukkah_Ever; "Grandma Got Run Over by a Reindeer," *Grey's Anatomy* (2005–2010), season 2, episode 12, aired 11 December 2005, ABC. An example with multiple possible interpretations, Papi invites a Jewish woman to celebrate Christmas with his family and she brings her menorah, on "Be Shure," *Ugly Betty* (2006–2010), season 4, episode 9, aired 11 December 2009, ABC.

204. *Ira and Abby* (Magnolia, 2006), color, 105 min.

205. Amy Klein, "Whither Art Thou, Oh Elusive American Male: Jason Segel's Character in *The Five-Year Engagement* Signals Evolution of the Jewish Leading Man," *Forward,* 18 May 2012, 16.

206. "Turning Nasty Was No Stretch for Sarah Marshall's Jason Segel," *Sydney Morning Herald,* 2 September 2010, accessed 22 May 2012, http://en.wikipedia.org/wiki/ Jason_Segel.

207. Nathan Burstein, "'The Simpsons' Tackle Jewish Intermarriage," *Forward,* 22 January 2010.

208. Michael Medved, "Hollywood's Mixed Message: Jews in Film Today," *Reform Judaism* 19, no. 3 (Spring 1991): 21–22.

209. For an interesting discussion about representations of Jewishness in Canada, see Michele Byers, "Post-Jewish? Theorizing the Emergence of Jewishness in Canadian Television," in "The Jews of Canada," special issue, *Contemporary Jewry* 31, no. 3 (2011): 247–271. Thanks to Randal Schnoor for editing this issue . . . and making sure I didn't miss it.

CONCLUSION

Epigraph: Samuel Osherson, *Finding Our Fathers* (Chicago: Contemporary Books, 1986), viii.

1. Anne-Marie Slaughter, "Why Women Still Can't Have It All," *Atlantic*, July/August 2012, 102.

2. Laurence Kotler-Berkowitz et al., *The National Jewish Population Survey 2000–01: Strength, Challenge and Diversity in the American Jewish Population* (New York: United Jewish Communities, 2003), 18.

3. See discussion about an apparent association between Taglit-Birthright Israel participation and marrying someone Jewish in chapter 2.

4. Thanks to Sarah Imhoff for raising this important point. See Imhoff, "All in the Family? Jewish Intermarriage in America," *Religious Studies Review* 34, no. 4 (December 2010): 263–266.

5. Nancy J. Chodorow, *The Reproduction of Mothering: Psychoanalysis and the Sociology of Gender*, 2nd ed. (Berkeley: University of California Press, 1999), 7. I am deeply grateful to Mari Jo Buhle for introducing me to Chodorow's work and countless women's/gender history lessons.

6. Greg Marin, interview by author, digital recording, 6 January 2009, Ann Arbor, MI.

7. "Breadwinner Moms," *Forward*, 7 June 2013, 8.

8. See, for example, at http://www.fathermag.com/; http://www.dadstayshome.com/; http://www.fathers.com/; http://strongfathers.com/; http://www.fatherhood.org/.

9. Diane Ehrensaft, *Parenting Together: Men and Women Sharing the Care of Their Children* (Urbana: University of Illinois Press, 1990), 93–96.

10. Larry Rush, interview by author, digital recording, 15 December 2008, Ann Arbor, MI.

11. Allan Benjamin, interview by author, digital recording, 21 November 2008, Ann Arbor, MI.

12. Charles Revkin, interview by author, digital recording, 11 January 2009, Ann Arbor, MI.

13. Robert L. Griswold, *Fatherhood in America: A History* (New York: Basic Books, 1993), 3.

14. Nathan Bloomer, interview by author, digital recording, 22 January 2009, Ann Arbor, MI.

15. Revkin, interview.

16. Kalman Long, interview by author, digital recording, 4 December 2008, Ann Arbor, MI.

17. Gary Michaels, interview by author, digital recording, 5 March 2009, Ann Arbor, MI.

18. Josh Lipowsky, "JFS Focuses on Jewish Men in Interfaith Relationships," *New Jersey Jewish Standard*, 13 August 2010, accessed 5 October 2011, http://joi.org/blog links/jfs_focuses_on_jewish_men_in_interfaith_relationships.htm.

19. Morton Langfeld, interview by author, digital recording, 13 March 2009, Ann Arbor, MI.

20. Keren R. McGinity, *Still Jewish: A History of Women and Intermarriage in America* (New York: NYU Press, 2009), 175; see 279n104.

21. Sylvia Barack Fishman and Daniel Parmer, *Matrilineal Ascent/Patrilineal Descent: The Gender Imbalance in American Jewish Life* (Waltham: Brandeis University, 2008).

22. Alvin Mitchells, interview by author, digital recording, 4 December 2008, Ann Arbor, MI.

23. Ben Gose, "Differences in Pay for Men and Women in Top Charity Jobs," *Chronicle of Philanthropy*, 11 November 2004; "Advancing Women: Closing the Salary Gap," accessed 3 March 2011, http://www.advancingwomen.org/advancing/closing/.

24. "The Wage Gap Over Time: In Real Dollars, Women See a Continuing Gap," National Committee on Pay Equity, accessed 6 October 2009, http://www.pay-equity .org/info-time.html.

25. I emphasize "white" here because women of different race and ethnic groups earned different percentages when compared to their direct male counterparts. For example, in 2009, Asian women earned 82 percent as much as Asian men, black women 94 percent as much as black men, and Hispanic women 90 percent as much as Hispanic men. *Women in America: Indicators of Social and Economic Well-Being*, prepared by the U.S. Department of Commerce, Economics and Statistics Administration, and the Executive Office of the President Office of Management and Budget for the White House Council on Women and Girls, March 2011, 32.

26. Steven M. Cohen and Judith Schor, *Gender Variation in the Careers of Conservative Rabbis: A Survey of Rabbis Ordained since 1985* (New York: Rabbinical Assembly, 2004); Julie Schonfeld, "Gender Equity in the Rabbinate," *Sh'ma: A Journal of Jewish Responsibility* 35, no. 615 (November 2004): 15–16; Alexandra Halpern, "Reform Female Rabbis Are Paid Less Than Male Counterparts, Study Finds," *JTA*, 20 June 2012; Stewart Ain, "Major Pay Gap for Female Rabbis in Reform Movement," *NY Jewish Week*, 12 July 2012.

27. Cohen also mentions the work of Advancing Women Professionals and the Jewish Community, "to fully utilize the talents of all of our professionals, men *and* women, and lead to a better work life for all of us." "Women negotiate for other benefits and are willing to take lower salaries to realize those benefits." Steven Cohen, "Cohen's Comments: The Gender Salary Gap," posted 18 February 2011, accessed 3 March 2011, http://www .bjpa.org/blog/index.cfm/2011/2/18/Cohens-Comments-The-Gender-Salary-Gap.

28. I disagree with Cohen's contention that "intermarriage does indeed constitute the greatest single threat to Jewish continuity today." Steven M. Cohen quoted by Niraj Warikoo, *USA Today*, 14 October 2010, accessed 24 October 2013; and Steven M. Cohen, Marshall Sklare Award Lecture, 42nd Conference of the Association for Jewish Studies, 19 December 2010, Boston, MA. I also oppose his portrayal of intermarriage as a "disaster for individuals." Steven M. Cohen, "Why Intermarriage May Not Threaten Jewish Continuity," *Moment*, Decermber 1994, 54.

29. Fred Stevens, interview by author, digital recording, 12 December 2008, Ann Arbor, MI.

30. Jennifer A. Thompson, "'He Wouldn't Know Anything': Rethinking Women's Religious Leadership," *Journal of the American Academy of Religion*, 25 April 2013, 9–10.

31. Susan Faludi, *Backlash: The Undeclared War against American Women* (New York: Crown, 1991); Susan Faludi, *Stiffed: The Betrayal of the American Man* (New York: William and Morrow, 1999), 602.

32. Sheryl Sandberg with Nell Scovell, *Lean In: Women, Work, and the Will to Lead* (New York: Knopf, 2013), 103, 108–109, 114–115, 120; Rebecca J. Rosen, "Why Men Need to Read 'Lean In,' Too," *Atlantic*, 14 March 2013, accessed 25 October 2013, http://www.theatlantic.com/sexes/archive/2013/03/why-men-need-to-read-lean-in-too/273984/. I am grateful to Ellen Jawitz for many conversations about this topic and so much else.

33. Alison Leigh Cowan, "Poll Finds Women's Gains Have Taken Personal Toll," *New York Times*, 21 August 1989.

34. Arlie Russell Hochschild with Anne Machung, *The Second Shift: Working Parents and the Revolution at Home* (New York: Viking, 1989).

35. Tom Gantert, "Husbands Add Seven Hours to Women's Housework Load Each Week, University of Michigan Study Says," *MLive.com*, 4 April 2008, accessed 24 January 2011, http://blog.mlive.com/annarbornews/2008/04/husbands_add_seven_hours_to_wo.html. See also *Chore Wars: Men, Women, and Housework: Study Confirms Wives Do Most Household Chores*, National Science Foundation, 28 April 2008, accessed 24 April 2011, http://www.nsf.gov/discoveries/disc_summ.jsp?cntn_id=111458.

36. Ruth Davis Konigsberg, "Chore Wars: Let It Go. Make Peace. Men and Women, It Turns Out, Work the Same Amount," *Time*, 8 August 2011, 44–49.

37. Slaughter, "Why Women Still Can't Have It All," 101, 102.

38. Brad Harrington, Fred Van Deusen, and Beth Humberd, *The New Dad: Exploring Fatherhood in a Career Context* (Chestnut Hill, MA: Boston College Center for Work & Family, 2010).

39. Harrington, Fred Van Deusen, and Beth Humberd, *The New Dad: Caring, Committed and Conflicted* (Chestnut Hill, MA: Boston College Center for Work & Family, 2011), 13–14.

40. Harrington et al., *The New Dad: Caring, Committed and Conflicted*, 15.

41. Jeremy Adam Smith, *The Daddy Shift: How Stay-at-Home Dads, Breadwinning Moms, and Shared Parenting Are Transforming the American Family* (Boston: Beacon Press, 2009), xi.

42. Michael S. Kimmel, "Abandoning the Barricades: Or How I Became a Feminist," in *Men Speak Out: Views on Gender, Sex, and Power*, ed. Shira Tarrant (New York: Routledge, 2008), 171. See also Michael Kimmel and Michael Kaufman, *The Guy's Guide to Feminism* (Berkeley, CA: Seal Press, 2011).

43. Chodorow, *The Reproduction of Mothering*, 218–219.

Suggested Reading

NONFICTION

Benvenuto, Christine. *Shiksa: The Gentile Woman in the Jewish World*. New York: St. Martin's Press, 2004.

Berman, Harold, and Gayle Redlingshafer Berman. *Doublelife: One Family, Two Faiths and a Journey of Hope*. New York: Longhill Press, 2013.

Blazina, Christopher. *The Secret Lives of Men: What Men Want You to Know about Love, Sex, and Relationships*. Deerfield Beach, FL: Health Communications, 2008.

Boteach, Shmuley. *The Broken American Male: And How to Fix Him*. New York: St. Martin's Press, 2008.

Boyarin, Daniel. *Unheroic Conduct: The Rise of Heterosexuality and the Invention of the Jewish Man*. Berkeley: University of California Press, 1997.

Brod, Harry, ed. *A Mensch among Men: Explorations in Jewish Masculinity*. Freedom, CA: Crossing Press, 1988.

Cantor, Aviva. *Jewish Women/Jewish Men: The Legacy of Patriarchy in Jewish Life*. San Francisco, CA: HarperCollins, 1995.

Chudacoff, Howard. *The Age of the Bachelor: Creating an American Subculture*. Princeton, NJ: Princeton University Press, 1999.

Cohen, Edward. *The Peddler's Grandson: Growing Up Jewish in Mississippi*. New York: Dell Publishing, 2002.

Cohen, Shaye D. *The Beginnings of Jewishness: Boundaries: Varieties, Uncertainties*. Berkeley: University of California Press, 1999.

Cohen, William S. *Love in Black and White: A Memoir of Race, Religion, and Romance*. Lanham, MD: Rowman & Littlefield, 2007.

Cott, F. Nancy. *Public Vows: A History of Marriage and the Nation*. Cambridge, MA: Harvard University Press, 2000.

Ehrensaft, Diane. *Parenting Together: Men and Women Sharing the Care of Their Children*. Urbana: University of Illinois Press, 1987.

Epstein, Helen. *Children of the Holocaust: Conversations with Sons and Daughters of Survivors*. New York: Penguin, 1979.

Friedes, Sally Srok. *The New Jew: An Unexpected Conversion*. Winchester, UK: O Books, 2009.

Fuchs, Lawrence H. *Beyond Patriarchy: Jewish Fathers and Families*. Hanover, NH: Brandeis University Press, 2000.

Griswold, Robert L. *Fatherhood in America: A History*. New York: Basic Books, 1993.

Hartman, Harriet and Moshe Hartman. *Gender and American Jews: Patterns in Work, Education, and Family in Contemporary Life*. Waltham, MA: Brandeis University Press, 2009.

Holzman, Michael G., ed. *The Still Small Voice: Reflections on Being a Jewish Man*. New York: URJ Press, 2008.

Hyman, Paula E. *Gender and Assimilation in Modern Jewish History: The Roles and Representation of Women*. Seattle: University of Washington Press, 1995.

Kaplan, Marion A., and Deborah Dash Moore, eds. *Gender and Jewish History*. Bloomington: Indiana University Press, 2011.

Keen, Jim. *Inside Intermarriage: A Christian Partner's Perspective on Raising a Jewish Family*. New York: URJ Press, 2006.

Kimmel, Michael, and Michael Kaufman. *The Guy's Guide to Feminism*. Berkeley, CA: Seal Press, 2011.

Leavitt, Judith Walzer. *Make Room for Daddy: The Journey from Waiting Room to Birthing Room*. Chapel Hill: University of North Carolina Press, 2009.

Mayer, Egon. *Love and Tradition: Marriage between Jews and Christians*. New York: Schocken Books, 1985.

McGinity, Keren R. *Still Jewish: A History of Women and Intermarriage in America*. New York: NYU Press, 2009.

Meers, Sharon, and Joanna Strober. *Getting to 50/50: How Working Couples Can Have It All by Sharing It All*. New York: Bantam, 2009.

Meszler, Joseph B. *A Man's Responsibility: A Jewish Guide to Being a Son, a Partner in Marriage, a Father and a Community Leader*. Woodstock, VT: Jewish Lights Publishing, 2008.

Olitzky, Kerry M. *From Your Father's House . . . Reflections for Modern Jewish Men*. Philadelphia: Jewish Publication Society, 1998.

Osherson, Samuel. *Finding Our Fathers: How a Man's Life Is Shaped by His Relationship with His Father*. New York: Contemporary Hill, McGraw Books, 2001 [1986].

Person, Hara E., et al., eds. *The Gender Gap: A Congregational Guide for Beginning the Conversation about Men's Involvement in Synagogue Life*. New York: URJ Press, 2009.

Pittman, Frank. *Man Enough: Fathers, Sons, and the Search for Masculinity*. New York: Berkley Publishing Group, 1993.

Prell, Riv-Ellen. *Fighting to Become Americans: Jews, Gender, and the Anxiety of Assimilation*. Boston: Beacon Press, 1999.

Salkin, Jeffrey K., ed. *The Modern Men's Torah Commentary: New Insights from Jewish Men on the 54 Weekly Torah Portions*. Woodstock, VT: Jewish Lights Publishing, 2009.

———. *Searching for My Brothers: Jewish Men in a Gentile World*. New York: Berkley Publishing Group, 1999.

Sandberg, Sheryl. *Lean In: Women, Work, and the Will to Lead*. New York: Knopf, 2013.

Sarna, Jonathan D. *American Judaism: A History*. New Haven and London: Yale University Press, 2004.

Smith, Jeremy Adam. *The Daddy Shift: How Stay-at-Home Dads, Breadwinning Moms, and Shared Parenting Are Transforming the American Family*. Boston: Beacon Press, 2009.

Spickard, Paul. *Mixed Blood: Intermarriage and Ethnic Identity in Twentieth-Century America*. Madison: University of Wisconsin Press, 1989.

Sweeney, Jon M. and Michal Woll. *Mixed-Up Love: Relationships, Family, and Religious Identity in the 21st Century*. New York: Jericho Books, 2013.

Thompson, Jennifer A. *Jewish on Their Own Terms: How Intermarried Couples are Changing American Judaism*. New Brunswick, NJ: Rutgers University Press, 2014.

Zevin, Dan. *Dan Gets a Minivan: Life at the Intersection of Dude and Dad*. New York: Scribner, 2012.

FICTION

Appel, Allan. *Club Revelation*. Minneapolis: Coffee House Press, 2001.

Asch, Sholem. *East River: A Novel of New York*. New York: G. P. Putnam's Sons, 1946.

Bartlett, Barbara. *The Shiksa: A Novel*. New York: William Morrow, 1987.

Brinig, Myron. *Footsteps on the Stair: A Novel*. New York: E. P. Dutton, 1950.

Brudno, Ezra. *The Tether*. Philadelphia: J.B. Lippincott, 1908.

Golding, Joshua. *The Conversation: A Novel*. Jerusalem: Urim Fiction, 2011.

Goodman, Allegra. *Paradise Park*. New York: Dial Press, 2001.

Gornick, Vivian. *Fierce Attachments: A Memoir*. New York: Farrar Straus Giroux, 1987.

Graham, Gwethalyn. *Earth and High Heaven*. Philadelphia: J.B. Lippincott, 1944.

Halberstam, Joshua. *A Seat at the Table: A Novel of Forbidden Choices*. Naperville, IL: Sourcebooks, 2009.

Hecht, Ben. *A Jew in Love*. New York: Triangle Books, 1939.

Henkin, Joshua. *Matrimony*. New York: Vintage Books, 2007.

———. *Swimming Across the Hudson*. New York: G.P. Putnam's Sons, 1997.

Jong, Erica. *Fear of Flying*. New York: Holt, Rinehart and Winston, 1973.

Katkov, Norman. *Eagle at My Eyes*. Garden City, NY: Doubleday, 1948.

Kaufman, Myron S. *Remember Me to God*. Philadelphia: J.B. Lippincott, 1957.

Kellerman, Faye. *The Ritual Bath: The First Decker/Lazarus Novel*. New York: William Morrow, 1986.

Kirshenbaum, Binnie. *A Disturbance in One Place: A Novel*. New York: HarperCollins, 1994.

Levi, Lia. *The Jewish Husband: A Story of Love and Secrets in Fascist Italy*. New York: Europa Editions, 2009.

Lewisohn, Louis. *The Island Within*. New York: Harper & Brothers, 1928.

Litwack, B. H. *The Last Shiksa*. New York: Putnam, 1978.

Malamud, Bernard. *The Assistant*. New York: Farrar, Straus, and Cudahy, 1957.

Pollak, Eileen. *Paradise, New York*. Philadelphia: Temple Press, 1998.

Roth, Philip. *Portnoy's Complaint*. New York: Random House, 1967.

Schaeffer, Susan Fromberg. *Mainland*. New York: Simon and Schuster. 1985.

Segal, Lore. *Her First American*. New York: Knopf, 1985.

Weidman, Jerome. *In the Enemy Camp*. New York: Random House, 1958.

Wolf, Emma. *Other Things Being Equal*. Chicago: A.C. McClurg, 1892.

Zangwill, Israel. *The Melting Pot*. New York: Macmillan, 1909.

INTERNET

Be'Chol Lashon (In Every Tongue), http://www.bechollashon.org

Dad Stays Home, http://www.dadstayshome.com/

Fathering Magazine, http://www.fathermag.com/
Federation of Jewish Men's Clubs, http://fjmc.org/
InterfaithFamily, http://interfaithfamily.com
Jewish Outreach Institute, http://joi.org
J-Journey, http://www.j-journey.org
Love & Tradition, http://loveandtradition.com
Men of Reform Judaism, http://www.menrj.org/
Moving Traditions, http://www.movingtraditions.org
MyJewishLearning, http://www.myjewishlearning.com
National Center for Fathering, http://www.fathers.com/
National Committee on Pay Equity, http://www.pay-equity.org/info-time.html
National Fatherhood Initiative, http://www.fatherhood.org
ShalomLearning, http://www.shalomlearning.org
The Shiksa in the Kitchen, http://theshiksa.com
Strong Fathers, http://strongfathers.com/

Index

Page numbers in italics refer to illustrations.

Affiliation: in *Are You There God? It's Me, Margaret,* 252n201; choice, 113; a dearth of positive associations as a kind of Jewish affiliation, 86; intermarried Jewish women's affiliations, 194; Jewish denominational shifts, 47–49; "love often ignores the dictates of religious affiliation," 184; men's at birth, 32; multiple Jewish, 17; original, 123; rabbinical impact, 59; in relation to marital satisfaction, 93; rise of the "nones," 64; synagogue affiliation helpful, 196; "We need to reverse the disaffiliation of men . . . ," 79; where no one questions his Jewishness or that of his child, 72

Alba, Richard, 34–35, 208n15, 216nn14–15

Alcohol, 36, 67–68, 78

Allen, Woody, 119, 170–171, 186, 190, 247n104, 250n165. *See also* films

Ann Arbor, 10, 14–22, 134–135, 138; Hebrew Day School, 17, 211n47; Jewish Community Center (JCC), 17, 57, 70, 127; open marital environment, 18

Antler, Joyce, 146, 176

Asian-Jewish. *See* Jewish-Asians

attitudes: Ann Arbor's transience, 17; contributing to interfaith romance, 40–42; differences in faith or disharmonious cultural differences, 92; husbands' and influence on Christian-born women's

religious journeys, 135; Jewish men's, 63, 71–72; parental attitude of Holocaust survivors, 46; Reform rabbi and cantor's, 135; toward celebrating Shabbat, 240n116; women's about work and career, 38–39

Avey, Tori, *110, 111*

baby boomers, 28, 32, 38, 46

bar mitzvahs, 76–77, 204. *See also* sports

Barrymore, Drew and Will Kopelman, 116

battle of the sexes. *See* gender; identity

Benor, Sarah Bunim, 112

Biden, Ashley and Howard Krein, 4–5

Birthright, 57–58, 94, 193

Blumberg, Stuart and Rena Joy Blumberg Olshansky, 184–185

B'nai Moshe, 31

breadwinning, 9; "breadwinner mom," 195; co-breadwinning, 90; equal ranking with providing discipline, 203; husband-provider and dependent wife model, 39; male breadwinner ethic, 60; male breadwinning ideology, 196; primary breadwinners, 28, 30, 200; size of paycheck, 36–38; women as secondary breadwinners, 39

Bronner, Simon, 76

Brooks, Mel and Anne Bancroft, 100–102; Max Brooks, 102

Bush, Lauren and David Lauren, 4

Case, Edmund, 81

Catholicism/Catholics: Amy Chua, 25; Anne Bancroft, 100; Anne Page Alvarado, 160; "blue-eyed blond," 114; Christiane Amanpour, 46; Christine Taylor, 181; Church in *Boston Legal,* 190; Cokie Roberts, 54; dating women who were not very religious, 65; daughter of wealthy Irish Catholics in *Bridget Loves Bernie,* 171; daughter-in-law and grandchild in *East River,* 163–164; David Doyle, 173; divorce rate, 91; "enough Irish Catholics," 131; "Father Says 'Catholic,' Mother Says 'Jewish,'" 96; house of worship, 16; husband against raising, 127; "I always felt like a misfit," 121–122; Irish Catholic Eileen, 175; Irish Catholic family, 117; Jewish woman prevented from marrying, 244n60; Joan Perry Cohn, 161; joke, 58; Joseph Reyes, 96; Ludwig Lewisohn, 157; marriages with Protestants, 33, 35; Meg Ryan in *When Harry Met Sally,* 176; priest in *Keeping the Faith,* 184; reinvigorated Catholic raising Jewish children, 127; ruling about education classes, 97; socioeconomic status, 114; stories of lower-class Jewish-Catholic marriages, 161; Violet in *The Five-Year Engagement,* 191; women more accepting of traditional familial role expectations and responsibilities, 39; women's backgrounds, 113

children of intermarriage: 25, 27, 32, 51, 56, 72, 73, 76, 93–94, 122–123, 125, 127; custody and religious upbringing, 97–98; descent, 109; Ela Shapiro Reyes, 96; how men raised their children, 52, 70; impact of visiting Israel on importance of marrying a Jew and raising Jewish children, 94; influence of gender on transmission of Jewish identity to children, 198, 201; Jewish interfaith families raising children with a Jewish identity, 221nn104–105, 222nn107–109; marriage begins when a child is born (or adopted) concept, 120; men's ability

to raise Jewish, 80–81; "Will my grandchildren be Jewish?" 118. *See also* Birthright; Saxe, Leonard; Sasson, Theodore

Christian women, 36, 54, 113, 114, 117; experience with prejudice, 129–130; feelings about the Holocaust, 131; lack of experience with Jews, 116–117; passing as Jews, 130; physical appearance and social construction of Jewish identity, 128–129; seeking Jewish partners on JDate, 36. *See also* Protestants

Christmas: in "The Best Christmukkah Ever," 190; Chinese restaurants, 26; Christmas tree, 97, 116, 124, 128, 145, 182, 189; difficult time of year for women, 128, 150, 189–190, 252n203; Eve, 58; refused to celebrate, 98; Santa Claus, 70; Spielberg family, 145. *See also* December Dilemma

civil rights movement, 15, 74–75

Clinton, Bill and Monica Lewinsky, 29

Clinton, Chelsea and Marc Mezvinsky, 4

Cohen, Edward, 59

Cohen, Steven: "work-life balance," 200, 254n28

Cohen, William S., 55

Cohn, Harry, 160–161

Comedians: Dan Zevin, 76; Jon Fisch, 58; Jon Stewart, 71; Steve Solomon, 57–58; Yisrael Cambell, 58

Comics: "Bucky Shvitz: Sociologist for Hire" (Eli Valley), 27; *"Just Married"* (Charlton Comics), 175; "Vader: Half-Jew" (Eli Valley) 108; *"Why I Only Date Shiksas"* (Adam Mutterperl), 107

comparison of intermarried Jewish men and intermarried Jewish women: 7, 29–30, 42, 51, 59, 65, 145, 148, 188–189, 193–194, 201, 207n2, 207n4, 222n109, 231n109

Congregation Beth Israel, 17, 72, 80, 238n84

Conservative Judaism: denominational shifting, 47–49, 55–56, 58–60, 72, 75; Federation of Jewish Men's Clubs, 78–79; Jewish youth post b'nai mitzvah, 77; leadership, 54; men's affiliations at birth, 32; patrilineal descent, 56–57; percent of American Jewish adults, 48; "That was the end of me being a Conservative Jew," 59; World Wide Wrap, 85. *See also* Simon, Rabbi Charles

continuity, Jewish, 3, 27, 51, 53, 60, 65, 77, 98, 102–103, 109, 129, 136, 138, 164, 178, 188, 200, 204, 254n28

conversion, 12, 32, 52, 53, 54, 70, 71, 102–103, 112, 113; Anne Meara, 180; convert treated better than "Jewish seekers," 85; Elizabeth Taylor, 54; Françoise Mouly, 66; Joseph Reyes, 96; Kate Capshaw, 145; reason for wanting to, 121–123, 125–126; Sharon Bak, 120; Susie Elkins, 143; women who chose not to, 127; women's desires for children to marry Jews, 133. *See also* Christian women; Friedes, Sally Srok

cooking: Jewish cuisine and mainstream American culture, 132; kugel, 132; *parve*, 108; "Why doesn't the house smell like a Jewish home should?" 198–199; working women doing more than half, 202

co-parenting, 89–90

December Dilemma, 71, 190. *See also* Christmas

DellaPergola, Sergio, 215n107

Desser, David, 149

Detroit: automakers, 11; intermarriage compared with Ann Arbor, 18, 211n50; Jewish community and marriage, 211n50; Jewish population, 16–17; population decrease, 15; suburbs, 18, 20–21

Diamond, Neil, 178, 185–186, 251n184

Diner, Hasia. *See* Holocaust

divorce, 9, 141–142, 160–161, 173–174, 178, 186, 193–194, 196, 231n109, 231n111, 231n113, 232n125, 236n36; escalating national rates, 64, 84, 86, 90–98; of Rebecca Shapiro and Joseph Reyes, 96; of Ronald Perelman and Patricia Duff, 98

Easter, 71, 98, 170

Education: adult, 49; Catholic, 97; children, 137; Eddie Fisher, 145; good

husband theory, 115; graduate, 134; Hebrew Day School, 17–18; inadequate, 84; interfaith differences, 92; Jewish cultural emphasis on educational aptitude, 28, 38; Jewish day school, 20, 24, 126, 196; Jewish education and Japanese language instruction, 26; Jewish education as responsibility of Christian-born wives, 193, 196; responsibility of men but without substantial Jewish education, 198; opportunities for cross-religious romance, 40; post-b'nai mitzvah, 77; potential influence of Jewish education, 94; religious education and first intermarriage, 13; women earned less, 200; women's employment in, 90; women's success in higher education, 203. *See also* Birthright

Emanuel, Rahm, 29

Faludi, Susan, 201

family: dual career, 39; "family values," 205; new ways to integrate work and family, 202–203; traditional, 39; work-life balance, 200

fatherhood, 6–7, 9; *The Daddy Shift* (Jeremy Adam Smith), 204; Father's Day, 7, 9; involved, 9, 195; Jewish, 29; more access to newborn children, 88; movement, 90, 205; National Fatherhood Initiative, 8–9; *The New Dad: Caring, Committed and Conflicted*, 203–204; "new fatherhood" of the 1970s and 1980s, 61; sperm donor and provider, 39; stalled men's movement, 203; stay-at-home dads, 88, 90

feelings: 1, 9, 54, 56, 67–68, 71, 76–77, 84–85, 95, 123, 131–132, 157, 194, 203, 247n104

feminism: enabling of intermarriage for Jewish men, 204; second-wave, 39

"feminization of Judaism," 78

Fiedler, Leslie, 36, 149

films: *Abie's Irish Rose*, 150–153, 190; *Along Comes Polly*, 179; *Annie Hall*, 119, 170; *The Benny Goodman Story*, 166; *Breaking Upwards*, 188; *A Child of the Ghetto*, 153; *The Cohens and Kellys*, 150; *Exodus*,

166–168, 190; *Fiddler on the Roof,* 168; *The Five-Year Engagement,* 190–191; *Gentleman's Agreement,* 164–166, 190, 247n108; *The Heartbreak Kid* (1972), 40, 141–142, 169, 184; *The Heartbreak Kid* (2007 remake) 179, 183; *Home Before Dark,* 166; *Ira and Abby,* 190; *The Jazz Singer,* 153–155, 158, 169, 184–186; *Keeping the Faith,* 179, 184–186; *Little Fockers,* 179; *Meet the Fockers,* 179, 183; *Meet the Parents,* 179; *Minnie and Moskowitz,* 168; *Mrs. Skeffington,* 162, 166; *None So Blind,* 150; *Prime,* 186–187; *Star Trek,* 57; *A Stranger Among Us,* 176–177; *Surrender,* 150; *Tevye,* 189; *Transamerica,* 189; *Two Lovers,* 187–188; *The Way We Were,* 169; *When Harry Met Sally,* 176–177; *The Young Lions,* 166

Fisher, Eddie and Elizabeth Taylor, 11
Fishman, Sylvia Barack, 78, 146, 207n2, 207n4, 232n125
Freedman, Samuel G., 82
Friedes, Sally Srok, 120, 125–126
Friedman, Edwin H., 138

gender: American gender during postwar decades, 52, 60–61; American women as purveyors of domestic religion, 126; "battle of the sexes," 192, 201, 204; both genders . . . full-fledged parents, 200; career-family balance benefits both genders, 203; "chore wars," 202; communal participation of men and women different, 77, 79; composition of intermarriage fluctuates with age, 145; dynamics, 10, 28; equal parenting, 61; equality, 204; ethnic gender, xi; gender against gender, 82; gender role socialization, 195; gender roles more powerful than religious identification, 131; gendered ethnicity, 7, 14; gendered meaning of intermarriage, 29; gendered notions of assimilation, 148; "gendered undertone . . . judgment against men," 23; "inequity in American society . . . and Jewish communal world," 199–200;

influence on transmission of Jewish identity, 201; intersection between religion and gender, 9; Jewish gender, 193; relationship between intermarriage and gender roles, 64, 198; representations of a gender disparity in intermarriage, 29, 147–148, 188, 190; roles, 30, 187; *The Second Shift,* 202; Sheryl Sandberg's *Lean In,* 201; socially constructed and engrained, xi; traditional family structures and ongoing disparity in workforce and home, 61–62, 90, 98, 134, 136, 194, 204; trumps ethnicity, 192. *See also* comparison of intermarried Jewish men and intermarried Jewish women; feminism; masculinity

Glenn, Susan A., 129
Golding, Joshua, 187
Goldstein, Eric L., 155
Gordon, Milton M., 10, 14, 52
Greenblum, Joseph, 185

halacha (Jewish law), 12, 51, 56, 60, 73, 82
Halberstam, Joshua, 187
Hartman, Harriet, 92
Harvard, 24, 65
Holocaust: "American Jews . . . forged a memorial culture," 45; *Boston Legal,* 190; Christian's women's perspectives, 131–132, 135; ethnic profiling, 152; "Jewish enough for Hitler," 72–73, 114; *Schindler's List,* 145, 178; Second Gens, 44–47. *See also* comparison of intermarried Jewish men and intermarried Jewish women
homogeneity, 25, 126–127, 139
homosexuality: "coming out of the closet" analogy, 130; gay men's desires to be fathers, 88; gay rights, 56; Keshet, Boston Pride Parade, 13; LGBT couples, 13; Meredith Baxter, 173
Horowitz, Bethamie, 59
Humanist Jews, 57

identity, 204; acceptance of in raising Jewish children, 48; American Jewish

Identification Survey (AJIS), 232n125; and antisemitism, 73; "authentic," 37; choice, 113; Christian wife as "best Jew in the family," 54; denominational, 48, 60, 193; difficult in formation of, 44; distinct from other American men, 67–68; family identity, 122; fathering Jewish offspring, 32; and gender, 7; *gemilut hasadim* (acts of kindness), 63, 204; "gender roles are more powerful than religious identification," 131; Holocaust, 45–46; impact of rabbi on, 59, 75; interwoven with professional success and income, 86; "invention of ethnicity," 6; Jewish . . . by religion, millennials', 51; "Jewish identity complex . . . Christian identity is purely religious," 137; Jew-o-meter, 82; as a journey, 47–48, 84–85, 98, 120, 125, 127, 135, 138, 157, 185, 187; linked to being a provider, 68; Matthew Boxer and effects of Jewish community size, 18; "more Jewish," 60; "the more restrictive our definition for 'who is a Jew,' the more we will shrink," 55; "Mudblood," 57; Vulcan, 57; nation, 45; new model, 192, 204–205; as nurtured, 30; paternal connection, 58–59; Paul Golin, 27; physical appearance, 128–129; politics and patrilineal descent, 54–58; reawakening of, 63, 69–70; Russian refugee, 56; as a set of beliefs and behaviors, 137; spectrum, 11; transmission of, 13, 52; *The Vanishing American Jew*, 2; visiting Israel, 124. *See also* affiliation; bar mitzvah; children; films; Holocaust; novels; *tikkun olam*

intermarriage: between Catholics and Protestants, 33, 35, 165; between Jews and Christians, 35; couples rate and individuals rate, 18, 211n50; definition, 12–13; global perspective, 215n107; patterns of seven largest European ancestry groups, 34–35; rates for each gender converge, 65

interracial marriage, 12, 22, 28, 33, 134, 155, 212n70

Israel: 2–3, 17, 32, 35, 47, 57, 87, 106, 123–124, 145, 166, 171, 190. *See also* Birthright

JDate, 24, 36, 116, 217n25

Jewish community: men's involvement in, 192–193, 199–200

Jewish fathers, 36, 205; "I haven't got a father," 45; men's criticism of their fathers, 43–44; redefining Jewish fatherhood, 204

Jewish masculine mystique, xii, 6–7, 37. *See also* masculinity

Jewish mothers: 13, 35, 205, 214n98; Christian women, 131, 134, 136, 139; in *East River, Eagle at My Eyes, Generation of Vipers, Footsteps on the Stair,* and *Portnoy's Complaint,* 163; in *The Jazz Singer,* 154–155; man moved back to Ann Arbor to live near his mother, 198; "the mother wound," 42–43; in *Prime, Keeping the Faith,* and *Two Lovers,* 184, 186, 188; Rebekah's lament to her husband Isaac, 117; in "Seven Candles," 156; single, 87; support from, 128; threatened to kill herself, 28, 100. *See also* children of intermarriage; matrilineal descent; stereotypes

Jewish Outreach Institute, 26, 56, 197, 198, 221n105

Jewish-Asians, 24–26; Ethan, Miho, and Naomi Segal, 26; Jed Rubenfeld and Amy Chua, 25–26; Jewpanese, 22, 27; Josh, Jamie, and Shari Mae Narva, 26, 214n91; Mark Zuckerberg and Priscilla Chan, 22–23 Nat Lehrman and Kazuko Miyajima, 27–28, 214n98; Noah Feldman and Korean American fiancée, 24; Paul and Yurika Golin, 26–27; *Soy Vay,* 26; *See also* novels

Kennedy, Caroline and Edwin Schlossberg, 5

Keysar, Ariela, 77, 232n125

Kim, Helen and Noah Leavitt, 25–26, 28

King, Larry, 37

Kosmin, Barry A., 77

Kranson, Rachel, 37
Kugelmass, Jack, 173

labor: compensation gaps between men and women rabbis, 200; domestic division of labor, 133–134; domestic labor after divorce, 196; gender equity in the workplace and in the home, 62; pay disparity, 40, 199–200; women with young children working outside the home, 39–40
Lambert, Josh, 157
Lefkovitz, Lori, 168
Lehrman, Nat and Kazuko Miyajima, 27–28, 214n98
Levy, Rabbi Bob, 49–50, 80, 127, 135
Lewisohn, Ludwig, 70, 156–158, 244n60, 245n61

Marder, Rabbi Janet: blessing for non-Jewish spouses, 137–138
masculinity: American, 6–7, 9; association with earning power, 32, 36, 68, 196; bar mitzvah, 76; breadwinning model and justification for men's less-than-equal commitment to childcare, 196; *Fiddler on the Roof*, 168; "freaking cajones," 71; Israeli, 37, 167–168; "It was easier to cave to my wife than to grow a pair," 96; Jewish, xii, 7; "kosher rebellion," 76; "pussydick" 183; size of homes, 196; strong in body as well as in mind, 68; tumultuous history, 208n18. *See also* bar mitzvah
matrilineal descent, 55–56, 65, 73, 109, 137, 178
May, Lary, 155
Mayer, Egon, 213n80
Mayyim Hayyim, 78
McDavit-Aron, Janice, 93
melting pot: marriages, 147–149; Zangwill's, 157
Melved, Michael, 191
Merton, Robert, 162
methodology, 215n2
Miller, Arthur and Marilyn Monroe, 103
Mormons, 16, 37, 69

Moving Traditions, 78
Muslims, 16, 69

Names, 71–73, 84, 251n188
National Fatherhood Initiative, 8, 9, 73
National Jewish Population Survey (NJPS), 48, 65, 92, 145, 208n8, 215n5, 220n88, 221n104, 222n109, 225n5, 242n24
National Marriage Project, 87, 91
North American Jewish Data Bank, 91
novels: *Are You There God? It's Me, Margaret*, 189; *Club Revelation*, 187; *Confessions of a Nervous Shiksa*, 106; *The Conversation*, 187; *Eagle at My Eyes*, 163; *Earth and High Heaven*, 161; *East River*, 163; *The Enemy Camp*, 163; *In Search of the Golden Shiksa*, 40; *The Island Within*, 157–158, 162; *A Jew in Love*, 162; *Mona in the Promised Land*, 28; *Portnoy's Complaint*, 163; *Remember Me to God*, 157; *A Seat at the Table*, 187; *The Shiksa*, 144; *The Shiksa Syndrome*, 106

Obama, Barack, 7, 9
Oppenheimer, Mark, 76
Orthodox: affiliation shift, 47–48, 59–60, 75; Asian-Jewish couples, 25; Chabad House/Orthodox Minyan, 17; conversion, 57–58, 135; day school, 20; denominational preference, 220n88; Einstein Medical School, 81; "Elisha" character in *A Seat at the Table*, 187; father character in *East River*, 163, 246n96; "intermarriage" between Jews, 12; Jared Kushner, 4; mingling among Ann Arbor Jews, 17–18; men in study, 11, 32; mother character in "Seven Candles," 156; "Orthodox Paradox" and Maimonides School, 24; Orthodox Union, 24, 26; Rabbi Asher Lopatin, Rabbi Avi Weiss, Yeshivat Chovevei Torah, and first female "rabba," 82; Rabbi J. Simcha Cohen, 55; rabbinate survey on the officiation issue, 229n67; "Rena" character in *Club Revelation*, 187; Ronald Perelman, 98; single motherhood, 87;

Steven Spielberg's family, 143; tension between "unity" and "pluralism," 83; uphold matrilineal descent, 54–55, 57; wedding, 108; *With Roots in Heaven* and *Doublelife*, 230n83; yeshiva, 44. *See also under* identity: Jew-o-meter

Osherman, Samuel, 76–77

outreach: "How Should I Know?," 197–198, 197; and in-reach, 220n93; and Jewish interfaith families, 221n100, 221n105; Jewish Outreach Institute, 26, 198; Keruv Initiative, 79; "The key to being inclusive," 50; Mothers Circle, 131; movement, 49; "similar levels of engagement," 56; Union for Reform Judaism, 85

Passover, 54, 71, 98, 134, 181

patrilineal descent, 51–58, 65, 78, 136–137, 180, 189

Pew Research Center, 22, 48, 69, 208n8, 220n90, 221n105, 225n4, 239n98

Phillips, Jetskalina H., 124, 238n74

Poderantz, Norman, 37

politics: Adlai Stevenson and Franklin Delano Roosevelt, 74; Ann Arbor, 15; Human Rights Party, 16; and identity, 54; men focused on, 68; New Right, 39; progressive, 19; radical, Communist, and Socialist parties, 33; in *The Way We Were*, 169

Prell, Riv-Ellen, 148, 152

prenuptial agreements, 97

Protestants: in all-white communities, 41; divorce rates, 91; Episcopalian, 98, 113–114, 191; Jews could marry into the upper social echelons of Protestant America, 161; loss of ethnic exclusiveness, 114; Methodist, 4, 16, 93, 113–114, 134; St. Clare's Church, 19; work ethic, 36; women more accepting of traditional familial role expectations and responsibilities, 39; women's backgrounds, 113

race: American Jews married blacks, 33; Asian women "abandoned," 27; banning discrimination based on race, 16; bind men across race, 9; black president, 200; "blackface," 155; "'brown fever,'" 42; earnings by race, 254n25; father remarried a black woman, 93; intermarriage rates by race, 212n70; "lily white town," 116; *Love in Black and White*, 55; mixed-race in Ann Arbor, 15; *The New Yorker*, 66; races in Ann Arbor, 210n34; "'schvartze,'" 111; "Shiksa is the 'N' word," 109; whiteness, 244n50

Reconstructionist Judaism, 17, 54, 57, 60, 82, 229n67

Reform Judaism: Central Conference of American Rabbis, 50, 138; Doug Barden, 79; Hebrew Union College-Jewish Institute of Religion, 138; Men of Reform Judaism, *The Men's Seder*, 78; most affluent, 48; "most popular denominational preference," 48; Rabbi Nadia Siritsky, 55; rabbis, 49–50; Union for Reform Judaism, 8; Union of American Hebrew Congregations, 171

Reinharz, Shulamit, 215n107

Riley, Naomi Schaefer, 57, 93

Roberts, Steve and Cokie, 54

Rogin, Michael, 154–155

Rosh Hashanah, 54, 138

Roth, Philip, 36. *See also* novels

Rubin, James. *See* Holocaust

Sandberg, Sheryl: *Lean In*, 201–202

Sarna, Jonathan, 213n80, 215n107

Sasson, Theodore, 51

Saxe, Leonard, 77, 94

Sex: "getting the girl," 42; Kinsey Reports, 42; *Playboy*, 67, 226n9; satisfaction, 42; sexual liberation movement, 39; thong, 67

Sex and the City. See television

Shabbat, 2, 49, 70, 83, 103, 125, 127, 136, 138, 159, 171, 186, 240n116

Shatner, William, 11

shaygets, 109

Sheskin, Ira, 18, 211n50

shiksa: Christine Benvenuto, 103; comparison with *shaygets*, 109; Deuteronomy, 108; discussion of the terms "shiksa," "shikse," "shaygets," and "shekketz," 106; "false Aphrodite," 157; *The Last Shiksa* (B. H. Litwack), 103; literature, 105–106; *Merriam-Webster Dictionary*, 108; *Moment* magazine cover, 104; "the 'N' word of the Jewish community," 109; *Portnoy's Complaint* (Philip Roth), 103, 163, 235n9; "See, I told you not to marry a shiksa!" joke, 102–103; The Shiksa in the Kitchen, 110; "shiksappeal," 29, 105; *The Shiksa's Guide to Yiddish* (Christy Potter Kass), 111; "shiksas are for practice," 106; "Why I Only Date Shiksas" (Adam Mutterperl), 107; Yiddish saying, 106–107. See also Avey, Tori

shiva, 118

Simchat Torah, 135, 178

Simon, Rabbi Charles, 79, 230n85

Sklare, Marshall, 10, 41, 92, 218n52

Slaughter, Anne-Marie, 192

social justice. See *tikkun olam*

socioeconomic class, 9, 21; American middle class, 37–38; in *The Cohens and the Kellys,* 150; difference between Jewish immigrant and Mayflower descendant, 117–118; impoverished, 27; *The Jazz Singer,* 155; Jewish upward mobility, 37; lower-class Jewish-Catholic marriages, 161; median income, 210n33; "middle-class gentile princess," 168; "newer immigrants . . . lower," 114; Reform Judaism is the most affluent, 48; suburbs, 41

Spickard, Paul R., 27

Spiegelman, Art: *The New Yorker,* 66, 225n8

Spielberg, Steven and Kate Capshaw, 141, 143–145

sports: bar mitzvah decorations, 76; importance of playing sports, 68; and post-b'nai mitzvah boys, 77; sports bars and drinking, 67

Staub, Michael, 173

stereotypes: Christian girls don't wear underpants, 108; "danger" of the "shiksa," 103, 109, 156; "frumpy, frizzy, and a loud-mouth," 178; Jewish American Princess, 109; Jewish men like Asian women, 23; Jewish men do not commit domestic violence, 35, 217n18, 236n43; Jewish men do not drink, 78; Jewish men do not gamble or cheat on their wives, 36; Jewish men make good husbands, 32, 35, 100, 115–116, 186, 192; Jewish mothers, 109, 116, 163; Jews as loud, overbearing, complaining, self-serving, 85; *real* Jewish men intermarried, 184

Stern, Rabbi Keith, 49–50, 221n97

Stewart, Jon and Tracey McShane, 71, 181

Stiller, Ben and Christine Taylor, 179–181, 183–184, *185,* 250n166

Stiller, Jerry and Anne Meara, 179–181, *180, 181,* 182–183

Synagogue Council of America, 171

tefillin, 85

television: *The Bachelorette,* 5; *Boston Legal,* 189; *Bridget Loves Bernie,* 171–173; *Curb Your Enthusiasm,* 178–179; *The Daily Show,* 181; *The Ed Sullivan Show,* 182; *Glee,* 178; *The Good Wife,* 88; *Grey's Anatomy,* 190; *Little House on the Prairie,* 153; *Mad about You,* 174, 176; *Northern Exposure,* 176; *The O.C.,* 190; *Orange is the New Black,* 178; *Saturday Night Live,* 180; *Seinfeld,* 181–182, *181; Sex and the City,* 1–2, *2; The Simpsons,* 191; *thirtysomething,* 176; *Ugly Betty,* 252n203; *Will and Grace,* 177

Temple Beth Emeth, 17, *19,* 49–50, 72, 117, 127–128, 130, 135, 137

Thompson, Jennifer, 131, 201, 215n3, 231n11

tikkun olam, 23, 62–63, 73–75

Torah, 48, 57, 75–76, 80, 83, 107, 121, 135–136, 180, 243n37; Deuteronomy, 108, 143; Genesis, 117

Trump, Ivanka and Jared Kushner, 4

tzedakah, 23, 86

Union of American Hebrew Congregations, 171

University of Michigan, 14–17, 19–20, 22, 31, 37, 125, 128, 202

Valley, Eli: comment on "Just Married" comic series, 176; "The Japanese Menace," 27; "Vader: Half-Jew," 108
Vietnam, 15, 39

Warner Brothers: 153–154, 158–160, 169, 243n48
Waxman, Chaim, 68–69
Weintraub, Jerry, 142–143
Wise, Rabbi Stephen S., 157–158
women, Jewish, 30

World War II, 27; "most important phase of modern life," 76; Pearl Harbor, 28. *See also* Holocaust
Wylie, Philip, 43, 163, 219n61

Yom Kippur, 57, 137, 180

Zingermans, 17; Ari Weinzweig, 74–75
Zoss, Betty, 173
Zuckerberg, Mark. *See* Jewish-Asians
Zurawik, David, 176

Photo by Goings Photography/D. C. Goings

KEREN R. McGINITY is affiliated with the Hadassah-
Brandeis Institute and the Cohen Center for Modern
Jewish Studies at Brandeis University. She was the
inaugural Berman Postdoctoral Research Fellow in
Contemporary American Jewish Life at the University
of Michigan's Frankel Center for Judaic Studies in Ann
Arbor. McGinity earned her PhD in history from Brown
University, where she was also appointed as visiting
assistant professor. She is author of *Still Jewish: A History
of Women and Intermarriage in America* (2009), a National
Jewish Book Award finalist. She lives in Boston. Learn
more and contact her at www.loveandtradition.com.